Check for
2 CD's:
Front and
Back Covers

BEGINNER'S
CHINESE
WITH 2 AUDIO CDs
SECOND EDITION

Yong Ho

Hippocrene Books, Inc.
New York

For information, address:
HIPPOCRENE BOOKS
171 Madison Avenue
New York, NY 10016
www.hippocrenebooks.com

Character stroke charts reproduced with permission from
Jinmei Liao and hanlexon.com.

Library of Congress Cataloging-in-Publication Data

Ho, Yong.
Beginner's Chinese with 2 audio cds / Yong Ho. -- 2nd ed.
    p. cm.
Includes bibliographical references.
ISBN 978-0-7818-1257-3 (alk. paper)
  1. Chinese language--Textbooks for foreign speakers--
English. 2. Chinese language--Spoken Chinese. 3. Chinese
language--Sound recordings for English speakers. I. Title.
PL1129.E5H6 2010
495.1'82421--dc22

                                                    2010019885

Printed in the United States of America

CONTENTS

If the 19ᵗʰ century belonged to Britain, and the 20ᵗʰ century to the United States, then the 21ˢᵗ century will surely belong to China. My advice: Make sure your kids learn Chinese.

—Jim Rogers, *Worth Magazine*

The future belongs to Mandarin.

—Martin Jacques, author of *When China Rules the World*

Mandarin is the national tongue of one in five people in the world, and it is rapidly edging out English as the preferred second language in Asia. In the early days of the Web, the language of cyberspace was English. But the explosion of Internet use in China will tip the balance to Mandarin before long.

—Joseph Kahn, former New York Times Beijing bureau chief

CD ACCOMPANIMENT TRACK LIST

DISC ONE

PINYIN PRACTICE (See pp. 301-308)

Vowels
1. Simple Vowels
2. Compound Vowels

Consonants
3. "B" syllables
4. "P" syllables
5. "M" syllables
6. "F" syllables
7. "D" syllables
8. "T" syllables
9. "N" syllables
10. "L" syllables
11. "G" syllables
12. "K" syllables
13. "H" syllables
14. "J" syllables
15. "Q" syllables
16. "X" syllables
17. "Z" syllables
18. "C" syllables
19. "S" syllables
20. "ZH" syllables
21. "CH" syllables
22. "SH" syllables
23. "R" syllables

DISC TWO

LESSONS FOR BEGINNER'S CHINESE

1. Lesson One
2. Lesson Two
3. Lesson Three
4. Lesson Four
5. Lesson Five
6. Lesson Six
7. Lesson Seven
8. Lesson Eight
9. Lesson Nine
10. Lesson Ten

INTRODUCTION

Congratulations on the two right choices you have made. You decided to study Chinese and you picked the right book.

The decision to study Chinese is a good one because it is a language of the twenty-first century, as Jim Rogers observed. Believe it or not, there are more people in the world speaking Chinese than English or any other language, with 800 million speakers in China and 200 million elsewhere in the world. Chinese is one of the six official languages for the United Nations. Above all, the ability to speak and write Chinese goes a long way to the understanding of 5,000 years of Chinese civilization, the exchanging of ideas with its people, and the conducting of business in or with China.

This is an exciting time to learn Chinese, as China is now the focus of the world. According to an analysis performed by the Global Language Monitor, the rise of China has been determined to be the top news story of the first decade of this century, topping the Iraq War, the 9/11 terrorist attacks, and the election of Obama to the U.S. presidency. While a large part of the world is experiencing an economic meltdown, the economy in China is developing at a neck-breaking speed. More and more Americans are heading for China to seek employment. The ability to speak the language will certainly afford you a competitive edge.

The selection of this book for your study of Chinese is a good one because it is unique and it fills a void. This book is written for the adult learner who has no background in Chinese, and for travelers who want to take a quick course on Chinese. The majority of courses offered to these students in the United States (variously called elementary, beginning, or "level 1" Chinese) consists of ten to twelve sessions, yet most textbooks used for such courses contain thirty to forty lessons. It would take at least three or four levels or semesters to finish such a book. Obviously, by the time the students reach the end of the book, they are no longer beginners. For beginning students of Chinese, such textbooks are unwieldy and intimidating. *Beginner's Chinese* consists of ten lessons. Each lesson is comprised of the following components: basic sentence patterns, a series of conversations that illustrate the communicative use of these patterns, words and expressions, supplementary words and expressions, language points, exercises, and cultural insights about the topic of the lesson. The book has been written in such a way that it is teachable and learnable during one academic semester for adult students. By the time students finish this book, they will have learned about ninety basic sentence patterns, three hundred characters, basic grammar, and basic communicative skills.

This book is based on the premise that less is more. When presented with only the basic and most crucial words and patterns, students will be able to start talking and communicating immediately without being concerned about the intricacies of grammar and vocabulary. For this reason, *Beginner's Chinese* is truly a beginner's guide.

CHINESE LANGUAGE:
ITS PROMINENT FEATURES

S tudents come to my Chinese classes for different reasons. Some are looking for a tool to gain an in-depth understanding of Chinese culture and society. Others, primarily those of the Chinese descent, try to connect, through the language, with their roots and cultural heritage, and still others want to learn the language to communicate with their Chinese friends, parents of their spouses and business partners. Interestingly, there are also students who come to study Chinese just for the thrill of taking up an academic challenge by learning a language drastically different from English.

If learning a drastically different language is one's sole motivation, the choice of Chinese is definitely a right one. Although similarities do exist between the two languages, Chinese differs from English significantly in sounds, grammar and writing. I should hasten to add that these differences are not insurmountable hurdles. With enough practice and exposure, they will ultimately prove to be aids in gaining access to the perceptions and conceptions of the people whose language they are learning. Didn't some philosopher once say that learning a second language is like gaining a second soul?

Chinese is the language spoken by more people in the world than any other language, yet in the West it is often categorized as a less-commonly-taught language. Poor knowledge and misinformation have produced an abundance of myths and misconceptions about the language. Hopefully, the following discussion will help dispel some of the mysteries that shroud Chinese.

Like any other language in the world, Chinese is a member of a language family. It belongs to the family of Sino-Tibetan languages. As the world's second largest language family (next only to the Indo-

European family), the Sino-Tibetan family is comprised of more than 300 languages that are spoken over a vast geographic area extending from Northeastern India to Southeast, South and East Asia. Other members of the family include Tibetan, Burmese and a number of lesser known languages. These languages share a number of common features, which include, among others, monosyllabism, tonality and the use of classifiers. While tonality will be discussed in the next chapter on Chinese phonetics, let us first take a look at monosyllabism and the use of classifiers.

Monosyllabism refers to a language phenomenon where each morpheme is represented by a syllable. While the syllable may be easy to understand, the morpheme may not. A quick explanation is therefore in order. The morpheme has been traditionally regarded as the minimal unit of meaning, although modern linguists have distinguished finer units. In languages like English, a morpheme can consist of one or more syllables such as *kind* (one syllable, one morpheme) and *monosyllable* (5 syllables and two morphemes -*mono* and *syllable*) and it can even be realized by a consonant, such as -s in *cats*. Morphemes in English are often bound, meaning that individual morphemes cannot stand alone and have to be strung together to form a word. In a monosyllabic language, syllables are coterminous with morphemes. In other words, a syllable is a morpheme. In this sense, Chinese is truly monosyllabic, because each morpheme is indeed represented by a syllable and most morphemes in the language are free rather than bound, meaning they can stand alone as independent words. However, it would be wrong to assume the reverse: a word always consists of a morpheme and thus a syllable. The majority of words used in modern Chinese are disyllabic or polysyllabic, consisting of two or more morphemes/syllables. What is noteworthy in this regard is that most of these disyllabic and polysyllabic words are formed by free-standing rather than bound morphemes. Juxtaposing two free-standing morphemes/words doesn't mean that the meaning of the new word is the sum total of the meanings of the component words. They can be very different. Note should also be taken that most of the more frequently used words in Chinese today remain monosyllabic.

The use of classifiers is another feature that characterizes Chinese, most other Sino-Tibetan and Southeast Asian languages. Basically, a classifier is a word that comes in between a number or a demonstrative pronoun (e.g. this, that) and a noun. Classifiers are also referred to as measure words. They are occasionally used in English (*a **piece** of paper*, *a **school** of fish*, and *two **heads** of cauliflower*), but in Chinese the use of classifiers is the rule rather than the exception. What the classifiers do is to help disambiguate homophones and supply additional semantic rather than quantitative information about the nouns that they are used with. For this reason, it is inappropriate to refer to them as measure words. Refer to Lesson Four for a detailed discussion of classifiers.

Besides these characteristics that Chinese shares with other Sino-Tibetan languages, there are other features that are unique to Chinese. These include morphological simplicity, syntactic economy, meaning taking precedence over the form, and the topic-comment sentence structure, which will be discussed in turn in the following.

Morphological simplicity. As compared with English and other Indo-European languages, Chinese grammar is very simple. It is considered by some people to be so simple that they say Chinese does not have grammar. These people would be right if grammar were equated to inflection, but unfortunately for them, it is not. Grammar is a system of rules that govern the use of language. For this reason, every language has grammar. It is true that Chinese is for the most part not inflectional. Words are invariable, unaltered and allow no internal changes. Affixes signaling lexical or grammatical meaning do exist, but they do not figure very large in the language. Syntactic and lexical meanings are not indicated through the manipulation of word forms, but through word order, specific particles and vocabulary items.

Syntactic economy. Many syntactic distinctions that are made in English are not made in Chinese. These include the distinctions between singular and plural (such as *book* vs. *books*), between nominative case and objective case (such as *I* vs. *me*), between first/second person and third person (such as *I speak* vs. *he speaks*), between active voice and passive voice (such as *call* vs. *be called*), between the positive degree and comparative degree (such as *pretty* vs. *prettier*), between past time and present time (such as *I was a teacher* vs. *I am a teacher*). Tense serves as another example. For non-native speakers, verbs are usually the most difficult part of an inflectional language. The concept of tense has two components: time and aspect. Since time is conceived of differently in different languages, let's confine ourselves to English, where time can be divided into past, present, future and future in the past (e.g. when you reflect on a comment about a future event that you made on a past occasion). Aspect refers to the manner in which an action takes place. Distinctions of aspects are made in English into indefinite, continuous/progressive, perfect, perfect continuous/progressive. These four times and four aspects form a matrix that generates a total of 16 different verb forms such as *I write a letter, I wrote a letter, I will write a letter, (I said) I would write a letter, I am writing a letter, I was writing a letter, I will be writing a letter, (I said) I would be writing a letter, I have written a letter, (I thought) I had written a letter, I will have written a letter, (I said) I would have written a letter, I have been writing a letter, (I thought) I had been writing a letter, I will have been writing a letter, (I said) I would have been writing a letter*.

Notwithstanding the controversies that abound as to whether some of these structures are really tenses, the sheer number and complexity of these verb forms are daunting. How can we expect non-native speakers of English to easily master these? Fortunately for students of Chinese, verbs do not present a major problem as time is expressed lexically and aspect makers are few and far between in Chinese. There are only two aspects distinguished in Chinese: complete and continuous. Another case in point is the gender distinction in nouns, which is absent in Chinese. *Fuwuyuan* can be both waiter and waitress, and *yanyuan* can be both actor and actress. Many of the problems that beset English and other languages in relation to gender simply do not exist in Chinese. I once gave a talk on the relationship between language and thought. The original title was *Linguistic Shaping of Thought: Man at the Mercy of His Language*. You may quickly notice that this is not a very appropriate title because of the use of *man* to represent both genders. It didn't seem to sound right either if I changed it to *Linguistic Shaping of Thought: Person/People at the Mercy of His/Her/Their Language*. Fortunately, my Chinese came to the quick rescue. The final title became *Language and Thought*: Ren *at the Mercy of* Tade *Language*. *Ren* (person or people) and *tade* (his or her) did their job and no one was offended.

Syntactic economy is prominently manifested in what I would call a single-signal system. In other words, Chinese is so stingy with linguistic resources that it only allows one signal for one meaning. To illustrate this point, let me give some examples. In the English sentence *I have two books*, the plural meaning of the word *book* is indicated by two signals: two and the suffix -s. This would not be economical to the Chinese people who would simply say (equivalent to English) *I have two book*. Since two already specifies the quantity, why is it necessary to use another signal? The negative of the sentence *wo baba qu le Zhongguo* (my father has gone to China) is *wo baba meiyou qu Zhongguo*, where the aspect marker *le* has to be dropped because the negative word *meiyou* already signals an action that has not completed. *-Men* is one of the few suffixes used in Chinese. It is used after personal pronouns and human nouns to indicate plurality such as *xueshengmen dou hen hao* (the students are all good). However, when there is another signal present in the sentence indicating plurality, *-men* has to be dropped. For example, we cannot say *wo you san ge Zhongwen laoshimen* (I have three Chinese teachers), we have to say *wo you san ge Zhongwen laoshi*, since *san ge* (three) already signals plurality. Similarly we cannot say *tamen shi laoshimen* (they are teachers), because *tamen* (they) already makes the number clear. Yes/no questions are formed in Chinese by either using the sentence final particle *ma* or repeating the verb using its negative form such as *ni shi Zhongguoren ma* (are you a Chinese) or *ni shi bu shi Zhongguoren*. If you have had some exposure to Chinese before, you will know that in the second form *ma* is not to be used. But do you know why? *Ma* is not to be used because the verb plus its negative form is only used in Chinese to indicate a yes/no question. We cannot have two signals in one sentence. In all these cases, we are not missing any information, are we?

Meaning takes precedence over form. Since morphological changes are non-extant and conjunctions are sparingly used, word order becomes a matter of paramount importance in indicating meaning. In stringing sentence constituents together, Chinese is characterized by parataxis whereby grammatical elements such as phrases or clauses are coordinated without the use of conjunctions. This is different from English, which relies on hypotaxis whereby grammatical elements are joined with connectives. Sentences in paratactic languages such as Chinese are necessarily simpler and less embedded than those in hypotactic languages such as English. The most noticeable feature of word order in Chinese is the natural iconicity between syntactic structure and temporal sequence or chronological succession of events. Basically it means that what happens earlier in time and what exists earlier in concept comes earlier in the sentence. Expressions of time and place precede the verb in Chinese, because they provide the scene and setting for the action. Modifiers, be they adjectives, adverbs, phrases, or clauses, always come before the modified, be they nouns or verbs. Lacking an article system, Chinese resorts to word order to indicate definiteness or indefiniteness. Generally, nouns with definite or specific reference are placed at the beginning of the sentence, whereas those with indefinite or unspecified reference are placed towards the end of the sentence. Word order is so important to Chinese that the renowned linguist Yuen Ren Chao once said that all Chinese grammar is syntax, all Chinese syntax is word order, and therefore all Chinese grammar is word order.

Topic-comment sentence. About 50% of sentences in Chinese are of a particular sentence structure where there is a binary division of two parts between topic and comment. The topic is what the speaker chooses to take as his point of departure and the comment is a statement on that topic. This structure is frowned upon in some languages

(English is possibly one) as a substandard or sloppy way of expression characteristic of impromptu or careless speech such as "John, I like him." "That book, don't read," whereas in other languages such as Chinese, it is quite normal and standard. Examples of topic-comment sentences include (topic and comment are separate by |): *wo | duzi e le* (I'm hungry; literally, I stomach hungry); *ta mama | shenti hen hao* (her mother enjoys good health; literally, her mother health good); *Yingyu | wo hui nüli* (I will work hard on my English; literally, English I will work hard on).

A particular type of favored linguistic structure reflects a particular cognitive process. The Chinese topic-comment structure characterizes a type of thinking wherein the speaker, in communicating an idea, would first of all dwell on a topic without considering the syntactic representation of the assertion on the topic. This is made possible by the freedom in the language from abiding by the subject-verb agreement. If you are interested in the corollary of this two-step cognitive organization, you may want to refer to my book *Aspects of the Discourse Structure in Mandarin Chinese*, which is listed in the bibliography.

You are about to study the Chinese language and you should know the word for Chinese language in Chinese. Instead of one, there are two terms—*Hanyu* and *Zhongwen*. The term *Hanyu*, which is widely used in China to refer to the Chinese language and is adopted as the title for most Chinese language textbooks, literally means "the language of the *Han*." If you have some familiarity with Chinese history, you will know that *Han* was the second imperial dynasty of China (the first imperial dynasty was *Qin*, which was formerly spelt as *Chin* from which the word "China" may have derived). Due to its importance in history, the name *Han* came to be used to refer to the ethnic Chinese. It is not difficult to see that *Hanyu* is not a politically correct term to use, because Chinese is also spoken by most of the minority groups in China as the second language and some of them as the first language. For this reason, *Zhongwen* would be a better term. It simply means the language of the Chinese people.

As one of the seven major dialect groups in China, Mandarin is spoken by over 900 million or 70% of the Chinese people in northern and parts of southern China, but more importantly, it is understood by 94% of the population. Mandarin, which is referred to in China as *beifanghua* (northern speech), has its own sub-varieties of northern Mandarin, northwest Mandarin, southern Mandarin and southwest Mandarin. The standard Mandarin, called *guoyu* or *putonghua*, is based on, but not equivalent to, the Beijing dialect. The term *guoyu*, which means "national language," is used in Taiwan, Hong Kong and overseas Chinese communities and the term *putonghua*, which means "common speech," is used in mainland China. This standard form has become an administrative and official medium. It is used on television, in radio broadcasts and in movies. More importantly, it has been promoted to be the language of instruction in primary and secondary schools. As such, *guoyu/putonghua* is the prestige form of speech that most people try to emulate. The reason that *guoyu/putonghua* has been chosen as the standard dialect is its sheer number of speakers. With a complex situation in China of a multitude of mutually unintelligible dialects, particularly in the south, there is a need for a *lingua franca* through which speakers of various dialects can communicate. If you speak Mandarin, chances are you may not understand people who speak a different dialect, but they may understand you. Besides China, Mandarin is also spoken by more than one million people in such Asian countries as Singapore, Malaysia, Indonesia, Brunei, Mongolia, Thailand and the Philippines.

People outside China are often under the impression that there are two languages in China: Mandarin and Cantonese, but this is far from being the case. Cantonese, which is spoken by only 5% of the population in China, is popular in the United States and elsewhere primarily due to the fact that many of the earlier immigrants to the United States were from Canton, which is coastal and its residents have easy access to the sea. When they immigrated to the West, they brought along with them their dialect. Until about 30 years ago, the dominant variety of Chinese spoken by immigrants in the United States was Cantonese, as few Mandarin speakers immigrated to this country. However the linguistic picture has completely changed since then, with more and more people from the Mandarin-speaking areas in China finding new homes in this and other countries.

Since Chinese is not a phonetic language and the characters do not bear any resemblance to the actual pronunciation, a system of transcribing Chinese phonetics was thus needed to assist people in learning to read words in Chinese. There are two systems currently in use. One is the Wade-Giles system and the other is the *pinyin* system. The Wade-Giles system was developed by Sir Thomas Francis Wade in the mid-19th century and modified by the Cambridge professor Herbert Allen Giles at the beginning of last century. This system makes it easier, particularly for English speakers, to pronounce Chinese sounds, but it is not the accurate representation of the sounds. For example, the Wade-Giles system often uses one symbol to represent different sounds and different symbols to represent the same sound. In mainland China, the Wade-Giles system has been replaced by the *pinyin* (which literally means *putting sounds together*) system which was developed in 1958 using the Latin alphabetic with the purpose of introducing standard pronunciation of Mandarin to school children. This system has been practically adopted worldwide since the late 1970s. The *pinyin* system is a more accurate reflection of the actual sounds in Chinese, but you need to know *pinyin* before you can use it. The *pinyin* system is used in this course.

CHINESE PHONETICS

There are 6 vowels and 21 consonants in Mandarin Chinese. As we discussed in the previous chapter, the majority of Chinese morphemes are monosyllabic. That is, they consist of one syllable only. The syllabic structure in Chinese is such that a syllable always consists of a vowel (V) or a consonant with a vowel (CV), such as ba, fo, ne. Consonant clusters—two or more consonants used in succession—are not permitted in Chinese. Syllabic combinations common in English such as VC (e.g. up, at), CVC (e.g. big, pat, map), CCVC (e.g. bred, dread, stone), CVCC (e.g. mask, best, sand), CCV (e.g. fly, blue, grow), CCCV (e.g. screw, spray, stray), VCC (old, and, ink), VCCC (e.g. Olds, ants, amps), CCVCC (e.g. brand, trains, swings), CVCCC (e.g. tests, tenths, lunged), CVCCCC (e.g. thirsts, texts, worlds), CCVCCC (e.g. slurps, prints, flirts), CCCVC (e.g. street, squat, strut), CCCVCC (e.g. struts, squats, sprained), CCCVCCC (e.g. scrimps, sprints, squelched) are not possible in Chinese. There is, however, a possible CVC structure in Chinese, but the final C can only be the nasal sounds -n and -ng and the retroflex -r, such as *jing*, *nan*, *yong* and *er*. Consonants are often called initials because they invariably appear initially in a syllable with the exception of the final -n or -ng which can appear finally. Vowels and VC combinations are also called finals because they always appear finally in a syllable. Vowels can stand by themselves when no initial consonant is present.

The 6 vowels are: a, o, e, i, u, ü.

Try to learn these 6 vowels in this sequence for two important reasons. First of all, this sequence shows a pattern or regularity of articulation. When you pronounce *a*, the mouth is open the widest,

Possible Sound Combinations in Mandarin Chinese

	a	ai	ao	an	ang	o	ou	ong	e	ei	en	eng	i	ia	iao	ie	iu	ian	in	ing	iang	iong	u	uo	ui	un	uan	ua	uai	uang	ü	üe	üan	ün
b	ba	bai	bao	ban	bang	bo				bei	ben	beng	bi		biao	bie		bian	bin	bing			bu											
p	pa	pai	pao	pan	pang	po	pou			pei	pen	peng	pi		piao	pie		pian	pin	ping			pu											
m	ma	mai	mao	man	mang	mo	mou		me	mei	men	meng	mi		miao	mie	miu	mian	min	ming			mu											
f	fa			fan	fang	fo	fou			fei	fen	feng											fu											
d	da	dai	dao	dan	dang		dou	dong	de	dei	den	deng	di		diao	die	diu	dian		ding			du	duo	dui	dun	duan							
t	ta	tai	tao	tan	tang		tou	tong	te			teng	ti		tiao	tie		tian		ting			tu	tuo	tui	tun	tuan							
n	na	nai	nao	nan	nang		nou	nong	ne	nei	nen	neng	ni		niao	nie	niu	nian	nin	ning	niang		nu	nuo			nuan				nü	nüe		
l	la	lai	lao	lan	lang		lou	long	le	lei		leng	li	lia	liao	lie	liu	lian	lin	ling	liang		lu	luo		lun	luan				lü	lüe		
g	ga	gai	gao	gan	gang		gou	gong	ge	gei	gen	geng											gu	guo	gui	gun	guan	gua	guai	guang				
k	ka	kai	kao	kan	kang		kou	kong	ke	kei	ken	keng											ku	kuo	kui	kun	kuan	kua	kuai	kuang				
h	ha	hai	hao	han	hang		hou	hong	he	hei	hen	heng											hu	huo	hui	hun	huan	hua	huai	huang				
j													ji	jia	jiao	jie	jiu	jian	jin	jing	jiang	jiong									ju	jue	juan	jun
q													qi	qia	qiao	qie	qiu	qian	qin	qing	qiang	qiong									qu	que	quan	qun
x													xi	xia	xiao	xie	xiu	xian	xin	xing	xiang	xiong									xu	xue	xuan	xun
z	za	zai	zao	zan	zang		zou	zong	ze	zei	zen	zeng											zu	zuo	zui	zun	zuan							
c	ca	cai	cao	can	cang		cou	cong	ce		cen	ceng											cu	cuo	cui	cun	cuan							
s	sa	sai	sao	san	sang		sou	song	se		sen	seng											su	suo	sui	sun	suan							
zh	zha	zhai	zhao	zhan	zhang		zhou	zhong	zhe	zhei	zhen	zheng											zhu	zhuo	zhui	zhun	zhuan	zhua	zhuai	zhuang				
ch	cha	chai	chao	chan	chang		chou	chong	che		chen	cheng											chu	chuo	chui	chun	chuan	chua	chuai	chuang				
sh	sha	shai	shao	shan	shang		shou		she	shei	shen	sheng											shu	shuo	shui	shun	shuan	shua	shuai	shuang				
r			rao	ran	rang		rou	rong	re		ren	reng											ru	ruo	rui	run	ruan	rua						

Visit http://www.quickmandarin.com/chinesepinyintable/ to hear each of the sound combinations pronounced in four tones.

and the tongue is the lowest. As you move down the list, the mouth gradually closes and the tongue gradually rises. By the time you pronounce *ü,* the mouth is almost closed and the tongue reaches the highest point. Second, the tone mark used in *pinyin* always falls on the vowel, but two or three vowels can be combined to form a compound vowel, such as: ao, ai, ou, ei, ia, iao, ie, iu, ua, uo, ue, ui, uai. When this happens, the tone mark will fall on the vowel that comes earliest in the sequence. Let's put a tone mark on these compound vowels and see where it falls:

ào, āi, ōu, èi, iā, iào, iě, ǒu, uā, uǒ, uè, uài

The 21 consonants are:

b, p, m, f, d, t, n, l, g, k, h, j, q, x, z, c, s, zh, ch, sh, r

A question that I like to ask students in my introductory class is what kind of problem they can envision for a language that has only 6 vowels, 21 consonants and is of the CV (with limited CVC possibilities) syllabic structure. It doesn't take them very long to come up with the answer: there is a poverty of possible sound combinations to express all the meanings that we have. Simple math will tell us that there are only about 400 possible sound combinations in Chinese. Can anybody name the number of meanings that we have in this world? The result of this poverty is the proliferation of homophones, words that are pronounced the same but have different meanings, because a single sound combination is called upon to express many meanings. This is not convenient or effective. To alleviate this problem, Chinese resorts to a variety of means, chief among them is the use of four tones. By introducing four tones, the total number of possible sound combinations is quickly boosted to around 1600. It is still not enough, but it is a tremendous relief.

Another question that I like to ask my beginning student is how much space they think is needed to plot all the possible sound combinations in Chinese. Again, this is not a tall order. It takes only one page. See page 14 for proof. Does anyone know how much space is needed to plot all the possible sound combinations in English? Keep in mind, what I said is *possible*, not *meaningful*. For example, *pright* is a possible sound combination in English, although there is no meaning associated with it. Maybe some day when we run out of words in English, we can resort to it. According to the Danish grammarian Jespersen, there are 158,000 possible sound combinations in English. The answer to the previous question is that any attempt to plot all of these possible sound combinations would result in a sizable book.

Although the severely restricted number of possible sound combinations poses a hindrance to effective communication, there is at least a bright side to it and this is for you, the non-native speakers of Chinese only. You don't have to learn too many sound combinations and you will know at the outset exactly how many sound combinations need to be learned. If you have learned all the possible sound combinations together with the four tones, there is not a single other sound combination that you will need to learn. Can the same thing be said of English? To help you practice the Chinese phonetics, a list of all the possible sound combinations in Mandarin is provided in the back of the book with the four tones marked (pages 301-308). There is a CD that accompanies the book with the readings of all the sound combinations. Follow the CD and practice until you have a firm grasp of the sounds and the tones. You can also visit www.quickmandarin.com/chinesepinyintable where you will see a *pinyin* chart listing all the sound combinations with the four tones. You can click on any sound combination to hear its pronunciation in four tones.

Tones

As mentioned above, tones are an effective means to reduce homophones and, consequently, ambiguity. Tones are variations of pitch contours. Such variations also occur in English, but they are only phonetic, not phonemic, in that they may change the pragmatic meaning of a word but they do not change the lexical or basic meaning of the word. For example, there may be a variety of ways to say the word *yes* in English, but *yes* will never become *desk* or *horse*.

In Mandarin however, pitch change is not only phonetic, but also phonemic in that tones distinguish meaning. By varying the pitch of a sound combination, you get a totally different word. Here are some examples:

mā (*mother*), má (*hemp*), mǎ (*horse*), mà (*scold*)
yī (*one*), yí (*move*), yǐ (*chair*), yì (*hundred million*)
wū (*house*), wú (*none*), wǔ (*five*), wù (*fog*)

In Mandarin Chinese, there are four tones, which are referred to as the first tone, the second tone, the third tone, and the fourth tone:

The **first tone** is called high level tone. As the name suggests, it should be high, almost at the upper limit of your pitch range, and level, without any fluctuation. A common mistake observed among students is that it is not high enough. The key to getting this tone right is that if you feel there is still room at the top of your pitch range, you should go for it.

The **second tone** is called rising tone. It starts from the middle of your pitch range and rises. This is usually not a difficult tone.

The **third tone** is called falling-rising tone. As such, it has two parts: first falling and then rising. Although this tone is represented by the graph v, the two sides of the v are not of equal length. A better representation would be a check mark. It moves down from the lower half of the pitch range and moves up to a point near the top. A common mistake is that students often start too high. It is only natural that if you start too high, it would be very difficult to maneuver the bend at the bottom of the valley when you need to rise. What you should do is to try to start low. In fact, it doesn't matter very much how low you start. Start as low as you can. If you still have trouble, try to lower your chin as you produce the tone as long as you don't get into an irreversible habit.

The **fourth tone** is also called falling tone. It falls precipitously all the way down from the top of the pitch level. It is interesting to observe that although we use this tone from time to time in English, particularly when we put our foot down by saying Yes! or No!, when it comes to pronouncing the fourth tone in Mandarin, a lot of students suddenly become indecisive and ineffectual. The key to getting this tone right is to try to be resolute.

The **neutral tone**: In addition to the four tones, Mandarin Chinese has a "fifth" tone, which is actually a toneless tone. As such it is usually called the neutral tone. Its pronunciation is soft and quick. The neutral tone is not diacritically marked. It occurs either on grammatical particles or the second character of some words that do not receive stress. For example:

    Grammatical particles:
        Nǐ hǎo ma? (How are you?)
        Nǐ ne? (How about you?)
        wǒde shū (my book)
        Tā qù le xuéxiào. (He has gone to the school.)

    Second character of some words:
        xièxie (thank you)
        māma (mother)
        bàba (father)
        xuésheng (student)

Tone Change

The juxtaposition of two tones may sometimes result in a tone change known as *tone sandhi*. This happens when:

1. A third tone becomes a second tone when immediately followed by another third tone, for example,

    nǐ hǎo → ní hǎo (hello)
    wǒ hěn hǎo → wó hén hǎo (I'm very good)

2. When a third tone is followed by the first tone, the second tone, the fourth tone and the most neutral tones, it becomes a half-third tone. A half-third tone is a modified third tone that falls but not rise, for example,

    wǒ māma (my mother), nǐ máng ma ? (Are you busy?)

It is clear from the above that the third tone is seldom used in full in Chinese unless it falls on a word in isolation or followed by a long pause. Please also note even though the third tone undergoes changes in connection with other tones, it is still given the original tone mark in print by convention.

There are a number of other conventions and rules that need to be noted:

i is written as *y* when it occurs at the beginning of a syllable, e.g. *ie* → *ye*, *ian* → *yan*. Exceptions are *in* and *ing*. With these two syllables, *y* is added at the beginning: *yin* and *ying*. When standing alone as a syllable by itself, *i* is written as *yi*.

u is written as *w* when it occurs at the beginning of a syllable, e.g. *uo* → *wo*, *uan* → *wan*. *u* is written as *wu* when it forms a syllable by itself, e.g. *u* → *wu*.

ü is written as *yu* when it occurs at the beginning of a syllable or forms a syllable by itself, e.g. *üe* → *yüe*, *üan* → *yüan*, *ü* → *yu*.

i does not have any phonetic value when it follows *z*, *c*, *s*, *zh*, *ch*, *sh* and *r*. It is placed there to fulfill the syllabic requirement. That is, there must be a vowel in every syllable.

When preceded by a consonant, *uei* and *uen* become *ui* and *un*.

ü is written as *u* after *j*, *q*, *x*, and *y*.

When a syllable beginning with *a*, *o*, and *e* is juxtaposed with another syllable, the mark (') is often used to demarcate the boundary between two syllables, e.g. nǚ'ér (daughter) and pèi'é (quota).

In Mandarin, an extra syllable is often attached to another syllable to make it retroflexed. This extra syllable is phonetically transcribed as "r" instead of "er," e.g. yìdiǎnr (a little bit), xiǎoháir (child), and should not be pronounced separately.

WRITTEN CHINESE

Of all the major writing systems in the world, Chinese is the only one that did not develop a phonetic alphabet. Its writing system is neither alphabetic nor phonetic, because it does not use romanization and its form does not bear any resemblance to the actual sound. The Chinese writing system uses a logographic script in the form of characters.

Mention was made in a previous chapter that most of the major dialect groups in China are not mutually intelligible, but the written form is the same. People in China who cannot communicate through speech can communicate through the written language. A commonly heard expression in China is "qǐng xiě xiàlai (please write it down)." This linkage can even facilitate to some extent communication between Chinese and Japanese and Koreans, who use Chinese characters extensively. It may be reasonable to assume that this unified writing system has helped preclude China from disintegration through the last two millennia. If anything, the writing system is definitely a link for the Chinese to connect to their literary tradition and cultural past. There have been debates about whether Chinese should abandon its characters and adopt romanization as its writing system. These discussions are fruitless and serve no purpose. If you followed our discussion in the previous chapter on Chinese phonetics, you would have already noticed the limited number of possible sound combinations and the abundance of homophones in Chinese. Although the use of tones and classifiers, and dissyllabizing words can help alleviate the situation to some extent, characters are the ultimate and the only way to distinguish words. Ten words may be pronounced exactly the same, but they will all be written differently. There is simply no way that characters can give way to romanization in Chinese.

Chinese characters are often thought of as pictures representing objects and concepts. This may be true of the earliest Chinese writing traceable to the 14th century BC when it was largely pictographic in nature, using line drawings to represent concrete and familiar objects, but almost from the very beginning, pictograms were found inadequate to represent everything, especially abstract ideas. This is when ideograms came in. Ideograms are graphic representations of abstract and symbolic ideas. For those pictographic characters, centuries of refining and stylizing resulted in the almost total loss of images and graphic quality.

Seventy-five percent of Chinese characters are of a type that is composed of two parts, a left part and a right part or a top part and a bottom part. In either formation, one part, called *radical*, usually appears on the left or the top. Radicals are category labels or specifiers that provide clues to the semantic classification of words such as person, food, metal, plant, animal, water, gender, feeling, language, etc. If you know the radical of a character, but do not know the character itself, you can get a general idea of its meaning. As such, radicals are also referred to as *significs*.

There are 214 such radicals in Chinese, which are also used in Chinese dictionaries to index words. The other component of the character, usually appearing on the right or the bottom, provides phonetic clues. However, the phonetic clue is only a rough one. It won't become useful unless you have already learned a substantial number of characters to make the prediction. Besides, tones may be very different.

Students of Chinese often wonder how many characters they need to learn in order to have a reading knowledge of Chinese materials other than classical literature. Various estimates have been given, ranging from 3,000 to 5,000. Statistics shows that the average high school graduate in China knows between 3,500 and 4,500 characters. I would think a knowledge of 2,000 to 2,500 characters is adequate to tackle reading contingencies that are non-academic and non-technical. This would probably be equivalent to the vocabulary of the average students beginning their junior high school in China. Please note that the majority of words used in contemporary Chinese are disyllabic or polysyllabic, consisting of two or more syllables or characters. The actual words you learn from these 2,000 to 2,500 characters are enormous, because juxtaposing two or more characters results in new words with different meanings.

Since characters are not phonetic and the emphasis of this or any other beginning course for adult learners is on speaking or communicating, character learning and writing are not given priority. To spend too much time on character writing at this stage would consume too much time that should be spent building a solid foundation in pronunciation and the basic sentence patterns used for various communicative functions. It is advisable that serious study of characters for adult students should follow a comfortable command of pronunciation, basic vocabulary and basic sentence patterns. In spite of all this, you may find it very hard to resist learning some characters when you study the language. Feel free to pursue if you have the urge as long as you do not lose sight of the main goal at this stage.

In writing a character, it is not only important to get the end product right, but also to follow the proper stroke order. Failure to follow proper sequence is the first sign of illiteracy. That is why teachers and parents in China keep a very close look at how children write and take pains to correct them when they make a wrong move. To that end, I would strongly suggest that students take advantage of the multitude of software programs that teach the writing of characters. You will find a list of character tutoring programs in the appendix of this book. Most of these programs will take you by the hand, showing you the basic strokes and stroke order. In addition, they usually come with quizzes, on-screen flashcards, and a bi-directional dictionary. Some of the programs even have the ability to display *pinyin* for any character by clicking on it. You can also view a list of stroke order rules at:

www.archchinese.com/arch_stroke_order_rules.html

Characters are also referred to as square characters, because each one is shaped like a square. Irrespective of the complexity of strokes and structures, each character occupies the same amount of space as the next one. To help with balancing and orienting strokes, it is a good idea therefore that when you practice writing characters, you should use an exercise book with grid pages.

Complex characters are formed by components. These components are either independent characters when used alone or blocks that recur in many other characters. For this reason, you should try to memorize these components rather than individual strokes. This is very much like building a house. It is easier to build a house using prefabricated materials than individual bricks and loose sands.

A cursory look at any older Chinese dictionary will reveal that many of the characters are very complex in structure, consisting of up to twenty or more strokes. They are complicated to write and difficult to remember. This also explains why illiteracy had been widespread in China up to the mid-20th century. In response to the pressing need to simplify the writing system, the Chinese government has introduced a total of 2,515 simplified characters since 1956. The most common form of simplification is the reduction of strokes in certain characters and assignment of a component to stand for the whole. Contrary to the thinking of many people outside China that the simplification was an imposition by the Chinese government on its people, what the government did was in response to the pent-up grassroots demand and in many cases was standardizing the simplified forms that had already been in wide use for hundreds of years. Without the government's legislation, common people would take the matter into their own hands and start to simplify characters for easy use anyway. Simplification proved to be a boon for millions of people, particularly for those who were struggling to shake off illiteracy. This process has gone a long way towards helping eradicate illiteracy. Studies have found that the literacy rate in China has been raised from 20 to 30% in the early 1950s to 80 to 90% in the 1990s. Simplification definitely has played a major part in this improvement. Favorably received as it has been, simplification of characters also created new problems. Since the decision to simplify characters was unilaterally made by the Chinese government, people in Taiwan, Hong Kong, and overseas Chinese communities are experiencing tremendous difficulty reading materials from mainland China and children in mainland China are also having trouble reading classical materials.

Beginning students often struggle with the decision whether to study the simplified characters or traditional characters. Unfortunately there is no easy solution, as there is no consensus among teachers of Chinese as to which form to teach. Although I've used simplified characters in this book, I would suggest that you make the decision based on your purpose. Study simplified characters if you need to read literature from mainland China, traditional characters if you plan to read materials from Taiwan (simplified characters are increasingly adopted in Hong Kong and overseas Chinese communities). There are teachers of Chinese who suggest that students should learn to read both forms, but write in the simplified form only. Many of the software programs and all the Chinese word-processing programs listed in the appendix of this book can be great aids in cross-referencing between traditional and simplified characters. With a click of a button, most of these programs will convert all the simplified characters that you input to traditional characters or the other way around. For your easy reference, those characters that appeared in this book that have a traditional version are listed with their traditional counterparts are listed in the glossary section at the back of this book.

For practice purposes, I listed a worksheet with 10 characters at the end of each lesson in this book, complete with pinyin and the stroke-by-stroke demonstration of their sequences. These are among the simplest and most frequently used characters in Chinese. For each character, there are three of them printed in gray so that students can trace before they attempt to produce on their own. These worksheets were generated using a free application provided at http://www.hanlexon.org. If you wish to produce worksheets for additional characters, you can do so at the website.

GRAMMATICAL TERMS EXPLAINED

Adverbial
A word, phrase or clause that functions to modify a verb, an adjective or another adverb, providing such information as time, place, manner, reason, condition and so on.

Aspect
Manner in which an action takes place. English distinguishes four aspects: indefinite, continuous, perfect and perfect continuous, whereas Chinese distinguishes indefinite, continuous and perfect. The indefinite aspect indicates the habitual or repeated action. The continuous aspect indicates the continuation or progression of the action. The perfect aspect indicates the completion of an action.

Classifier
A word used between a numeral and a noun to show a sub-class to which the noun belongs.

Object
A noun, pronoun, phrase or clause that is used after, and affected in some way by, a transitive verb. If it is affected in a direct way, it is called the direct object. If it is affected in an indirect way, it is called the indirect object. In the sentence *he gave me a book*, *a book* is the direct object and *me* is the indirect object.

Particle
A word that has only grammatical meaning, but no lexical meaning, such as 吗 ma, 呢 ne, and 吧 ba in Chinese.

Predicate
The part of a sentence that states or asserts something about the subject. This role is only assumed by the verb in English, but can also be assumed by the adjective in Chinese.

Predicative adjective
An adjective used after the verb *to be* in English, as in *the book is interesting*, which is opposed to an attributive adjective used before a noun, as in *this is an interesting book*. The predicative adjective in Chinese is used without the verb *to be*, and functions as the predicate of the sentence.

Subject
Something about which a statement or assertion is made in the rest of the sentence.

Transitive and intransitive verb
A transitive verb is one that needs to take an object such as *we study Chinese*. An intransitive verb is one that does not take an object such as *walk, run* and *go*.

LESSON 1
GREETINGS

SENTENCE PATTERNS

你好!
Nǐ hǎo!

Hello!

你好 吗?
Nǐ hǎo ma?

How are you?

你呢?
Nǐ ne?

How about you?

这 是 王 先生。
Zhè shì Wáng Xiānsheng.

This is Mr. Wang.

你怎么样?
Nǐ zěnmeyàng?

How is everything with you?

我 也很 好。
Wǒ yě hěn hǎo.

I'm also fine.

认识 你, 我很 高兴。
Rènshí nǐ, wǒ hěn gāoxìng.

It's a pleasure to know you.

CONVERSATIONS

A: 你好!   Hello!
   Nǐ hǎo!
B: 你好!   Hello!
   Nǐ hǎo!

A: 你好 吗?   How are you?
   Nǐ hǎo ma?
B: 我 很 好, 你呢?   I'm fine. And you?
   Wǒ hěn hǎo, nǐ ne?
A: 我 也很 好。   I'm fine, too.
   Wǒ yě hěn hǎo.

A: 你爸爸好 吗?   How is your father?
   Nǐ bàba hǎo ma?
B: 他很 好。   He is fine.
   Tā hěn hǎo.
A: 你妈妈 呢?   How about your mother?
   Nǐ māma ne?
B: 她也很 好。   She is also fine.
   Tā yě hěn hǎo.

A: 王 先生,   你好 吗?   How are you, Mr. Wang?
   Wáng Xiānsheng, nǐ hǎo ma?
B: 马马虎虎。你呢, 张   So-so. How about you,
   Mǎmahūhu.   Nǐ ne, Zhāng   Miss Zhang?
   小姐?
   Xiǎojiě?
A: 我 也马马虎虎。   I'm so-so, too.
   Wǒ yě mǎmahūhu.

A: 你怎么样?
   Nǐ zěnmeyàng?

How's everything with you?

B: 不 错。你呢?
   Bú cuò. Nǐ ne?

Not bad. And you?

A: 我 也不错。
   Wǒ yě bú cuò.

Not bad, either.

A: 这 是 张 小姐。
   Zhè shì Zhāng Xiǎojiě.

This is Miss Zhang.

   这 是 王 先生。
   Zhè shì Wáng Xiānsheng.

This is Mr. Wang.

B: 认识 你, 我很 高兴。
   Rènshi nǐ, wǒ hěn gāoxìng.

It's a pleasure to know you.

A: 认识 你, 我 也很 高兴
   Rènshi nǐ, wǒ yě hěn gāoxìng.

It's a pleasure to know you too.

WORDS AND EXPRESSIONS

Pronouns

我	wǒ	I, me
你	nǐ	you
他	tā	he, him
她	tā	she, her
这	zhè	this

Nouns

爸爸	bàba	father
妈妈	māma	mother
先生	xiānsheng	Mr., husband
小姐	xiǎojiě	Miss

Verbs

是	shì	be
认识	rènshi	know

Adjectives

好	hǎo	good
错	cuò	bad, wrong
马马虎虎	mǎmahūhu	so-so
高兴	gāoxìng	glad, happy

Adverbs

很	hěn	very
也	yě	also
不	bù	not

Grammatical particles

| 吗 | ma |
| 呢 | ne |

Expressions

| 怎么样 | zěmeyàng | how is ...? |

SUPPLEMENTARY WORDS AND EXPRESSIONS

Nouns

老师	lǎoshī	teacher
学生	xuésheng	student
哥哥	gēge	older brother
弟弟	dìdi	younger brother
姐姐	jiějie	older sister
妹妹	mèimei	younger sister
医生	yīshēng	doctor
律师	lǜshī	lawyer
中国	Zhōngguó	China
美国	Měiguó	United States
日本	Rìběn	Japan

Pronouns

| 它 | tā | it |

Verbs

来	lái	come
去	qù	go
喜欢	xǐhuan	like

Adjectives

| 累 | lèi | tired |
| 忙 | máng | busy |

LANGUAGE POINTS

1. 你好 (nǐ hǎo)

你好 (nǐ hǎo) is the most common form of greeting in Chinese. It can be used at any time during the day and on any occasion. 你好 (nǐ hǎo), equivalent to *Hello* or *Hi* in English, does not require any specific answer except 你好 (nǐ hǎo) in return.

2. 是 (shì)

Although Chinese has a verb *to be* in the form of 是 (shì), it is not used the same way as verb *to be* in English. In most cases, 是 (shì) is only used when the subject and predicative have the same referent or refer to the same person or object such as:

| 我　是　老师。 | I am a teacher. |
| Wǒ　shì　lǎoshī. | |

| 他　是　学生。 | He is a student. |
| Tā shì　xuésheng. | |

When the predicative is an adjective or a prepositional phrase, 是 (shì) is not used at all in Chinese. Adjectives and prepositional phrases thus used are conditions, locations or descriptions of the subject. For example, sentences such as *I am happy*, *the book is on the table*, *she is there* and *they are home* would be rendered into Chinese without 是 (shì). It is evident that a Chinese sentence can consist of a subject and an adjective or prepositional phrase only. In such a case, adjectives function as quasi-verbs.

3. 你好吗 (nǐ hǎo ma)?

你好吗 (nǐ hǎo ma) is used when you really want to know how things are with the other person. The expression literally means *are you good* and requires either an affirmative or negative answer. Responses to this greeting usually include 我很好 (wǒ hěn hǎo), 我不

错 (wǒ bú cuò), and 马马虎虎 (mǎmahūhu). While 我很好 (wǒ hěn hǎo) is probably the most frequently heard, keep in mind that 很 (hěn) in the expression is indispensable, as adjectives tend not to stand alone when used as predicatives. Native speakers usually do not respond by saying 我好 (wǒ hǎo).

4. The pronunciation of 不 (bu)

The dictionary form of 不 is the fourth tone (bù), but it becomes the second tone when followed by a fourth-tone word. Compare:

不来 bù lái	not come	不去 bú qù	not go
不好 bù hǎo	not good	不认识 bú rènshi	not know

5. Yes/no questions

Yes/no questions are questions that require either a yes answer or a no answer. As such, they are also called polar questions. Yes/no questions are formed in English by either reversing the subject and the verb in the case of verb *to be* or one of those modal verbs like *can* and *may*, or by using a dummy word such as *do* before the subject in the case of a regular verb. In Chinese, however, we do not switch around sentence constituents to form a yes/no question. Such a question is indicated rather by adding the sentence final particle 吗 (ma) to an affirmative sentence. For example:

你 好 吗? Nǐ hǎo ma?	How are you (are you good)?
你 爸爸 忙 吗? Nǐ bàba máng ma?	Is your father busy?
你 妈妈 来 吗? Nǐ māma lái ma?	Is your mother coming?

It may come as a surprise that in Chinese there is no single equivalent to *yes* or *no* in English. In other words, there is not a single specific word that we can use all the time to respond to various yes/no questions. Equivalents to *yes* and *no* are actually the verbs or predicative adjectives in the questions. For this reason, they vary from sentence to sentence. To give positive and negative answers to the following questions in English:

1. Do you speak Chinese?
2. Do you like Japanese food?
3. Are you a doctor?
4. Can you cook?

All you need to do is to answer by using the verb or the verb-like adjective in the question. Positive and negative answers to the above questions would be:

1. Speak / not speak.
2. Like / not like.
3. Am / am not.
4. Can / can not.

Now, let's look at some real Chinese yes/no questions and answers:

你 来 吗?   Are you coming?
Nǐ lái ma?
 来。   Yes, I am.
 Lái.
 不 来。   No, I am not.
 Bù lái.

你 是 老师 吗?   Are you a teacher?
Nǐ shì lǎoshī ma?
 是。   Yes, I am.
 Shì.
 不 是。   No, I am not.
 Bú shì.

你 爸爸 忙   吗?   Is your father busy?
Nǐ bàba máng ma?
　　很 忙。   Yes, he is.
　　Hěn máng.
　　不 忙。   No, he is not.
　　Bù máng.

You may have already noticed that in answering a yes/no question in Chinese, you can practically drop everything in the sentence including the subject except the verb or the verb-like adjective.

6. 呢 (ne)

As a sentence final particle, 呢 (ne) is used to avoid repeating a question previously asked. It basically means *what about ...?* or *how about ...?* For example:

你哥哥 是 学生   吗?   Is your older brother a student?
Nǐ gēge shì xuésheng ma?
　　是。   Yes, he is.
　　Shì.

你姐姐 呢?   What about your older sister?
Nǐ jiějie ne?
　　不是。   No, she is not.
　　Bú shì.

Without using this short-hand device, you would have to repeat the whole question. In this instance, you would have to say "你姐姐是学生吗" (nǐ jiějie shì xuésheng ma)?

7. 怎么样 (zěnmeyàng)

怎么样 (zěnmeyàng) is a colloquial expression of greeting, meaning *how is it going* or *how are things*. It is used between people who know each other very well. It requires the same answers as 你好吗 (nǐ hǎo ma).

8. Sibling terms

There are a number of principles people in different cultures adhere to in addressing their siblings and relatives. These principles include linearity (direct line of descent or collateral extension), collaterality (father's side or mother's side), generation, sex and seniority. Distinctions made in one culture are very often not made in another culture. Kinship terms often provide clues to how relatives are perceived and treated in various cultures. Cultures that make more distinctions have more terms for their kin than those that make fewer distinctions. Since Chinese is one of those languages that recognize all the above distinctions, it is to be expected that the system of kinship terminology in the language is very complicated. There are two major differences between English and Chinese in this regard. First, the English system does not distinguish relatives on the father's side and relatives on the mother's side, while the Chinese system does. Second, English does not recognize seniority among siblings, while the distinction is important in Chinese. Thus older brothers and younger brothers are called by different terms and so are older sisters and younger sisters. There is no way in Chinese to ask, "Do you have a brother/sister?" You must specify whether he or she is an older one or a younger one.

9. Address forms

先生 (xiānsheng, *Mr.*), 太太 (tàitài, *Mrs.*) and 小姐 (xiǎojiě, *Miss*) had been used in China as polite forms of address prior to 1949 when they were replaced by 同志 (tóngzhì, *Comrade*), which was considered revolutionary. However, with the opening of the country to the outside world that began in the late 70s, 先生 (xiānsheng), 太太 (tàitai) and 小姐 (xiǎojiě) have staged a comeback and re-emerged as the popular address forms. Keep in mind when using these forms of address with the family names, the rule is: the name precedes the title, instead of following it as in English. Examples are 王先生 (Wáng Xiānsheng, *Mr. Wang*) and 李小姐 (Lǐ Xiǎojiě, *Miss Li*). 太太 (tàitai) is not used very often to address people simply because it is difficult to determine if the addressee is married or not and even if the addressee is married, she may still prefer to be addressed as 小姐 (xiǎojiě). Another reason that 太太 (tàitai) is not often used as an address form is that women in contemporary China do not take their husbands' family name after their marriage. To use 太太 (tàitai) after a woman's own name is therefore not appropriate.

10. 也 (yě)

English uses two different adverbs, *too* and *either*, to indicate that one situation also applies to another. *Too* is used in the affirmative sentence, while *either* is used in the negative sentence. Chinese, however, uses only one word 也 (yě) in both affirmative sentences and negative sentences. This is very similar to *also* in English. As an adverb, 也 (yě) is always placed before the verb or the quasi-verb (adjective).

11. Punctuation marks

They are for the most part the same as those in English except that the period is in the form of a small circle "。" instead of a dot, and the ellipsis consists of six dots (......) instead of three. An extra mark in Chinese is "、", which is variously translated as the enumerative comma, half-comma, listing comma and series comma. It is used after items in an enumeration.

EXERCISES

I. Respond to the following:

1. 你好！
   Nǐ hǎo!   _____

2. 你好 吗?
   Nǐ hǎo ma?   _____

3. 你怎么样?
   Nǐ zěnmeyàng?   _____

4. 你爸爸 好 吗?
   Nǐ bàba hǎo ma?   _____

5. 你妈妈 呢?
   Nǐ māma ne?   _____

6. 你是 学生   吗?
   Nǐ shì xuésheng ma?   _____

7. 你爸爸是老师 吗?
   Nǐ bàba shì lǎoshī ma?   _____

8. 你妈妈 是 医生   吗?
   Nǐ māma shì yīshēng ma?   _____

9. 认识 你, 我很 高兴。
   Rènshi nǐ, wǒ hěn gāoxìng.   _____

10. 你认识 我 妈妈 吗?
    Nǐ rènshi wǒ māma ma?   _____

II. Translate the following dialogs into Chinese:

1.
A: Hi, Mr. Zhao!   _____
B: Hi, Miss Huang!   _____
A: Are you busy?   _____
B: I'm not. How about you?   _____
A: I am very busy.   _____

2.
A: Is your father going to China?   _____
B: Yes, he is.   _____
A: What about your mother?   _____
B: She is going, too.   _____

3.
A: Is your older brother a teacher?   _____
B: Yes, he is.   _____
A: Is your younger sister also a   _____
   teacher?
B: No, she is not. She is a student.   _____

4.
A: This is Mr. Hua. This is   _____
   Miss Wang.   _____
B: It's a pleasure to know you.   _____
C: It's a pleasure to know you, too.   _____

III. Translate the following into Chinese:

1. Are you tired?

   _____

2. Mr. Hu is not a doctor. He is a lawyer.

   _____

3. My father is very busy, but my mother is not (you do not need
   to translate "but" in Chinese).

   _____

4. I don't know her.

   _____

5. His younger brother is very happy.

   _____

6. This is my father.

_____

7. My mother is not going to China. She is going to Japan.

_____

8. Mr. Li is a lawyer. Mrs. Li is also a lawyer.

_____

9. Her father and mother are coming to the United States.

_____

10. Does your older brother like my younger sister?

_____

IV. Change the following into yes/no questions and then give both affirmative and negative answers:

1. 我 妹妹 来 美国。
   Wǒ mèimei lái Měiguó.

_____

_____

2. 沈 小姐 是 老师。
   Shěn Xiǎojiě shì lǎoshī.

_____

_____

3. 他认识 我 爸爸。
   Tā rènshi wǒ bàba.

_____

_____

4. 我 妈妈 也是 医生。
Wǒ māma yě shì yīshēng.

_____

_____

5. 他 哥哥很 喜欢 中国。
Tā gēge hěn xǐhuan Zhōngguó.

_____

_____

6. 他 是 王　先生。
Tā shì Wáng Xiānsheng.

_____

_____

7. 张　小姐 很 高兴。
Zhāng Xiǎojiě hěn gāoxìng.

_____

_____

8. 她姐姐是学生。
Tā jiějie shì xuésheng.

_____

_____

9. 我 爸爸妈妈 很 忙。
Wǒ bàba māma hěn máng.

_____

_____

10. 你很 累。
Nǐ hěn lěi.

_____

_____

V. Recognize and practice writing the following characters:

yě   也 ㇄ 也 也
也 也 也 也

xiǎo   小 小 小 小
小 小 小 小

bù   不 不 不 不 不
不 不 不 不

tā   他 他 他 他 他 他
他 他 他 他

xiān   先 先 先 先 先 先 先
先 先 先 先

ma   吗 吗 吗 吗 吗 吗
吗 吗 吗 吗

tā   她 她 她 她 她 她 她
她 她 她 她

hǎo   好 好 好 好 好 好 好
好 好 好 好

mā   妈 妈 妈 妈 妈 妈 妈
妈 妈 妈 妈

nǐ   你 你 你 你 你 你 你 你
你 你 你 你

CULTURAL INSIGHTS

Over a century ago, the renowned anthropologist Bronislaw Malinowski coined the term "phatic communion" in his article "The Problem of Meaning in Primitive Languages" to refer to the non-referential use of language to establish social bonds or rapport rather than sharing information, a language act familiarly known as small talk. A typical example in English is the expression of "how are you", which is often automatically uttered in a social encounter. Although it is not necessarily an insincere greeting, the speaker more often than not uses it as a salutation without expectation of a detailed response. It is often observed that one speaker greets the other with "how are you" and receives "how are you" in return and then walks on. Other examples of phatic communion in English include telling someone to have a good day and making a clichéd comment about the weather.

Phatic communion takes different forms in different cultures and it is an area that can give rise to misunderstanding and misinterpretation by people new to the culture. In China, people very often do not greet each other with 你好 (nǐ hǎo) or 你好吗 (nǐ hǎo ma). Rather they will say "where are you going," "have you eaten," or "you should put on more clothes as the weather is cold." Such greetings of the personal nature sound very warm to the Chinese, showing care and concern, but foreigners may feel perplexed or even offended.

Asking about the obvious is another case of phatic communion in Chinese culture. For example, when someone arrives in the office to work, he or she is often greeted by his or her colleague with "you have come." When the wife sees her husband return from work, she often greets him by saying "you have returned."

The Chinese are not known for readily accepting compliments. When receiving compliments, the usual response is often denial, self-deprecation or saying that the opposite of the compliment is true. If you praise someone being good at cooking, they will respond by saying something didn't turn out right. If you comment on someone speaking good English, they tend to say far from being enough. This propensity extends to accepting gifts and invitation. When receiving gifts and invitations to meals, it is not unusal for the Chinese to decline or refuse. This doesn't mean that they don't want the gifts or they don't want to accept the invitations, but they can only accept them after much protest as prescribed by their culture.

Until relatively recently, there had been no equivalent in Chinese for the word "privacy." The word that is currently used as the equivalent, *yinsi*, actually has a pejorative connotation, as it implies that you have something to hide. Taboo questions in the West, such as a person's age, income, marital status, and cost for items purchased, are often asked in everyday conversation, even at the first meeting. The Chinese interpret these questions as an indication of concern and friendliness. However, there are topics considered innocent in the West that are treated as taboo, such as divorce and adoption. Although the divorce rate is on the rise in China, it is still considered humiliating by many. As for adoption, most parents won't tell their adopted children that they are not their biological parents if the children were adopted as infants.

Visit:
www.kwintessential.co.uk/resources/global-etiquette/china-country-profile.html
for information about Chinese customs and etiquette.

LESSON 2
NAMES

SENTENCE PATTERNS

您 贵 姓?
Nín guì xìng?

What is your family name?

我 姓 王。
Wǒ xìng Wáng.

My family name is Wang.

你姓 什么?
Nǐ xìng shénme?

What is your family name?

你叫 什么 名字?
Nǐ jiào shénme míngzi?

What is your name?

我 叫 马丁。
Wǒ jiào Mǎdīng.

My name is Martin.

你有 中国 朋友 吗?
Nǐ yǒu Zhōngguó péngyou ma?

Do you have Chinese friends?

没 有。
Méi yǒu.

No, I don't.

CONVERSATIONS

A: 您 贵 姓?
　　Nín guì xìng?

What is your family name?

B: 我 姓 王。 你呢?
　　Wǒ xìng Wáng. Nǐ ne?

My family name is Wang.
　And yours?

A: 我 姓 张。
　　Wǒ xìng Zhāng.

My family name is Zhang.

A: 你姓 什么?
　　Nǐ xìng shénme?

What is your family name?

B: 我 姓 李。你呢?
　　Wǒ xìng Lǐ.　Nǐ ne?

My family name is Li. And
yours?

A: 我 姓 黄。
　　Wǒ xìng Huáng.

My family name is Huang.

A: 你叫 什么　名字?
　　Nǐ jiào shénme míngzi?

What is your name?

B: 我 叫 马丁。你呢?
　　Wǒ jiào Mǎdīng. Nǐ ne?

My name is Martin. And
yours?

A: 我 叫 安。
　　Wǒ jiào Ān.

My name is Ann.

B: 认识 你我 很 高兴。
　　Rènshi nǐ wǒ hěn gāoxìng.

It's a pleasure to know you.

A: 认识 你我 也很 高兴。
　　Rènshi nǐ wǒ yě hěn gāoxìng.

It's a pleasure to know you,
too.

A: 你有 中国　　朋友　吗?　　　Do you have Chinese friends?
　　Nǐ yǒu Zhōngguó péngyou ma?

B: 没 有。你有 美国　　　　　No, do you have American
　　Méi yǒu.　Nǐ yǒu Měiguó　　　friends?
　　朋友　吗?
　　péngyou ma?

A: 我 有。　　　　　　　　　　Yes, I do.
　　Wǒ yǒu.

B: 他叫 什么　名字?　　　　　What is his name?
　　Tā jiào shénme míngzi?

A: 他叫 安迪。　　　　　　　　His name is Andy.
　　Tā jiào Āndí.

A: 你知道 她的 名字 吗?　　　Do you know her name?
　　Nǐ zhīdao tāde　míngzi ma?

B: 不 知道。你呢?　　　　　　No, I don't. And you?
　　Bù zhīdao.　Nǐ ne?

A: 我 也不知道。　　　　　　　I don't, either.
　　Wǒ yě bù zhīdao.

A: 你是 学生　　吗?　　　　　Are you a student?
　　Nǐ shì xuésheng ma?

B: 不是, 我 是 工人。　　　　No, I'm a worker.
　　Bú shì, wǒ shì gōngrén.

A: 你们的 公司 叫 什么　　　What is the name of your
　　Nǐmende gōngsī jiào shénme　　company?
　　名字?
　　míngzi?

B: 我们的　公司 叫 海尔。　　Our company is called Haier.
　　Wǒmende gōngsī jiào Hǎi'ěr.

A: **谢谢**。   Thank you.
  Xièxie.

B: **不客气**。   You are welcome.
  Bú kèqi.

A: **再见**。   Good-bye.
  Zàijiàn.

B: **再见**。   Good-bye.
  Zàijiàn.

WORDS AND EXPRESSIONS

Nouns

姓	xìng	family name
名字	míngzi	name
朋友	péngyou	friend
工人	gōngrén	factory worker
公司	gōngsī	company

Verbs

叫	jiào	call
有	yǒu	have
谢谢	xièxie	thank (you)
再见	zàijiàn	good-bye
客气	kèqi	be polite, be formal
知道	zhīdao	know

Pronouns

您	nín	you (*polite form*)

Adjectives

贵	guì	distinguished, expensive

Adverbs

没	méi	not

Interrogatives

什么	shénme	what

Particles

| 们 | men | *plural suffix* |
| 的 | de | *possessive marker* |

Conjunctions

| 但是 | dànshì | but |

SUPPLEMENTARY WORDS AND EXPRESSIONS

Nouns

银行	yínháng	bank
学校	xuéxiào	school
餐馆	cānguǎn	restaurant
人	rén	person, people
男朋友	nánpéngyou	boyfriend
女朋友	nǚpéngyou	girlfriend
同事	tóngshì	colleague
老板	lǎobǎn	boss
市长	shìzhǎng	mayor
校长	xiàozhǎng	principal, president (of a school)
经理	jīnglǐ	manager
儿子	érzi	son
女儿	nǚ'ér	daughter
问题	wèntí	question
中文	Zhōngwén	Chinese language
书	shū	book
面条	miàntiáo	noodles

Verbs

看	kàn	read
吃	chī	eat

Adverbs

都	dōu	both, all

LANGUAGE POINTS

1. 您 (nín)

您 (nín) is a polite form of 你 (nǐ), similar to *vous* in French and *usted* in Spanish. It is used primarily in the northern part of China by a younger person to an older person or between strangers irrespective of age. If the use of 您 (nín) turns out to be too complicated resulting from the consideration of age, rank and status of the person spoken to, you may just stick to 你 (nǐ) on all occasions. People won't get offended being addressed 你 (nǐ) instead of 您 (nín) by foreigners. Although you may not want to use 您 (nín) to address people, you yourself may hear people address you as 您 (nín).

2. 您贵姓 (nín guì xìng), 你姓什么 (nǐ xìng shénme) and 你叫什么名字 (nǐ jiào shénme míngzi)

您贵姓 (nín guì xìng) is a formula question about someone's family name. It is usually the first question asked when people inquire about each other's names. In this polite and formal expression, 贵 (guì) is an honorific, meaning *honorable* or *respectable*. The whole question literally means *what is your respectable family name?* Sometimes, the subject 您 (nín) can be left out. Refer to the *Cultural Insights* at the end of this lesson for more information on this subject.

你姓什么 (nǐ xìng shénme), literally meaning *you are last-named what*, is an informal question about someone's family name, where 姓 (xìng) is a verb. This expression is used between people who don't want to stand on ceremony or by an adult to a child.

In 你叫什么名字 (nǐ jiào shénme míngzi), the exact meaning of 名字 (míngzi) depends on the context or the listener's interpretation or preference. 名字 (míngzi) can be the full name or the given name alone, similar to *name* in *what's your name* in English. This question form is most useful because it can be used not only to ask people's names, but also to ask the names of places and things. It is advisable therefore for foreign students to stick to this expression whenever they want to ask people's names.

3. Wh-question forms

The term *wh-question* is borrowed from English grammar to refer to those questions that require specific, rather than yes/no answers. Wh-questions include *who, whose, what, which, when, where, why* and *how*. Contrary to English where these interrogative words are placed at the beginning of the questions, Chinese keeps them where they belong grammatically and logically in the sentence, thus *what is this* in English would be *this is what* in Chinese, and *what do you like to eat* in English would be *you like to eat what* in Chinese. The status of the sentence as a question is indicated not by placing the question word at the beginning of the sentence, but simply by the presence of this interrogative word. This syntactic feature actually makes it easier for nonnative speakers of Chinese. When asked a wh-question, you just need to address the question word, while keeping everything else intact. There is no need to move sentence constituents around:

你看 <u>什么</u>? Nǐ kàn shénme?	What are you reading?
我 看 书。 Wǒ kàn shū.	I'm reading a book.
你喜欢 吃 <u>什么</u>? Nǐ xǐhuan chī shénme?	What do you like to eat?
我 喜欢 吃 面条。 Wǒ xǐhuan chī miàntiáo.	I like to eat noodles.

4. 有 (yǒu)

In many languages, the verb *to have* is peculiar in some way. There is usually a separate chapter in English grammar books on *to have*, because conventional rules do not apply. This is also true of 有 (yǒu) in Chinese, although to a much lesser extent. In Chinese 有 (yǒu) is not negated by 不 (bù), but rather by 没 (méi), which is only used with 有 (yǒu). In other words, 不 (bù) is used with all the verbs and adjectives except one. The one exception is 有 (yǒu). Compare:

我 没 有 女朋友。　　　I don't have a girlfriend.
Wǒ méi yǒu nǚpéngyou.

她不是 我的 女朋友。　　She is not my girlfriend.
Tā bú shì wǒde nǚpéngyou.

5. 知道 (zhīdao) and 认识 (rènshí)

知道 (zhīdao) and 认识 (rènshí), which both appear in this lesson, are both translated as *to know* in English, but they are used quite differently in Chinese. Generally 知道 (zhīdao) is followed by things, while 认识 (rènshí) is followed by people. Examples are:

我 不认识他。　　　　I don't know him.
Wǒ bú rènshi tā.

我 不知道 他的名字。　I don't know his name.
Wǒ bù zhīdao tāde míngzi.

Sometimes however, 知道 (zhīdao) can be followed by people and 认识 (rènshí) can be followed by things. When this happens, 知道 (zhīdao) means *to know of* or *be aware of*, and 认识 (rènshí) means *to recognize, to be acquainted with* or *to acquire the knowledge through learning*, for example:

我 知道 他, 但是 我　　I know of him, but I don't
Wǒ zhīdao tā, dànshì wǒ　know him.
不认识 他。
bú rènshi tā.

他不认识 路。 Tā bú rènshi lù.	He does not know the way.
你认识 这个字吗? Nǐ rènshi zhè ge zì ma?	Do you know this character?

6. 谢谢 (xièxie)

谢谢 (xièxie) is not used as much or as excessively in Chinese as *thank you* in English. It is unimaginable to a Chinese that husband and wife, and parents and children say 谢谢 (xièxie) to each other. To the Chinese, to say thank you between husband and wife, between parents and children and between close friends is to treat them as strangers. The use of 谢谢 (xièxie) is often taken as being polite and formal. Thus the response to 谢谢 (xièxie) in Chinese is usually 不客气 (bú kèqi) or 不谢 (bú xiè). 不客气 (bú kèqi) means *don't stand on ceremony*, or *don't be polite* and 不谢 (bú xiè) is simply *do not have to say thank you* or *don't mention it*.

7. 们 (men)

们 (men) is a suffix used after personal pronouns and human nouns to form plurals. For example: 我们 (wǒmen, *we*), 你们 (nǐmen, *you*), 他们 (tāmen, *they*), 老师们 (lǎoshīmen, *teachers*), and 学生们 (xuéshengmen, *students*). In keeping with the single-signal feature of Chinese (refer to the introductorary chapter on the features of Chinese language), 们 (men) cannot be used when there is a number preceding the noun or when the subject is already plural such as:

三个 老师 sān ge lǎoshī	*not*	三个 老师们 sān ge lǎoshīmen
他们 是 学生。 Tāmen shì xuésheng.	*not*	他们 是 学生们。 Tāmen shì xuéshengmen.

8. 的 (de)

So far you might have been under the impression that the personal pronouns also double as possessive pronouns in Chinese, as seen in 我爸爸 (wǒ bàba, *my father*), 你妈妈 (nǐ māma, *your mother*) and 她姐姐 (tā jiějie, *her older sister*), but it is not the case. Chinese does have possessive pronouns formed by personal pronouns with the possessive marker 的 (de). For example:

我的 (wǒde, *my*)   **你的** (nǐde, *your*)
他的 (tāde, *his*)   **她的** (tāde, *her*)
我们的 (wǒmende, *our*)   **你们的** (nǐmende, *your*)
他们的 (tāmende, *their*)

It is interesting to note that when talking about family members, we generally drop 的 (de), as in 我爸爸 (wǒ bàba, *my father*) and 你妈妈 (nǐ māma, *your mother*). By dropping 的 (de), we make the family relationship even closer syntactically. This is an illustration of isomorphism between language and real life. It is not grammatically wrong nevertheless to include 的 (de) with family members, but the use of 的 (de) would imply a contrast or strong sense of possession. Thus, if you want to sound possessive (the pun is intended), you could say 她是我的太太 (tā shì wǒde tàitai, *she is MY wife*), which implies a contrast: *she is not YOUR wife*.

With relationships outside of the family, 的 (de) is optional, depending on the closeness of the relationship. 的 (de) is used when the relationship is distant or aloof and is dropped when the relationship is close.

When what is possessed is a place, 的 (de) is optional, but its presence or absence has an implied meaning. The absence of 的 (de) implies that the subject is either a member of, or is identified with, the place, whereas the presence of 的 (de) simply indicates a possessive relationship. For example, 这是我们中文系 (zhè shì wǒmen Zhōngwénxì) not only means that *this is our Chinese Department*, it also suggests that the speaker is a member of the department. 这是我们的中文系 (zhè shì wǒmende Zhōngwénxì) does not have the suggestion that the previous sentence does. The sentence could be said by anyone at the university to a visitor. This also explains why we never use 的 (de) when we say 我家 (wǒ jiā, *my home*) or 你家 (nǐ jiā, *your home*) unless we want to emphasize the possessive relationship or show contrast.

With objects, the use of 的 (de) is usually obligatory, such as 我的 书 (wǒde shū, *my book*), 他们的汽车 (tāmende qìchē, *their car*).

Apart from being used with personal pronouns to form possessive pronouns, 的 (de) is also used as a possessive similar to apostrophe *s* in English. While English has two possessive forms: apostrophe *s* and the *of* genitive, Chinese has only one form. 的 (de) is used after both animate nouns and inanimate nouns to show possessive relationships. For example:

学校 的老师 xuéxiào de lǎoshī	school's teacher(s)
老师 的书 lǎoshī de shū	teacher(s)'s book(s)
公司 的名字 gōngsī de míngzi	name of the company

EXERCISES

I. Answer the following questions:

1. 你姓 什么?
   Nǐ xìng shénme?

   _____

2. 你叫 什么 名字?
   Nǐ jiào shénme míngzi?

   _____

3. 你们的 中文 老师 叫 什么 名字?
   Nǐmende Zhōngwén lǎoshī jiào shénme míngzi?

   _____

4. 你认识 你们 中文 老师 的太太吗?
   Nǐ rènshi nǐmen Zhōngwén lǎoshī de tàitai ma?
   她叫 什么 名字?
   Tā jiào shénme míngzi?

   _____

5. 你的学校 / 公司 叫 什么 名字?
   Nǐde xuéxiào / gōngsī jiào shénme míngzi?

   _____

6. 你有 姐姐吗? 她叫 什么 名字?
   Nǐ yǒu jiějie ma? Tā jiào shénme míngzi?

   _____

7. 你有 中国　　朋友　吗?
   Nǐ yǒu Zhōngguó péngyou ma?
   他/她/他们 叫 什么　名字?
   Tā / tā / tāmen jiào shénme míngzi?

_____

8. 你的 中文　　书 叫 什么　名字?
   Nǐde　Zhōngwén shū jiào shénme míngzi?

_____

9. 你的 中文　　老师 忙　　吗?
   Nǐde　Zhōngwén lǎoshī máng ma?

_____

10. 你的 银行　叫 什么　名字?
    Nǐde　yínháng jiào shénme míngzi?

_____

II. Translate the following conversations into Chinese:

1. Do you know his girlfriend's name?

_____

   No. I don't.

_____

2. Do you know my Chinese teacher?

_____

   Yes, I do.

_____

3. Is your family name Wang?

_____

   No. My family name is Zhang.

_____

4. Do you know him?

I heard of him, but I don't know him.

5. Are you Mr. Zhao's wife?

Yes, I am.

It's a pleasure to know you.

It's a pleasure to know you, too.

III. Translate the following sentences into Chinese:

1. What is this?

2. She is my older brother's girlfriend.

3. I know of her, but I don't know her.

4. My wife's name is Lily.

5. His daughter doesn't have any Chinese friends.

IV. Change the following into negative sentences:

1. 她有 男朋友。
   Tā yǒu nánpéngyou.

   _____

2. 我 叫 大卫。
   Wǒ jiào Dàwèi.

   _____

3. 我们的 中文   老师 姓 王。
   Wǒmende Zhōngwén lǎoshī xìng Wáng.

   _____

4. 我 妈妈 很 高兴。
   Wǒ māma hěn gāoxìng.

   _____

5. 她有 儿子。
   Tā yǒu érzi.

   _____

6. 他太太有 哥哥。
   Tā tàitai yǒu gēge.

   _____

7. 我 认识她先生。
   Wǒ rènshí tā xiānsheng.

   _____

8. 他们 有 美国 朋友。
   Tāmen yǒu Měiguó péngyou.

   _____

9. 我 爸爸很 忙。
Wǒ bàba hěn máng.

_____

10. 我们 去中国。
Wǒmen qù Zhōngguó.

_____

V. Translate the following into English:

1. 我 有 哥哥, 也有 姐姐。哥哥叫 小华, 姐姐
Wǒ yǒu gēge, yě yǒu jiějie.   Gēge jiào Xiǎohuá, jiějie
叫 小红。
jiào Xiǎohóng.

_____

2. 我 认识 你妈妈 很 高兴。
Wǒ rènshi nǐ māma hěn gāoxìng.

_____

3. 她的 男朋友 不是 马丁, 是 大卫。
Tāde nánpéngyou bú shì Mǎdīng, shì Dàwèi.

_____

4. 你的中国 朋友 叫 什么 名字?
Nǐde Zhōngguó péngyou jiào shénme míngzi?

_____

5. 我 爸爸妈妈 都 姓 黄。
Wǒ bàba māma dōu xìng Huáng.

_____

VI. Recognize and practice writing the following characters:

rén　人人人

| 人 | 人 | 人 | 人 | | | | | | |

me　么么么么

| 么 | 么 | 么 | 么 | | | | | | |

gōng　工工工工

| 工 | 工 | 工 | 工 | | | | | | |

shén　什什什什什

| 什 | 什 | 什 | 什 | | | | | | |

men　们们们们们们

| 们 | 们 | 们 | 们 | | | | | | |

jiào　叫叫叫叫叫

| 叫 | 叫 | 叫 | 叫 | | | | | | |

míng　名名名名名名名

| 名 | 名 | 名 | 名 | | | | | | |

zì　字字字字字字字

| 字 | 字 | 字 | 字 | | | | | | |

yǒu　有有有有有有

| 有 | 有 | 有 | 有 | | | | | | |

méi　没没没没没没没没

| 没 | 没 | 没 | 没 | | | | | | |

CULTURAL INSIGHTS

Like English names, Chinese names also consist of two parts—a given name and a family name. In Chinese however, the family name precedes, instead of following, the given name. Traditionally, the given name consists of two characters, one of which is the generation name and the other one is what may be called the distinguishing given name. The generation name is shared by all the siblings in the family and all the people in the lineage who belong to the same generation. For example, in a Kong family with four children named Kong Ling Qi, Kong Ling Hua, Kong Ling Fei and Kong Ling Tao, Kong is the family name, Ling is the generation name that identifies where the siblings belong on the genealogical ladder and Qi, Hua, Fei and Tao are that part of the given name that distinguishes the siblings one from another. In addition, all the cousins on the father's side will have Ling as part of their given name. In other words, their names will also begin with "Kong Ling". In contemporary China and particularly in the urban area, more and more parents are breaking away from the tradition by leaving out the generation name. It has almost become a trendy thing for parents to give their children a one-character given name. If you recall the syllabic structure and limited possibility of sound combinations in Chinese discussed in the chapter on Chinese phonetics, it is not difficult to imagine that there are numerous namesakes in China. The United Press International (UPI) recently reported that a survey conducted by the Chinese Character Reform Committee revealed the severity of the problems: 4,800 people named 梁淑珍 (Liáng Shūzhēn) shared the exact same characters in the city of Shenyang alone. If there are so many namesakes with a two-character given name, the situation with a one-character given name is even worse. Now the Chinese government is calling on parents to give a two-character given name to their children to cut down the number of namesakes. When choosing a two-character given name, parents, particularly those in the urban area again, are no longer bound by the generation names that their ancestors or lineage elders prescribed for their children. They are free to pick any name to their liking.

Unlike people in the West, Chinese people are not very comfortable calling each other by their first or given names. First names are reserved only for family members and a selected number of close friends. Professional colleagues are seldom "on the first-name basis," even though they may be very close. Intimacy between them is not indicated by the use of the first name, but by other means. One of these means is to prefix the word 老 (lǎo, *old*) or 小 (xiǎo, *young*) to the family name such as 老王 (Lǎo Wáng) and 小马 (Xiǎo Mǎ). 老 (lǎo) is generally used for middle-aged or old people, while 小 (xiǎo) is used for young people. Since Chinese people are not used to addressing people other than their family members or very close friends by their given names, they are usually content with knowing the family names of the people they meet for the first time. Very often they do not even bother to ask their given name after they asked "您贵姓" (nín guì xìng) or "你姓什么" (nǐ xìng shénme). What's the use of knowing somebody's first name if you are never going to use it?

Want to have a Chinese name? Ask your Chinese teacher or Chinese friends to give you one. If they can't help, go to:
www.mandarintools.com/chinesename.html
where you enter your name in English in addition to your gender, birthdate and preference as to what you want your Chinese name to suggest and a name will be automatically generated for you.

LESSON 3
PLACES

SENTENCE PATTERNS

请问,……?
Qǐngwèn, ...?

May I please ask, …?

中国　银行　在 哪儿?
Zhōngguó yínháng zài nǎr?

Where is Bank of China?

你在 哪儿工作?
Nǐ zài nǎr　gōngzuò?

Where do you work?

你妈妈 在家 吗?
Nǐ māma zài jiā ma?

Is your mother home?

中国城　　有 中国
Zhōngguóchéng yǒu Zhōngguó
餐馆。
cānguǎn.

There are Chinese restaurants
in Chinatown.

哪儿 有 厕所?
Nǎr　yǒu cèsuǒ?

Where can I find a restroom?

这儿 有 中国　餐馆 吗?
Zhèr yǒu Zhōngguó cānguǎn ma?

Is there a Chinese restaurant
here?

你去哪儿?
Nǐ qù nǎr?

Where are you going?

CONVERSATIONS

A: 请问，你工作 吗?   May I please ask, do you work?
   Qǐngwèn, nǐ gōngzuò ma?

B: 工作。   Yes, I do.
   Gōngzuò.

A: 你的单位 在 哪儿?   Where is your workplace?
   Nǐde dānwèi zài nǎr?

B: 我的 单位 在 北京。   My workplace is in Beijing.
   Wǒde dānwèi zài Běijīng.

A: 你妈妈 在家吗?   Is mother home?
   Nǐ māma zài jiā ma?

B: 不在。   No, she is not.
   Bú zài.

A: 她在 哪儿?   Where is she?
   Tā zài nǎr?

B: 她在 公司。   She is at her company.
   Tā zài gōngsī.

A: 请问，中国   银行   Excuse me, where is Bank of
   Qǐngwèn, Zhōngguó yínháng   China?
   在哪儿?
   zài nǎr?

B: 中国   银行 在   Bank of China is in Chinatown.
   Zhōngguó yínháng zài
   中国城。
   Zhōngguóchéng.

A: 中国城   远 吗?   Is Chinatown far?
   Zhōngguóchéng yuǎn ma?

B: 不太 远。   Not too far.
   Bú tài yuǎn.

A: 请问，你在哪儿工作?　　　Excuse me, where do you
　　Qǐngwèn, nǐ zài nǎr　gōngzuò?　work?

B: 我 在 公司 工作。　　　　I work for a company.
　　Wǒ zài gōngsī gōngzuò.

A: 你在 什么 公司 工作?　　What company do you work
　　Nǐ zài shénme gōngsī gōngzuò?　for?

B: 我 在 电话 公司 工作。　I work for a telephone company.
　　Wǒ zài diànhuà gōngsī gōngzuò.

A: 请问，你在 哪儿 住?　　Excuse me, where do you live?
　　Qǐngwèn, nǐ zài nǎr　zhù?

B: 我 在 曼哈顿 住。　　　I live in Manhattan.
　　Wǒ zài Mànhādùn zhù.

A: 曼哈顿 在 哪儿?　　　　Where is Manhattan?
　　Mànhādùn zài nǎr?

B: 曼哈顿 在 纽约。　　　　It is in New York.
　　Mànhādùn zài Niǔyuē.

A: 你学 中文 吗?　　　　　Do you study Chinese?
　　Nǐ xué Zhōngwén ma?

B: 学。　　　　　　　　　　Yes, I do.
　　Xué.

A: 你在 哪儿 学 中文?　　Where do you study Chinese?
　　Nǐ zài nǎr　xué Zhōngwén?

B: 我 在 纽约 大学 学　　I study Chinese at New York
　　Wǒ zài Niǔyuē dàxué xué　University.
　　中文。
　　Zhōngwén.

A: 你的中文 老师 是　　　Is your Chinese teacher
　　Nǐde Zhōngwén lǎoshī shì　Chinese?
　　中国人 吗?
　　Zhōngguórén ma?

B: 是。　　　　　　　　　　　Yes.
　　Shì.

A: 他叫 什么　名字?　　　　　What is his name?
　　Tā jiào shénme míngzi?

B: 他叫 李华。　　　　　　　His name is Li Hua.
　　Tā jiào Lǐ Huá.

A: 请问，　这儿 有 厕所 吗?　Excuse me, is there a restroom
　　Qǐngwèn, zhèr　　yǒu cèsuǒ ma?　here?

B: 有，在那儿。　　　　　　　Yes, it's over there.
　　Yǒu, zài nàr.

A: 谢谢。　　　　　　　　　　Thank you.
　　Xièxie.

B: 不客气。　　　　　　　　You are welcome.
　　Bú kèqi.

A: 请问，　这儿 有 中国　　　Excuse me, is there a Chinese
　　Qǐngwèn, zhèr　　yǒu Zhōngguó　restaurant here?
　　餐馆 吗?
　　cānguǎn ma?

B: 没 有。　　　　　　　　　No, there is not.
　　Méi yǒu.

A: 哪儿 有 中国　　餐馆?　　Where can I find a Chinese
　　Nǎr　yǒu Zhōngguó cānguǎn?　restaurant?

B: 中国城　　　有 中国　　　There are Chinese restaurants
　　Zhōngguóchéng yǒu Zhōngguó　in Chinatown.
　　餐馆。
　　cānguǎn.

A: 中国城　　　有 日本　　　Are there Japanese restaurants
　　Zhōngguóchéng yǒu Rìběn　in Chinatown?
　　餐馆 吗?
　　cānguǎn ma?

B: 没 有。　　　　　　　　　No, there are not.
　　Méi yǒu.

WORDS AND EXPRESSIONS

Nouns

单位	dānwèi	workplace
家	jiā	home, family
电话	diànhuà	telephone
大学	dàxué	university
人	rén	person, people
厕所	cèsuǒ	restroom
城	chéng	town, city
曼哈顿	Mànhādùn	Manhattan
纽约	Niǔyuē	New York

Pronouns

| 这儿 | zhèr | this place |
| 那儿 | nàr | that place |

Verbs

工作	gōngzuò	work
住	zhù	live
学	xué	study

Adjectives

| 远 | yuǎn | far |

Prepositions

| 在 | zài | in, at |

Adverbs

| 太 | tài | too |

Interrogatives

哪儿	nǎr	what place

Expressions

请问	qǐngwèn	May I ask ...

SUPPLEMENTARY WORDS AND EXPRESSIONS

商店	shāngdiàn	store
电影院	diànyǐngyuàn	movie theater
医院	yīyuàn	hospital
邮局	yóujú	post office
公园	gōngyuán	park
图书馆	túshūguǎn	library
办公室	bàngōngshì	office
公安局	gōngānjú	police station
博物馆	bówùguǎn	museum
教堂	jiàotáng	church
汽车站	qìchēzhàn	bus stop
火车站	huǒchēzhàn	train station
飞机场	fēijīchǎng	airport
饭店	fàndiàn	hotel

北京	Běijīng	Beijing
上海	Shànghǎi	Shanghai
南京	Nánjīng	Nanjing
旧金山	Jiùjīnshān	San Francisco
洛杉矶	Luòshānjī	Los Angeles
加州	Jiāzhōu	California

LANGUAGE POINTS

1. 请问 (qǐngwèn)

请问 (qǐngwèn) is a polite attention-getter. It literally means *may I please ask*. However, confusion may arise due to its frequent translation into *excuse me* in English. To translate the expression into *excuse me* is fine in this context, but to apply it to situations where you caused somebody inconvenience, such as stepping on his toes, is totally inappropriate. In other words, 请问 (qǐngwèn) is only equivalent to one of the meanings of *excuse me* in English. It is generally used when you would like to ask somebody his or her name, directions, or a question.

2. 中国银行在哪儿 (Zhōngguó yínháng zài nǎr)

The pattern used to ask where something or some place is "_____ 在哪儿 (zài nǎr)?" In this pattern, 在 (zài) is a preposition, meaning *in* or *at*, and 哪儿 (nǎr) means *what place*. 中国银行在哪儿 (Zhōngguó yínháng zài nǎr) literally means "Bank of China is in what place". It would be wrong to add 是 (shì) in the sentence: 中国银行是在哪儿 (Zhōngguó yínháng shì zài nǎr), although you may be tempted to do so as an English speaker. If you recall, we only use 是 (shì) for the most part when the words at either side of it are both nouns and have the same referent.

Note also that the noun placed at the beginning of the pattern is specific and definite. This is the most important way in Chinese to indicate specificity and definiteness:

书 在哪儿?   Where is the book?
Shū zài nǎr?

餐馆   在哪儿?   Where is the restaurant?
Cānguǎn zài nǎr?

厕所 在 哪儿?   Where is the restroom?
Cèsuǒ zài nǎr?

书 (shū, *book*), 餐馆 (cānguǎn, *restaurant*) and 厕所 (cèsuǒ, *restroom*) refer to a specific book, restaurant and restroom instead of unspecified, general or indefinite ones.

3. 你在哪儿工作 (nǐ zài nǎr gōngzuò)

This sentence consists of three parts: subject 你 (nǐ, *you*), adverbial phrase 在哪儿 (zài nǎr, *where*) and verb 工作 (gōngzuò, *work*). The only difference between English and Chinese in this sentence is that the adverbial of place precedes the verb in Chinese instead of following it as in English.

4. 中国城有中国银行 (Zhōngguóchéng yǒu Zhōngguó yínháng)

This is a so-called existential sentence similar to the "there is/are" structure in English. The pattern for existential sentences in Chinese is Adverbial of Place + 有 (yǒu, *there is/are*) + Subject. Again the adverbial of place precedes, instead of follows, the verb 有 (yǒu). *There is a Bank of China in Chinatown* is thus expressed in Chinese as 中国城有中国银行 (Zhōngguóchéng yǒu Zhōngguó yínháng). Please note that whenever 在 (zài) appears at the beginning of an existential sentence, it is usually dropped. The result of the deletion in the following sentences is:

(在) 这儿有 日本餐馆。
(zài)   Zhèr yǒu Rìběn cānguǎn.
There is a Japanese restaurant here.

(在) 那儿 有 女厕所。
(zài) Nàr   yǒu nǚcèsuǒ.
There is a ladies' room there.

(在)学校　　有 学生。
(zài) Xuéxiào yǒu xuésheng.
There are students in the school.

If we compare this pattern with the pattern in 银行在哪儿 (yínháng
zài nǎr), we'll find that the noun phrase in the former is not specified
or definite, whereas the noun phrase in the latter is definite and specified, as discussed earlier on. This word order feature conforms to
the tendency of human languages to place definite or specified items
at or towards the beginning of the sentence, and indefinite or unspecified items at or towards the end of the sentence. Indefinite or
unspecified items at the beginning of a sentence would appear
abrupt, bearing no cohesive tie with the previous discourse and leaving little room for the listener to make necessary connections and
respond. The awkwardness immediately disappears as soon as we
push the indefinite item towards the end of the sentence by adding
there is before it. The following are perfect English existential
sentences:

> There is a book on the desk.
> Compare: A book is on the desk.
>
> There are many universities in Beijing.
> Compare: Many universities are in Beijing.

This principle is even more strictly adhered to in Chinese because
it does not have the flexibility of an article system to indicate
definteness except by word order whereby a definite item is placed
first in the sentence, and an indefinite item is placed later in the
sentence.

5. 哪儿有中国银行 (nǎr yǒu Zhōngguó yínháng)

If you have read the last point, it won't be difficult to understand the
question "哪儿有中国银行" (nǎr yǒu Zhōngguó yínháng). The pattern explained in #2 above is used when we need to know where
something or some place is, whereas the pattern illustrated in this

question is used when we want to get confirmation whether there is something or some place in some particular place. Sometimes, however, we simply want to know where (i.e. in any place) we can find a certain object or place. In this case, we are actually questioning the first part of the pattern: location + 有 (yǒu) + object. Since we are questioning a location, the interrogative word that we use is naturally 哪儿 (nǎr). Thus we have 哪儿有中国银行 (nǎr yǒu Zhōngguó yínháng). To respond to the question, all we need to do is to supply the answer where the interrogative word is in the question such as 中国城有中国银行 (Zhōngguóchéng yǒu Zhōngguó yínháng).

Again, keep in mind that 在 (zài), which would otherwise precede 哪儿 (nǎr), is dropped because it would appear at the beginning of an existential sentence.

EXERCISES

I. Answer the following questions:

1. 你在 哪儿 住?
   Nǐ zài nǎr   zhù?

   _____

2. 你工作   吗? 你在 哪儿工作?
   Nǐ gōngzuò ma? Nǐ zài nǎr   gōngzuò?

   _____

3. 你的单位 叫 什么   名字?
   Nǐde dānwèi jiào shénme míngzi?

   _____

4. 你的单位   远   吗?
   Nǐde dānwèi yuǎn ma?

   _____

5. 你 在 哪儿学 中文?
   Nǐ zài nǎr   xué Zhōngwén?

   _____

6. 纽约   有 中国城   吗?
   Niǔyuē yǒu Zhōngguóchéng ma?

   _____

7. 哪儿有 日本城?
   Nǎr   yǒu Rìběnchéng?

   _____

8. 曼哈顿　在　哪儿?
   Mànhādùn　zài　nǎr?

_____

9. 你　妈妈　在　医院　工作　　吗?
   Nǐ　māma　zài　yīyuàn gōngzuò　ma?

_____

10. 你的学校　有　中国　　老师　吗?
   Nǐde　xuéxiào yǒu Zhōngguó lǎoshī ma?

_____

II. Fill in the blanks with appropriate words:

1. 你家 _____ 哪儿?
   Nǐ jiā _____ nǎr?

2. _____ 有　医院?
   _____ yǒu yīyuàn?

3. 这儿 _____中文　　学校　吗?
   Zhèr _____ Zhōngwén xuéxiào ma?

4. 你在 _____学　中文?
   Nǐ zài _____xué Zhōngwén?

5. 那儿 _____ 有　日本餐馆。
   Nàr _____ yǒu Rìběn cānguǎn.

6. 女厕所 _____ 那儿。
   Nǚcèsuǒ _____ nàr.

7. 我的 男朋友   在 上海 _____。
   Wǒde nánpéngyou zài Shànghǎi _____.

8. _____ 在 哪儿?
   _____ zài nǎr?

9. 哪儿 _____ 银行?
   Nǎr _____ yínháng?

10. 你去 _____?
    Nǐ qù _____?

III. Translate the following into Chinese:

1. Excuse me, where is the men's room?

   _____

2. Excuse me, is there an American town in Beijing?

   _____

3. My wife works in a school.

   _____

4. His girlfriend studies at Nanjing University.

   _____

5. There is no Chinese restaurant here.

   _____

6. My mother is not a doctor. She is a teacher.

   _____

7. Our Chinese teacher lives in San Francisco.

   _____

8. My mother is not home.

_____

9. Are your parents going to the restaurant?

_____

10. The hospital is not there.

_____

IV. Translate the following into English:

1. 北京　没 有 美国　银行。
   Běijīng méi yǒu Měiguó yínháng.

_____

2. 我 在学校　工作。我 太太也在 学校　工作。
   Wǒ zài xuéxiào gōngzuò. Wǒ tàitai yě zài xuéxiào gōngzuò.

_____

3. 纽约　没 有 日本城。 洛杉矶　有。
   Niǔyuē méi yǒu Rìběnchéng. Luòshānjī yǒu.

_____

4. 请问 ，　火车站　 在哪儿?
   Qǐngwèn, huǒchēzhàn zài nǎr?

_____

5. 请问 ， 哪儿 有 商店?
   Qǐngwèn, nǎr yǒu shāngdiàn?

_____

6. 你们的 学校　 叫 什么　 名字?
   Nǐmende xuéxiào jiào shénme míngzi?

_____

7. 纽约　的中国城　　　有　日本　餐馆　　吗?
Niǔyuē de Zhōngguóchéng yǒu Rìběn cānguǎn ma?

---

8. 我　不知道　厕所　在哪儿，他知道。
Wǒ bù zhīdao cèsuǒ zài nǎr,　　tā zhīdao.

---

9. 你去哪儿? 我　去飞机场。
Nǐ qù nǎr?　　Wǒ qù fēijīchǎng.

---

10. 我　爸爸妈妈　在加州　　住。
Wǒ bàba māma zài Jiāzhōu zhù.

V. Recognize and practice writing the following characters:

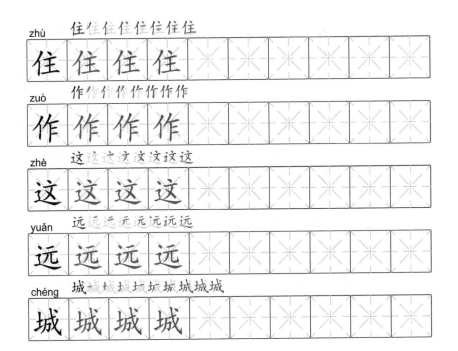

zhù 住住住住住住住住

住 住 住 住

zuò 作作作作作作作

作 作 作 作

zhè 这这这这这这这这

这 这 这 这

yuǎn 远远远远远远远远

远 远 远 远

chéng 城城城城城城城城城

城 城 城 城

CULTURAL INSIGHTS

It won't take observant travelers to China very long to find the attention given by the Chinese to 单位 *danwei* (workplace). The Chinese are obsessed with *danwei* for a simple reason. It is an inescapable part of their life. To be exact, *danwei* holds the reins of their life. As a basic organizational unit in the urban sector, *danwei* is not only the place where people report to work, but also the focal point in their domestic and social life. Many of the functions that are deemed social, individual, domestic, and governmental in other societies are assumed by *danwei*.

In many cases, *danwei* provides housing for its employees, often on its premises. Unless you are very wealthy and can afford to buy a private apartment that has become available in recent years, you are at the mercy of your *danwei*. Many young people have to shelve their plans for marriage simply because they have not been provided with an apartment due to their lack of seniority. Since *danwei* is the ultimate owner of the residential units, it collects rents and utility payments from its employees, often by deducting them from the employees' salary.

Danwei is the primary enforcer of the government's public policies. Take for example the family planning program, particularly the single-birth policy. *Danwei* gives rewards to those who comply and metes out punishment to those who don't. *Danwei* very often makes sure that newlyweds time their childbearing schedule so that it won't exceed the quota allocated them for the number of births in a given period. It is also the responsibility of *danwei* to distribute and monitor the use of contraceptive devices.

Danwei is also bound up with just about any other aspect of employees' domestic life. It runs nurseries, daycare centers, and even schools. *Danwei* has to give its stamp of approval before one registers with the government for a marriage certificate. When there is a domestic dispute, *danwei* often serves as the mediator or arbitrator. More importantly, *danwei* is the one that pays your medical bills, partially or fully depending on the nature of its ownership.

Deregulation and privatization over the last 30 years have created a polarity of wealth in the population. Many people, especially those who are in a "nonprofit" *danwei*, such as schools and government departments, are increasingly feeling uneasy, as their friends and relatives in other "profit" *danwei*s or the private sector are getting rich. These non-profit *danwei*s have been under tremendous pressure to improve the life of their employees by putting more money into their pockets in the form of bonuses on a regular basis. The additional money is usually generated by operating some sideline businesses. It is commonplace nowadays to see schools running stores and government services running shops.

It is evident that *danwei* is a self-contained or even self-sufficient community in the true sense of the word. As such, it has become an effective means of social control by the state to limit the mobility and maintain social stability in the urban sector. You depend on your *danwei* not just for a living; you depend on your *danwei* when you need to get married, when you are ready to have a child, when you are sick, and when you need to receive government benefits.

"Chinatowns" are found throughout the world and are usually major tourist attractions within the cities in which they are located. To see a list of the Chinatowns around the world and their descriptions, please visit:

www.chinatownology.com/
chinatowns_of_the_world.html

LESSON 4
FAMILY

SENTENCE PATTERNS

你家有 几口人?
Nǐ jiā yǒu jǐkǒu rén?

How many people are there in your family?

他们 是 谁?
Tāmen shì shéi?

Who are they?

你爸爸做 什么 工作?
Nǐ bàba zuò shénme gōngzuò?

What work does your father do?

你有 几本中文 书?
Nǐ yǒu jǐběn Zhōngwén shū?

How many Chinese books do you have?

她有 多少 学生?
Tā yǒu duōshao xuésheng?

How many students does she have?

他在 哪个学校 工作?
Tā zài nǎge xuéxiào gōngzuò?

Which school does he work in?

你女儿是 不是 大学生?
Nǐ nǚ'ér shì bu shì dàxuéshēng?

Is your daughter a college student?

你有 没 有 孩子?
Nǐ yǒu méi yǒu háizi?

Do you have any children?

CONVERSATIONS

A: 你家有 几口人?
Nǐ jiā yǒu jǐkǒu rén?

How many people are there in your family?

B: 我 家有 五口 人。
Wǒ jiā yǒu wǔkǒu rén.

There are five people in my family.

A: 他们 是 谁?
Tāmen shì shéi?

Who are they?

B: 他们 是我 爸爸, 我
Tāmen shì wǒ bàba, wǒ
妈妈, 我 姐姐, 我
māma, wǒ jiějie, wǒ
弟弟和我。
dìdi hé wǒ.

They are my father, my mother, my older sister, my younger brother, and myself.

A: 你家有 几口人?
Nǐ jiā yǒu jǐkǒu rén?

How many people are there in your family?

B: 我 家有 四口人。
Wǒ jiā yǒu sìkǒu rén.

There are four people in my family.

A: 他们 是谁?
A: Tāmen shì shéi?

Who are they?

B: 他们 是我 太太, 我
Tāmen shì wǒ tàitai, wǒ
女儿, 我儿子和我。
nǚ'ér, wǒ érzi hé wǒ.

They are my wife, my daughter, my son and myself.

A: 你女儿是不 是
Nǐ nǚ'ér shì bu shì
大学生?
dàxuésheng?

Is your daughter a college student?

B: 不是。她是中学生。
Bú shì. Tā shì zhōngxuésheng.

No, she is not. She is a middle school student.

A: 你儿子呢?   What about your son?
   Nǐ érzi ne?

B: 他 是 小学生。   He is an elementary school
   Tā shì xiǎoxuésheng.   student.

A: 你有 没 有 孩子?   Do you have any children?
   Nǐ yǒu méi yǒu háizi?

B: 有。   Yes, I do.
   Yǒu.

A: 你有 几个孩子?   How many children do you
   Nǐ yǒu jǐ ge háizi?   have?

B: 我 有 两 个孩子。   I have two, one boy and one
   Wǒ yǒu liǎng ge háizi.   girl.
   一个男孩，一个女孩。
   Yí ge nánhái, yí ge nǚhái.

A: 你儿子多 大?   How old is your son?
   Nǐ érzi duō dà?

B: 我 儿子七岁。   My son is seven years old.
   Wǒ érzi qī suì.

A: 你女儿几岁?   How old is your daughter?
   Nǐ nǚ'ér jǐ suì?

B: 她 五 岁。   She is five.
   Tā wǔ suì.

A: 你太太在 哪儿工作?   Where does your wife work?
   Nǐ tàitai zài nǎr gōngzuò?

B: 她在 学校 工作。   She works in a school.
   Tā zài xuéxiào gōngzuò.

A: 她做 什么 工作?   What work does she do?
   Tā zuò shénme gōngzuò?

B: 她是 老师。   She is a teacher.
   Tā shì lǎoshī.

A: 她忙 不 忙?　　　　　　Is she busy?
Tā máng bu máng?

B: 她很 忙。　　　　　　　Yes, she is.
Tā hěn máng.

A: 她有 多少 学生?　　　How many students does she
Tā yǒu duōshao xuésheng?　　have?

B: 她有 五十 个学生。　She has fifty students.
Tā yǒu wǔshí ge xuésheng.

A: 你有 哥哥吗?　　　　Do you have older brothers?
Nǐ yǒu gēge ma?

B: 有。　　　　　　　　　Yes, I do.
Yǒu.

A: 你有 几个哥哥?　　How many older brothers do
Nǐ yǒu jǐ ge gēge?　　　you have?

B: 我 有 一个哥哥。　I have one older brother.
Wǒ yǒu yí ge gēge.

A: 你哥哥工作 吗?　　Does your older brother work?
Nǐ gēge gōngzuò ma?

B: 他不 工作，他是学生。　He does not work. He is a
Tā bù gōngzuò,tā shì xuésheng.　student.

A: 他在 哪个学校 学习?　Which school does he study in?
Tā zài nǎ ge xuéxiào xuéxí?

B: 他在 纽约 大学 学习。　He studies at New York
Tā zài Niǔyuē dàxué xuéxí.　　University.

A: 他学 什么?　　　　　What does he study?
Tā xué shénme?

B: 他学 历史。　　　　　He studies history.
Tā xué lìshǐ.

A: 他喜欢 历史吗?　　Does he like history?
Tā xǐhuan lìshǐ ma?

B: 很 喜欢。　　　　　Very much.
Hěn xǐhuan.

WORDS AND EXPRESSIONS

Nouns

历史	lìshǐ	history
男孩	nánhái	boy
女孩	nǚhái	girl
大学生	dàxuésheng	university/college student
中学生	zhōngxuésheng	secondary school student
小学生	xiǎoxuésheng	elementary school student

Verbs

做	zuò	do
学习	xuéxí	study

Interrogatives

几	jǐ	*question word about numbers*
多少	duōshao	*question word about numbers*
谁	shéi/shuí	who
哪	nǎ	which
多	duō	how

Numerals

零	líng	zero
一	yī	one
二	èr	two
三	sān	three
四	sì	four
五	wǔ	five
六	liù	six
七	qī	seven

八	bā	eight
九	jiǔ	nine
十	shí	ten

Conjunctions

和	hé	and

Classifiers

个	ge
本	běn
口	kǒu

SUPPLEMENTARY WORDS AND EXPRESSIONS

Nouns

爷爷	yéye	paternal grandfather
奶奶	nǎinai	paternal grandmother
外公	wàigōng	maternal grandfather
外婆	wàipó	maternal grandmother

Numerals

百	bǎi	hundred
千	qiān	thousand
万	wàn	ten thousand

LANGUAGE POINTS

1. How to read numbers in Chinese

Numbers from 0 to 10 are given in *Words and Expressions*. To read the numbers beyond 10, just insert the place name after each number such as # + place name + # + place number + # + place name, etc. The place names for tens, hundreds and thousands are: 十 (shí), 百 (bǎi), and 千 (qiān). Please note that there is an important difference between English and Chinese in expressing 10,000. English doesn't have a place name for it, using a composite number instead. Chinese, on the other hand, does have a place for 10,000 called 万 (wàn). Thus, a number like 12,345 should be read as 一万二千三百四十五 (yī wàn èr qiān sān bǎi sìshí wǔ).

When zero appears in a number, the place name is not read since it does not have a value. For example 103, 4,056, and 70,809 should be read 一百零三 (yī bǎi líng sān), 四千零五十六 (sì qiān líng wǔshí liù), and 七万零八百零九 (qī wàn líng bā bǎi líng jiǔ).

Numbers in Chinese beyond 10,000 are very different from English. Please refer to the Cultural Insight section of Lesson 7 for more information.

2. Classifiers

Mention was made in the introductory chapter on Chinese that whenever we use a number in Chinese to quantify a noun such as a person, 20 books and 300 cars, we must use a classifier between the number and the noun, somewhat similar to *a piece of paper*, *two heads of lettuce* and *three cups of coffee* in English. This similarity, however, is very limited in that these "classifiers" are only used occasionally in English, but are always present in Chinese whenever a number and a noun come together. Another major difference between the two languages is that if the "classifiers" are used in English, they are actually measure words, but for the most part in Chinese, they do not indicate any measure. They serve a special function in the language by classifying particular nouns into semantic groups. For this reason, they should be called "classifiers" rather than "measure words" as in many textbooks. Please note that it is not true that for every noun in Chinese there is a specific classifier. A particular classifier is often shared by a number of nouns having the same underlying semantic feature. The most commonly used classifiers in Chinese amount to probably less than twenty. When you reach the end of this book, you may only come across seven or eight of them at the most. It may be a good exercise to ask a native speaker to give you a classifier and a number of nouns that use the classifier to see if you can find the underlying semantic feature. You may be surprised to find that most native speakers do not know the answers unless they are linguistically trained simply because they have been brought up speaking the language, not questioning about the language. Although classifiers seem to impose an extra burden on your memory, they do add precision to the language and reveal how certain things are perceived by native speakers. Two examples would suffice. The following nouns use the classifier 本 (běn): book, dictionary, photo album, magazine, and atlas. What is it that they have in common? They are all bound, printed, or book-like materials. The following words use the classifier 件 (jiàn): shirt, blouse (in fact there is only one word in Chinese for both shirt and blouse), sweater, blazer, jacket and coat. If you think that the classifier is used for clothing, you are very close, but not exactly right, because it is not used for pants, skirt and shorts. With this clue, you may finally come to the conclusion that 件 (jiàn) is used for clothing that you wear on the upper part of your body.

What happens if you do not use a classifier between a number and a noun? In most cases, native speakers simply do not understand you. This is because they are linguistically programmed to expect to hear something (a classifier) in that syntactic slot. What happens if you did use a classifier but it was a wrong one? In most cases, native speakers would understand you, but they would laugh, sometimes hysterically. This is because classifiers group nouns together according to certain underlying semantic features. As such they are usually associated with certain images. Some classifiers are used for animals, others indicate appearances and shapes. If you use the wrong classifier, you will conjure up wrong images that will make people laugh. In fact, the deliberate misuse of classifiers is a great source of humor in Chinese. Children make mistakes using classifiers all the time. What do you do if you want the native speakers to understand, but you don't want them to laugh when you use a wrong classifier? Fortunately, there is a way. Whenever you are stuck with any classifier, use 个 (ge) instead. This is because 个 (ge) is the most frequently used classifier in Chinese. It is used for people and most objects. Chances are the classifier that you are stuck for is 个 (ge) anyway. Second, the word 个 (ge), literally meaning "piece" or "entity," is not associated with any particular image. When there is no image association, people have no reason to laugh. In addition, native spekers often use 个 (ge) for nouns that should be used with some other specific classifiers. Please also note that 个 (ge) is usually pronounced in the neutral tone when used as a classifer, although its entry in the dictionary bears the fourth tone.

3. 你家有几口人 (nǐ jiā yǒu jǐ kǒu rén)

In most cases, the classifier 个 (ge) is used for people (e.g. older brother, teacher, student, doctor, and lawyer) when they are preceded by a number such as three people, four teachers, and two hundred students. However when we talk about the number of people in the family, we always use the classifier 口 (kǒu) instead. For example: 我家有五口人 (wǒ jiā yǒu wǔ kǒu rén). The word 口 (kǒu) means *mouth* in literary Chinese. When used for the number of people in the family, it actually implies that there are a certain number of mouths to feed in the family.

4. The pronunciation of number one

Number one is pronounced in the first tone (yī) when used as a pure number as in telephone numbers, ID numbers, zip codes, etc. When used in conjunction with a classifier and consequently a noun to indicate its quantity, it is pronounced in the second tone (yí) when followed by a fourth-tone word, and in the fourth tone (yì) when followed by a first, second, third or neutral tone. Compare: 一个哥

哥 (yí ge gēge, *an older brother*) and 一本书 (yì běn shū, *a book*). 一 is pronounced in the second tone in 一个哥哥 (yí ge gēge, *an older brother*) because 个 (ge) bears the fourth tone as a dictionary entry (refer to #2 above).

5. The pronunciation of number two

Number two can be pronounced in two ways in Chinese and each is written differently: 二 (èr) and 两 (liǎng). Generally, *two* is pronounced as *èr* when it is used as a meaningless number such as in a telephone number, zip code, social security number, or ID number. *Two* is meaningless in that it does not stand for a quantitative value, but rather a differentiating sign. Thus, a zip code with a higher number is not better than or superior to one with a lower number. *Two* is pronounced *liǎng* when it is meaningful. This happens when *two* is used to indicate a quantitative value of a noun, such as *two students* and *two books*. Please note that when we use a number with a noun, we must use a classifier. *Two students* and *two books* in Chinese are actually 两个学生 (liǎng ge xuésheng) and 两本书 (liǎng běn shū). In other words, *two* is always pronounced *liǎng* whenever a classifier is used after it.

6. 几 (jǐ) and 多少 (duōshao)

To ask questions about numbers, Chinese uses 几 (jǐ) and 多少 (duōshao). Although these two expressions are often translated into *how many* or *how much* in English, they are also used to ask questions about things that involve numbers such as telephone numbers, social security numbers, zip codes and so on. These are usually asked in English using *what*: what is your telephone number, zip code and so on. 几 (jǐ) and 多少 (duōshao) differ from each other in the following important ways:

First of all, there is some kind of assumption or expectation on the part of the questioner in using 几 (jǐ) that the answer will be a small number, usually not exceeding ten, or the answer is a number from a range of given choices. Such assumptions or expectations are not suggested by 多少 (duōshao), which is open or neutral. 多少 (duōshao) can be used to ask about a large number as well as a small number. So if you assume or expect the answers to the following questions will be small, you can safely ask using 几 (jǐ):

你家 有 几口 人?
Nǐ jiā yǒu jǐ kǒu rén?

How many people are there in your family?

你有 几本 中文 书?
Nǐ yǒu jǐ běn Zhōngwén shū?

How many Chinese books do you have?

中国城 有 几个
Zhōngguóchéng yǒu jǐ ge
日本 餐馆?
Rìběn cānguǎn?

How many Japanese restaurants are there in Chinatown?

However, if the number is large or if you are not sure, it would be better to use 多少 (duōshao) to avoid awkwardness or even offense. It may be all right for someone to ask you 你有几本中文书 (nǐ yǒu jǐ běn Zhōngwén shū, *how many Chinese books do you have*), knowing that you may not have many Chinese books, but it is inappropriate, even insulting, to ask a Chinese professor 你有几本中文书 (nǐ yǒu jǐ běn Zhōngwén shū), because you are suggesting he does not have many Chinese books. For this reason, whenever you know the answer won't be a small number such as students in a school or books in a library, or when you are not sure about the possible answer such as the number of employees in a company, it is better to use 多少 (duōshao) instead of 几 (jǐ).

There is an added advantage of using 多少 (duōshao). That is, when you use 多少 (duōshao) in the question, the classifier, whatever it is, can be left out. This option does not exist for 几 (jǐ). Compare the following:

你们 学校　的图书馆　有 多少　中文　　书?
Nǐmen xuéxiào de túshūguǎn yǒu duōshao Zhōngwén shū?
How many Chinese books does your school's library have?

你有 几本 中文　　书?
Nǐ yǒu jǐ běn Zhōngwén shū?
How many Chinese books do you have?

你们 公司 有 多少　人?
Nǐmen gōngsī yǒu duōshao rén?
How many people does your company have?

你们 公司 有 几个人?
Nǐmen gōngsī yǒu jǐ ge rén?
How many people does your company have?

Keep in mind that the classifier is optional after 多少 (duōshao), but obligatory after 几 (jǐ).

There are occasions, however, when only 几 (jǐ) can be used. This happens when we ask time (since we are only dealing with 12 numbers), days of the week (since we are only dealing with 7, or 6 to be exact, numbers) and the dates (again we are only dealing with a handful of given numbers).

7. 你女儿是不是大学生 (nǐ nǚ'ér shì bu shì dàxuésheng)

Yes/no questions in Chinese can be formed in two ways. In addition to the use of the sentence-final particle *ma*, yes/no questions can also be indicated by repeating the verb/adjective using its negative form. Compare:

你工作　吗?　　　　Do you work?
Nǐ gōngzuò ma?

你工作　不工作?　　Do you work?
Nǐ gōngzuò bu gōngzuò?

你忙　吗?　　　　　　　Are you busy?
Nǐ máng ma?
你忙　不忙?　　　　　　Are you busy?
Nǐ máng bu máng?

他是　中国人　　　吗?　　Is he Chinese?
Tā shì　Zhōngguórén ma?
他是　不是　中国人?　　Is he Chinese?
Tā shì　bu shì　Zhōngguórén?

As compared with *ma*, the affirmative and negative form of the verb/adjective is more favored not only because it is more colloquial and informal, but also because it unequivocally tells the listener up front that "this is a question, be prepared to give an answer." This is particularly so with a long sentence. With 吗 (ma), the listener has to wait until the end to know if the speaker is asking a question or is simply making a statement. By the time the end of the sentence is reached, the listener may already have forgotten what was asked at the beginning. An added advantage of using the affirmative and negative form of the verb/adjective is that the questioner clearly states the wording of the yes/no answer. For example:

你学　不学　中文?　　　Do you study Chinese?
Nǐ xué bu xué Zhōngwén?

The listener just has to answer 学 (xué) or 不学 (bù xué).

Note that 不 (bù) in this type of question is pronounced in the neutral tone. Also please note the following:

A. The negative word for 有 (yǒu) is 没 (méi), not 不 (bù), for example:

你有　没　有　男朋友?　　Do you have a boyfriend?
Nǐ yǒu méi yǒu nánpéngyou?

这儿有 没 有 医院?　　Is there a hospital here?
Zhèr yǒu méi yǒu yīyuàn?

B. When the affirmative and negative form of the verb/adjective is used, 吗 (ma) cannot be used anymore. This is because both of these two forms serve the same function of indicating the question status. To use both forms would be redundant and violate the single-signal principle.

C. The affirmative and negative form of the verb/adjective cannot be used when the verb or the adjective has a modifier. For example, it is not correct to say:

你妈妈 也去不去中国?
Nǐ māma yě qù bu qù Zhōngguó?
Is your mother also going to China?

We can only say:

你妈妈 也去中国　　 吗?
Nǐ māma yě qù Zhōngguó ma?
Is your mother also going to China?

8. 他在哪个学校学习 (tā zài nǎ ge xuéxiào xuéxí)

Besides numbers, a number of other words also require the presence of classifiers when used with nouns. These include the demonstrative pronouns 这 (zhè, *this*), 那 (nà, *that*), the interrogative word 哪 (nǎ, *which*) and the pronoun 每 (měi, *every* or *each*). These words require the use of classifiers because they are ultimately veiled forms of numbers. When we use these words, don't we really mean *this one*, *that one*, *which one* and *each one*? Let's now look at the following examples in which these words are used with classifiers:

这 个 商店　　 叫 什么　 名字?
Zhè ge shāngdiàn jiào shénme míngzi?
What's the name of this store?

我 不认识 那个人。   I don't know that person.
Wǒ bú rènshi nà ge rén.

哪 本 书 是 你的?   Which book is yours?
Nǎ běn shū shì   nǐde?

9. 学习 (xuéxí) and 学 (xué)

学习 (xuéxí) and 学 (xué) both mean *study*. Although they can be used interchangeably from time to time, there are two main differences between them. While 学 (xué) is always a verb, 学习 (xuéxí) can be used both as a verb and as a noun. For example:

他学习中文。   He studies Chinese.
Tā xuéxí Zhōngwén.

他的学习 很 好。   He is very good with his studies.
Tāde xuéxí hěn hǎo.

When both 学习 (xuéxí) and 学 (xué) are used as verbs, 学 (xué) is a transitive verb (one that takes an object) and 学习 (xuéxí) can be used both transitively and intransitively (i.e. taking no object). Compare:

我 哥哥学(习)中文。   My older brother studies Chinese.
Wǒ gēge xué (xí) Zhōngwén.

他在 纽约   大学 学习。 He studies at New York
Tā zài Niǔyuē dàxué xuéxí.   University.

In the second sentence, it is not grammatical to use 学 (xué) for 学习 (xuéxí).

10. 大学 (dàxué), 中学 (zhōngxué) and 小学 (xiǎoxué)

The differentiation of places of learning into universities, secondary schools and elementary schools is indicated in Chinese through the use of such adjectives as 大 (dà, *big*), 中 (zhōng, *middle*) and 小 (xiǎo, *small*) with 学 (xué), which is short for 学校 (xuéxiào, *school*). While 大学 (dàxué) and 小学 (xiǎoxué) are universities and elementary schools, 中学 (zhōngxué) comprises both junior high and high schools. Students in these schools are called 大学生 (dàxuésheng, *college students*), 中学生 (zhōngxuésheng, *middle school students*) and 小学生 (xiǎoxuésheng, *elementary school students*) respectively.

11. Asking age

There is more than one way to ask age depending on the person you ask. Basically, there are the following two ways, as shown in this lesson:

你几岁?
Nǐ jǐ suì?

你多 大?
Nǐ duō dà?

While both mean "how old are you," 你几岁 (nǐ jǐ suì) is used to ask the age of a child or youngster, as 几 (jǐ) suggests a small number; whereas 你多大 (nǐ duō dà) has a neutral reference and can be used for anyone. 多 (duō) in the sentence is used to question measurement and degree.

EXERCISES

I. Answer the following questions:

1. 你家有 几口 人?

   Nǐ jiā yǒu jǐ kǒu rén?

   _____

2. 他们 是 谁?

   Tāmen shì shéi?

   _____

3. 你爸爸工作 吗? 他在 哪儿工作?

   Nǐ bàba gōngzuò ma? Tā zài nǎr gōngzuò?

   _____

4. 你妈妈 工作 吗? 她在 哪儿工作?

   Nǐ māma gōngzuò ma? Tā zài nǎr gōngzuò?

   _____

5. 你是 学生 吗? 你在哪 个学校 学习?

   Nǐ shì xuésheng ma? Nǐ zài nǎ ge xuéxiào xuéxí?

   _____

6. 你在 学校 学 什么?

   Nǐ zài xuéxiào xué shénme?

   _____

7. 你有 哥哥吗? 你有 几个哥哥? 他们 多 大?

   Nǐ yǒu gēge ma? Nǐ yǒu jǐ ge gēge? Tāmen duō dà?

   _____

8. 你有 几本 中文   书?

   Nǐ yǒu jǐ běn Zhōngwén shū?

   _____

9. 你们 学校 有 多少 学生?

   Nǐmen xuéxiào yǒu duōshao xuésheng?

   _____

10. 你们 学校 有 中国 学生 吗? 有 多少

    Nǐmen xuéxiào yǒu Zhōngguó xuésheng ma? Yǒu duōshao

    中国 学生?

    Zhōngguó xuésheng?

   _____

II. Write the following numbers in pinyin:

32	_____
854	_____
3,020	_____
5,600	_____
4,798	_____
98,765	_____
10,304	_____

III. See if you can figure out the underlying semantic features for the following classifiers in Chinese from the nouns given that use these classifiers:

张 (zhāng)   stamp, picture, desk, table, bed, map, paper

条 (tiáo)   river, pants, street, tie, scarf, road, fish, bench

块 (kuài)   soap, cake, watch, brick, candy, loaf of bread

枝 (zhī)   pencil, pen, chopstick, cigarette, flower

只 (zhī)   cat, puppy, chicken, mouse, duck, tiger

IV. Rewrite the following yes/no questions using the affirmative and negative form of the verb/adjective:

1. 你是中国人   吗?
   Nǐ shì Zhōngguórén ma?

   _____

2. 她有 孩子吗?
   Tā yǒu háizi ma?

   _____

3. 你爸爸妈妈去 银行   吗?
   Nǐ bàba māma qù yínháng ma?

   _____

4. 这儿有 厕所吗?
   Zhèr yǒu cèsuǒ ma?

   _____

5. 你姓   王   吗?
   Nǐ xìng Wáng ma?

   _____

6. 他在 家吗?
   Tā zài jiā ma?

   _____

7. 他们 学 中文   吗?
   Tāmen xué Zhōngwén ma?

   _____

8. 你的中文   老师 是中国人   吗?
   Nǐde Zhōngwén lǎoshī shì Zhōngguórén ma?

   _____

9. 这 是你的书 吗?
   Zhè shì nǐde shū ma?

   _____

10. 你姐姐是 大学生   吗?
    Nǐ jiějie shì dàxuésheng ma?

    _____

V. Translate the following into Chinese:

1. There are four people in my family. They are my wife, my son,
   my daughter, and myself.

   _____

2. How many Chinese books does your Chinese teacher have?

   _____

3. How many people are there in Shanghai?

   _____

4. My wife does not work at a company. She is a school teacher.

   _____

5. I don't know that person. Do you know him?

   _____

6. My older sister is not a high school student. She is a college
   student.

   _____

7. What does your older sister study at college?

   _____

8. Which company do you work for?

_____

9. There are 1,500 students in our school.

_____

10. How old is younger sister?

_____

VI. Translate the following into English:

1. 我 在北京　大学学习 美国　历史。
   Wǒ zài Běijīng dàxué xuéxí Měiguó lìshǐ.

_____

2. 他们 学校　有 两　个中国　　老师。
   Tāmen xuéxiào yǒu liǎng ge Zhōngguó lǎoshī.

_____

3. 他们 公司 很 大, 有 一千　个人。
   Tāmen gōngsī hěn dà, yǒu yì qiān ge rén.

_____

4. 你有 几个中国　　朋友?
   Nǐ yǒu jǐ ge Zhōngguó péngyou?

_____

5. 我的 男朋友　　不喜欢　学 历史，他喜欢 学
   Wǒde nánpéngyou bù xǐhuan xué lìshǐ, tā xǐhuan xué
   中文。
   Zhōngwén.

_____

6. 我 妈妈 在 家 工作。
   Wǒ māma zài jiā gōngzuò.

   _____

7. 你知道 上海 有 多少 大学 吗?
   Nǐ zhīdao Shànghǎi yǒu duōshao dàxué ma?

   _____

8. 那个人 的哥哥是 我们的 中文 老师。
   Nà ge rén de gēge shì wǒmende Zhōngwén lǎoshī.

   _____

9. 我 家有 八口 人。你家呢?
   Wǒ jiā yǒu bā kǒu rén. Nǐ jiā ne?

   _____

10. 他是 加州 大学的学生。
    Tā shì Jiāzhōu dàxué de xuésheng.

    _____

VII. Write about yourself and your family. Include such information as the number of people in your family, who they are, what they do, where they work, where they live. If you want to mention their ages, it's fine too. You can substitute English for occupation or place names in Chinese that you don't know.

_____

_____

_____

_____

_____

_____

VIII. Recognize and practice writing the following characters:

CULTURAL INSIGHTS

Family has been the cornerstone of the Chinese society, both in the past and at present. To understand Chinese society, one has to understand the Chinese family. The family and the broader kinship organization play an extraordinarily important part in Chinese life. Family is held so important to the Chinese that it is considered inseparable from the state even in the literal sense of the word. The word for state in Chinese—国家 (guójiā)—is composed of 国 (guó, *state*) and 家 (jiā, *family*). This is not just a linguistic coincidence. In traditional China, the state and the society were basically modeled on the domestic organization in terms of the hierarchical and overarching relationships. The type of the relationship of subordination between the father and the son was also expected between the emperor and his subjects.

Family has always been the center of loyalty for individuals in China. Children are taught from the very beginning to have filial piety towards their parents and respect towards other senior members in the extended family. Such education and socialization prepare them from an early age in such a way that they would become, outside of their family, loyal subjects to the ruler and good citizens in society. Members of a family in traditional China were even responsible for each other's behaviors. Infraction of law by one member would bring punishment to all the other members. Such severity of punishment served as a major deterrent for the occurance of infraction by a member. If the crime warranted the death penalty, a whole family could be exterminated. Faced with such severe consequence, the family would impose strict internal discipline on its members, a move certainly welcomed by the ruler.

Families in China differ from those in the West in an important way. In traditional China, the ultimate goal of an individual is to perpetuate his family, whereas in the West, families exist to support the individuals. For this reason, in China family interests come before the individuals' interest. Where family interests are at stake, individual interests must be suppressed or compromised. This explains the prevalent practice of arranged marriage and child betrothal in traditional China. Since the purpose of marriage was to procreate, not to love, romance and affection became irrelevant and divorces were few and far between.

Family in China functions as a collective security system that provides help to the sick, disabled, and unemployed. It is also a cornerstone of social policy in the country. Only those who have no families to turn to for support can count on assistance from the state. This is unlike many countries in the world, particularly in the West, where the obligation between parents and children is uni-directional. Parents are responsible for bringing up their children, but children are not obligated to support their parents later on. In China, however, the obligation is mutual. Parents are responsible for the upbringing of their children and the children are obligated to take care of their parents in their old age. This is not just a moral issue. It is required by law and is clearly stipulated in the Chinese constitution. It is inconceivable and incomprehensible to the Chinese to see how people in the West, particularly those well-to-do, put their aged parents in nursing homes. To them, it is simply an unforgivable sin.

The Chinese family is very often thought of as being large, consisting of several generations living under the same roof. This is nothing more than pure myth. Chinese families have always been small, containing less than ten people in most cases. Part of the reason for this pervading myth stems from the literary portrayal of prominent families. In traditional China, the large family was the ideal, but few people except those that possessed ample wealth could attain it. Those who could afford to support a large family were usually landlords and wealthy businessmen, gentry and high-ranking officials. Landless peasants could not even afford to marry and start a family, to say nothing of maintaining a large family. In contemporary China, urban families are usually of the nuclear type, consisting of parents and their child only. In rural China, families are often of the stem type, where parents live with their married son.

Marriage in traditional China had always been patrilocal, meaning that daughters leave their parental home upon marriage and sons bring their wives into the family. This is because sons bear the ultimate responsibility of taking care of the aged parents and continuing the family line. For this reason, sons are preferred to daughters. For the same reason, relatives by marriage are not of equal status either. Those on the husband's side enjoy higher status and more privileges than the ones on the wife's side. In the urban area, more and more young people have become economically independent and thus can afford to purchase their own apartments and houses. As a result, young couples are increasingly living on their own instead of residing with their parents.

www.mandarintools.com/family.html
offers a quick lookup of kinship terms in Chinese. Enter a relationship in English and the site will generate the Chinese term automatically, no matter how complex the relationship is.

LESSON 5
TIME

SENTENCE PATTERNS

现在　几　点?
Xiànzài jǐ　diǎn?

What time is it?

对不起。
Duìbuqǐ.

Sorry.

没　关系。
Méi guānxi.

That's all right.

你每　天　几点　上班?
Nǐ měi tiān jǐ diǎn shàngbān?

What time do you go to
　work everyday?

你每　天　什么　　时间　下班?
Nǐ měi tiān shénme　shíjiān xiàbān?

What time do you get off
　work everyday?

我　有时　五　点　下班,
Wǒ yǒushí wǔ　diǎn xiàbān,
有时　五　点　半　下班。
yǒushí wǔ diǎn bàn xiàbān.

Sometimes I get off work at
　5, sometimes at 5:30.

今天　星期　几?
Jīntiān xīngqī jǐ?

What day is today?

你星期　几有　中文　　课?
Nǐ xīngqī jǐ yǒu Zhōngwén kè?

What days of the week do you
　have your Chinese class on?

今天　几号?
Jīntiān jǐ　hào?

What's the date today?

你什么　　时候　去中国
Nǐ shénme shíhou qù Zhōngguó
学习?
xuéxí?

When are you going to study
　in China?

CONVERSATIONS

A: 请问， 现在 几点?   Excuse me, what time is it?
Qǐngwèn, xiànzài jǐ diǎn?

B: 现在 七点 三十 分。   It is 7:30.
Xiànzài qī diǎn sānshí fēn.

A: 谢谢。   Thank you.
Xièxie.

B: 不 客气。   You are welcome.
Bú kèqi.

A: 请问， 现在 几点?   Excuse me, what time is it?
Qǐngwèn, xiànzài jǐ diǎn?

B: 对不起, 我没 有 表,   Sorry, I don't have a watch.
Duìbuqǐ, wǒ méi yǒu biǎo,   I don't know.
我 不 知道。
wǒ bù zhīdao.

A: 没 关系。   That's all right.
Méi guānxi.

A: 你每 天 几点 上班?   What time do you go to work
Nǐ měi tiān jǐ diǎn shàngbān?   everyday?

B: 我 每 天 八点 上班。   I go to work at 8 everyday.
Wǒ měi tiān bā diǎn shàngbān.

A: 你每 天 几点 下班?   What time do you get off
Nǐ měi tiān jǐ diǎn xiàbān?   work everyday?

B: 我 有时 五 点 下班,   I sometimes get off work at 5,
Wǒ yǒushí wǔ diǎn xiàbān,   sometimes at 5:30.
有时 五 点 半 下班。
yǒushí wǔ diǎn bàn xiàbān.

A: 你今天 上午　做 什么?　　　What are you going to do
　Nǐ jīntiān shàngwǔ zuò shénme?　　this morning?

B: 我 今天 上午　在 家　　　I'm going to read at home
　Wǒ jīntiān shàngwǔ zài jiā　　this morning.
　看书。
　kànshū.

A: 下午 呢?　　　　　How about this afternoon?
　Xiàwǔ ne?

B: 下午 我 去学校。　　I'm going to school this
　Xiàwǔ wǒ qù xuéxiào.　　afternoon.

A: 你昨天　晚上　　在　　Were you home last night?
　Nǐ zuótiān wǎnshang zài
　不在 家?
　bu zài jiā?

B: 不在。　　　　No, I was not.
　Bú zài.

A: 你在 哪儿?　　Where were you?
　Nǐ zài nǎr?

B: 我 在 图书馆。　　I was in the library.
　Wǒ zài túshūguǎn.

A: 今天 星期 几?　　What day is today?
　Jīntiān xīngqī jǐ?

B: 今天 星期三。　　Today is Wednesday.
　Jīntiān xīngqīsān.

A: 今天 几号?　　What is the date today?
　Jīntiān jǐ hào?

B: 今天 二十八号。　　Today is the 28th.
　Jīntiān èrshí bā hào.

A: 你的生日　是几月 几号?　　When is your birthday?
　Nǐde shēngri shì jǐ yuè jǐ hào?

B: 我的 生日 是 十二月　　　My birthday is December 4.
Wǒde shēngri shì shí'èr yuè
四号。
sì hào.

A: 你星期 几有 中文　　课?　What days of the week do you
Nǐ xīngqī jǐ yǒu Zhōngwén kè?　　have your Chinese class on?

B: 我 星期一, 三, 五 有　　　I have my Chinese class on
Wǒ xīngqīyī, sān, wǔ yǒu　　　Monday, Wednesday and
中文　　课。　　　　　　　Friday.
Zhōngwén kè.

A: 你什么　时候 去中国　　When are you going to study
Nǐ shénme shíhou qù Zhōngguó　in China?
学习?
xuéxí?

B: 明年。　　　　　　　　　Next year.
Míngnián.

WORDS AND EXPRESSIONS

Nouns

现在	xiànzài	now
点	diǎn	o'clock
分	fēn	minute
半	bàn	half
今天	jīntiān	today
明天	míngtiān	tomorrow
昨天	zuótiān	yesterday
天	tiān	day
时间	shíjiān	time
时候	shíhou	time
星期	xīngqī	week
号	hào	number
月	yuè	month
上午	shàngwǔ	morning
下午	xiàwǔ	afternoon
晚上	wǎnshang	evening
明年	míngnián	next year
生日	shēngri	birthday
课	kè	class, lesson
手表	shǒubiǎo	watch

Verbs

上班	shàngbān	go to work
下班	xiàbān	get off work
看书	kànshū	read

Adjectives

每	měi	every, each

Expressions

有时......	yǒushí	sometimes ... sometimes
有时	yǒushí	
对不起	duìbuqǐ	sorry
没关系	méi guānxì	that's all right

SUPPLEMENTARY WORDS AND EXPRESSIONS

Nouns

早上	zǎoshang	early morning
中午	zhōngwǔ	noon
夜里	yèli	night
早饭	zǎofàn	breakfast
中饭	zhōngfàn	lunch
晚饭	wǎnfàn	dinner
今年	jīnnián	this year
去年	qùnián	last year
周末	zhōumò	weekend

Verbs

起床	qǐchuáng	get up
睡觉	shuìjiào	sleep
开始	kāishǐ	begin
结束	jiéshù	end

Pronouns

那	nà	that

Adverbs

一般	yìbān	generally, usually

Days of Week

星期一	xīngqīyī	Monday
星期二	xīngqī'èr	Tuesday
星期三	xīngqīsān	Wednesday

星期四	xīngqīsì	Thursday
星期五	xīngqīwǔ	Friday
星期六	xīngqīliù	Saturday
星期天	xīngqītiān	Sunday

Months of Year

一月	yīyuè	January
二月	èryuè	February
三月	sānyuè	March
四月	sìyuè	April
五月	wǔyuè	May
六月	liùyuè	June
七月	qīyuè	July
八月	bāyuè	August
九月	jiǔyuè	September
十月	shíyuè	October
十一月	shíyīyuè	November
十二月	shí'èryuè	December

LANGUAGE POINTS

1. 几 (jǐ)

Remember 几 (jǐ) is the interrogative word used to ask questions about numbers. 几 (jǐ) is therefore used to ask about time, days of the week and dates since they are all expressed in numbers.

2. To tell the time

To tell the time, we use 点 (diǎn, *o'clock*) and 分 (fēn, *minute*). For example, the following times should be read as:

7:00	七点 (qī diǎn)
8:15	八点十五（分）(bā diǎn shíwǔ fēn)
9:40	九点四十（分）(jiǔ diǎn sìshí fēn)
10:05	十点零五（分）(shí diǎn líng wǔ fēn)
11:30	十一点三十（分）(shíyī diǎn sānshí fēn)

In all these expressions, 分 (fēn, *minute*) can be left out. Also, 11:30 can also be read as 十一点半 (shíyī diǎn bàn, *half past 11*).

Note also that time expressions can be directly used as an adverbial without having to be preceded by a preposition, for example:

我 每天 七点 起床。   I get up at 7 everyday.
Wǒ měitiān qī diǎn qǐchuáng.

3. 对不起 (duìbuqǐ) and 没关系 (méi guānxì)

对不起 (duìbuqǐ) is the most common expression of apology that can be used on all occasions when an apology is called for. The most common response is 没有关系 (méiyǒu guānxì), where the verb 有 (yǒu) is often left out. 关系 (guānxì) in this expression means *significance*. 没关系 (méi guānxì) therefore means that there is no significance. If there is no significance, it doesn't matter.

4. Word order involving several temporal units

Temporal units in Chinese indicating the time, the day, the week, the month and so on invariably follow each other according to their temporal scope. The general rule is that the unit that commands a larger scope precedes the one that commands a smaller scope. Thus, the proper temporal sequence in Chinese is *year-month-day-part of the day* (such as morning or afternoon) *-time*. This is exactly the reverse of English, where the smaller unit precedes the larger unit with the only exception of the relative positioning of month and day, which is the same as Chinese. In 你每天几点上班? (nǐ měi tiān jǐ diǎn shàngbān, *what time do you go to work everyday?*), 每天 (měi tiān, *everyday*) commands a larger scope than 几点 (jǐ diǎn, *what time*), which is part of 每天 (měi tiān, *everyday*). It is therefore placed before 几点 (jǐ diǎn).

Word order involving several spatial units parallels that with several temporal units, where larger places precede smaller places. To indicate a complete address, Chinese would start with the country followed by province, city, district, street, building number and finally the apartment number. This again is the reverse of the order in English.

5. Word order involving adverbials

One of the cardinal principles that govern word order in Chinese is that the modifier precedes the modified. For example, attributes, be they individual words, phrases, or clauses, always come before nouns, and adverbs always come before adjectives, verbs, and other adverbs. Many of the adverbials that we are going to encounter in this book have to do with time or place. They are usually placed immediately before the verb as in:

你每 天 几点 起床?
Nǐ měi tiān jǐ diǎn qǐchuáng?

What time do you get up everyday?

我 在中国 学 中文。
Wǒ zài Zhōngguó xué Zhōngwén.

I study Chinese in China.

This is one of the major difficulties for beginning students of Chinese in speaking, if not in writing, because adverbials of time and place usually follow, instead of preceding, verbs in English. Try to get used to this usage.

6. Days of the week and names of the months

Days of the week in Chinese are easy to learn, as they are all numbered except Sunday. The week in Chinese begins with Monday rather than Sunday as it does in the U.S. (doesn't the Bible say that Sunday is the seventh day of the week?). Thus we have 星期一 (xīngqīyī, *Monday*), 星期二 (xīngqī'èr, *Tuesday*), 星期三 (xīngqīsān, *Wednesday*), 星期四 (xīngqīsì, *Thursday*), 星期五 (xīngqīwǔ, *Friday*), 星期六 (xīngqīliù, *Saturday*), and 星期天 (xīngqītiān, *Sunday*). The word 星期 (xīngqī) means *week*, so don't mistake the above as week one, two, and so on.

Like days of the week, months in Chinese are also numbered. But unlike those, numbers are placed before, rather than after, the word 月 (yuè, *month*): 一月 (yīyuè, *January*), 二月 (èryuè, *February*), 三月 (sānyuè, *March*), 四月 (sìyuè, *April*), 五月 (wǔyuè, *May*), 六月 (liùyuè, *June*), 七月 (qīyuè, *July*), 八月 (bāyuè, *August*), 九月 (jiǔyuè, *September*) 十月 (shíyuè, *October*), 十一月 (shíyīyuè, *November*), and 十二月 (shí'èryuè, *December*).

7. Asking dates

To ask a particular date in Chinese is literally asking what the month is and what the number of the day in the month is. We are again dealing with numbers. So we need to use the interrogative word 几 (jǐ) as in 今天几月几号? (jīntiān jǐ yuè jǐ hào, *what is the date today?*) In addition, we usually know what month we are in before we ask the question. For this reason, people usually leave out 几月 (jǐ yuè) in the question. However, we must include 几月 (jǐ yuè) when we ask when someone's birthday is, since we have no idea what month his or her birthday is in.

8. 什么时间 (shénme shíjiān) and 什么时候 (shénme shíhou)

什么时间 (shénme shíjiān), like 几点 (jǐdiǎn), is similar to *what time* in English. It is used to ask a specific time. The answer must be a clock time, such as 7 o'clock or 8:30. 什么时候 (shénme shíhou) is similar to *when* in English in that the answer can be a clock time, or a general time such as *tomorrow, next week*, or even *next year*. Thus 什么时候 (shénme shíhou) can often be used in place of 什么时间 (shénme shíjiān), but the reverse is not true when the expected answer is a general time.

EXERCISES

I. Answer the following questions:

1. 现在　几点？
   Xiànzài jǐ diǎn?

   _____

2. 今天　星期　几？
   Jīntiān xīngqī jǐ?

   _____

3. 今天　几号？
   Jīntiān jǐ hào?

   _____

4. 你的生日　是几月　几号？
   Nǐde shēngri shì jǐ yuè jǐ hào?

   _____

5. 你妈妈　的生日　是几月　几号？
   Nǐ māmā de shēngri shì jǐ yuè jǐ hào?

   _____

6. 今天　是　星期天　吗？
   Jīntiān shì xīngqītiān ma?

   _____

7. 你明天　晚上　做　什么？
   Nǐ míngtiān wǎnshang zuò shénme?

   _____

8. 你星期六　下午　在　哪儿？
   Nǐ xīngqīliù xiàwǔ zài nǎr?

   _____

9. 你星期 几有 中文   课?
   Nǐ xīngqī jǐ yǒu Zhōngwén kè?

_____

10. 这 个星期五 是几号?
    Zhè ge xīngqīwǔ shì jǐ hào?

_____

II. Say the following times in Chinese:

7:05   12:30   4:15   9:43   10:59
3:28   6:32   1:30   8:04   11:16

III. Ask questions about the underlined parts in the following sentences:

1. 今天 星期四。
   Jīntiān xīngqīsì.

2. 昨天   四月五号。
   Zuótiān sìyuè wǔ hào.

3. 他明天   来。
   Tā míngtiān lái.

4. 我的 美国   朋友   今年   八月去 北京。
   Wǒde Měiguó péngyou jīnnián bāyuè qù Běijīng.

5. 今天 是 二月二十三号, 星期四。
   Jīntiān shì èryuè èrshí sān hào, xīngqīsì.

IV. Translate the following into Chinese:

1. Where were you last night?

_____

2. Sorry, I don't have a watch. I don't know what time it is now.

_____

3. On what days of the week do you have your Chinese class?

_____

4. What time do you get off work this afternoon?

_____

5. I usually eat dinner at a restaurant Saturday evening.

_____

6. My father gets up at six everyday.

_____

7. I don't eat breakfast.

_____

8. It is not good not to eat breakfast.

_____

9. What are you going to do tomorrow afternoon?

_____

10. When are you going to go to China? June next year.

_____

V. Translate the following into English:

1. 我 早上　　一般不吃 早饭。
Wǒ zǎoshang yībān bù chī zǎofàn.

2. 她中午　　有时 在 公司 吃饭, 有时 在家 吃饭。
Tā zhōngwǔ yǒushí zài gōngsī chīfàn, yǒushí zài jiā chīfàn.

_____

3. 下 星期三 是 我 太太的生日。
   Xià xīngqīsān shì wǒ tàitai de shēngri.

_____

4. 我 明天　　上午　九 点 去银行。
   Wǒ míngtiān shàngwǔ jiǔ diǎn qù yínháng.

_____

5. 你每　 天 几点　 睡觉?
   Nǐ měi tiān jǐ diǎn shuìjiào?

_____

VI. State the birthdays of your family members in complete sentences.

_____
_____
_____
_____

VII. Write your daily schedule such as when you get up, eat breakfast, go to work, have lunch, get off work, go home, have dinner and go to bed. You may also indicate things (e.g. having breakfast) that you don't do.

_____
_____
_____
_____
_____
_____
_____
_____
_____
_____

VIII. Recognize and practice writing the following characters:

shàng 上 上 上 上
上 上 上 上

xià 下 下 下 下
下 下 下 下

jīn 今 今 今 今 今
今 今 今 今

fēn 分 分 分 分 分
分 分 分 分

tiān 天 天 天 天 天
天 天 天 天

rì 日 日 日 日 日
日 日 日 日

yuè 月 月 月 月 月
月 月 月 月

hào 号 号 号 号 号 号
号 号 号 号

míng 明 明 明 明 明 明 明 明 明
明 明 明 明

diǎn 点 点 点 点 点 点 点 点 点
点 点 点 点

CULTURAL INSIGHTS

People of different cultures have different perceptions and categorizations of time. As a result, the way they use time may also be different.

Time is very often expressed in spatial terms. When asked to visualize the movement of time from past to present and then to future, most American students would say time moves horizontally from left to right, with left being the past, the midpoint that meets the eye the present and the right being the future. In Chinese however, time is perceived of as moving vertically from top to bottom, with the top being the past, the midpoint at the level of the eye the present and the bottom being the future. This explains the logic of these Chinese temporal expressions 上午 (shàngwǔ, *morning*), 上个星期 (shàng ge xīngqī, *last week*), and 上个月 (shàng ge yuè, *last month*), where 上 (shàng) means "up," and 下午 (xiàwǔ, *afternoon*), 下个星期 (xià ge xīngqī, *next week*), and 下个月 (xià ge yuè, *next month*), where 下 (xià) means "down."

For the English word "morning," there are two equivalents in Chinese: 早上 (zǎoshang) and 上午 (shàngwǔ). The difference between these two terms is that 早上 (zǎoshang) is the early part of the morning that usually lasts until one goes to work. When people meet each other during this part of the day, they often greet each other by saying 你早 (nǐ zǎo, *Good morning*) or simply 早 (zǎo, *Morning*), which literally means "You are early." 上午 (shàngwǔ) is that part of the day that extends to lunch time. In the West, noon is a point of time such that as soon as the clock strikes 12, it is afternoon. That's why we don't often hear expressions like *this noon, yesterday's noon* and so on. On the contrary, noon is a period of time in China that can extend two or three hours covering the time when people stop morning work, go home, prepare lunch, eat lunch, take a nap and head back to afternoon work. With the exception of stores, essential services and factory operations that cannot stop, government offices, schools and companies would come to a halt during this time so that people could go home to eat lunch (the most important meal of the day for a lot of people), and take a nap. Some years ago, the Chinese government imposed a ban on this midday break by limiting the lunch time allocation and thus eliminating the indispensable nap. This measure caused havoc in the population and created a major culturally conditioned physiological breakdown. The midday break is so culturally ingrained and biologically programmed that people simply could not do without it. When forced to abandon this time-honored indulgence, people would either fall asleep or doze off on the job. Heated debates arose and various theories were advanced. One argument for the midday break was that the Chinese diet, which is made of low calorie foods such as pork and vegetables, is not as sustaining as the Western diet, which is rich in beef and dairy products. Another theory along the same line was that Chinese people spent more time shopping for and preparing food. By the time people finished their lunch, they were exhausted and desperately needed a nap to recoup their energy. Although no consensus was reached, the government backed off and people went back to their nap. Interestingly enough, with the recent economic boom and increasing privatization in China, more and more people are voluntarily giving up their nap and making use of the precious midday time. It seems that economic incentives are the only force that could thwart any customary or even biological practice.

At www.mandarintools.com/calendar.html, you can find a Western-Chinese or Chinese-Western calendar converter as well as information about Chinese holidays, astrological signs, and historical eras.

LESSON 6

NATIONALITIES & LANGUAGES

SENTENCE PATTERNS

你是 哪国 人?
Nǐ shì nǎ guó rén?

Where are you from?

你是 哪儿人?
Nǐ shì nǎr rén?

What part of the country are you from?

你会 说 中文 吗?
Nǐ huì shuō Zhōngwén ma?

Do you speak Chinese?

会 一点儿。
Huì yìdiǎnr.

A little.

"**Mandarin**" 用 中文
"Mandarin" yòng Zhōngwén
怎么 说?
zěnme shuō?

How do you say "Mandarin" in Chinese?

"广东话" 是 什么
"Guǎngdōnghuà" shì shénme
意思?
yìsi?

What does "广东话" mean?

我 不懂 你的话。
Wǒ bù dǒng nǐde huà.

I don't understand what you say.

请 慢 一点儿说。
Qǐng màn yìdiǎnr shuō.

Please speak a little slowly.

CONVERSATIONS

A: 你是中国人　　吗?　　　　Are you Chinese?
Nǐ shì Zhōngguórén ma?

B: 是。你也是中国人　　吗?　Yes, are you also Chinese?
Shì.　Nǐ yě shì Zhōngguórén ma?

A: 我　不是, 我　是日本人。　No, I am not. I am Japanese.
Wǒ bú shì, wǒ　shì Rìběnrén.

B: 对不起。　　　　　　　　I'm sorry.
Duìbuqǐ.

A: 没　关系。　　　　　　　That's all right.
Méi guānxi.

A: 你是　哪国　人?　　　　Where are you from?
Nǐ shì　nǎ guó rén?

B: 我　是中国人。　　　　　I am Chinese.
Wǒ shì Zhōngguórén.

A: 你太太呢?　　　　　　　What about your wife?
Nǐ tàitai ne?

B: 她是　英国人。　　　　　She is British.
Tā shì　Yīngguórén.

A: 你从　哪儿来?　　　　　Where did you come from?
Nǐ cóng nǎr　lái?

B: 我　从　法国来。　　　　I came from France.
Wǒ cóng Fǎguó lái.

A: 你是　法国人吗?　　　　Are you French?
Nǐ shì Fǎguórén ma?

B: 不是。我　是德国人。　　No, I am not. I am German.
Bú shì.　Wǒ　shì Déguórén.

A: 你是 哪儿人？
Nǐ shì nǎr rén?
What part of the country are you from?

B: 我 是 上海人。
Wǒ shì Shànghǎirén.
I am from Shanghai.

A: 你太太也是上海人 吗？
Nǐ tàitai yě shì Shànghǎirén ma?
Is your wife also from Shanghai?

B: 不是。她是 广州人。
Bú shì. Tā shì Guǎngzhōurén.
No, she is from Guangzhou.

A: 你会 说 广东话 吗？
Nǐ huì shuō Guǎngdōnghuà ma?
Do you speak Cantonese?

B: 我 懂 广东话, 但是
Wǒ dǒng Guǎngdōnghuà, dànshì
不会 说。
bú huì shuō.
I understand Cantonese, but I don't speak it.

A: 你太太会 说 上海话
Nǐ tàitai huì shuō Shànghǎihuà
吗？
ma?
Does your wife speak the Shanghai dialect?

B: 她会。
Tā huì.
Yes, she does.

A: 你太太会 说 英语 吗？
Nǐ tàitai huì shuō Yīngyǔ ma?
Does your wife speak English?

B: 会。
Huì.
Yes, she does.

A: 你爸爸呢？
Nǐ bàba ne?
What about your father?

B: 他不会。
Tā bú huì.
No, he doesn't.

A: 你妈妈呢？
Nǐ māma ne?
What about your mother?

B: 她会一点儿。
Tā huì yìdiǎnr.
She speaks a little.

A: 你会 说 几种 语言?
Nǐ huì shuō jǐ zhǒng yǔyán?

How many languages do you speak?

B: 我 会 说 四种 语言。
Wǒ huì shuō sì zhǒng yǔyán.

I speak four languages.

A: 哪四种?
Nǎ sì zhǒng?

Which four?

B: 英语，法语, 西班牙语
Yīngyǔ, Fǎyǔ, Xībānyáyǔ
和一点儿中文。
hé yìdiǎnr Zhōngwén.

English, French, Spanish and a little Chinese.

A: 请问， "Mandarin"用
Qǐngwèn, "Mandarin" yòng
中文 怎么 说?
Zhōngwén zěnme shuō?

Excuse me, how do you say "Mandarin" in Chinese?

B: "Mandarin"用 中文 说
"Mandarin" yòng Zhōngwén shuō
是 普通话。
shì pǔtōnghuà.

"Mandarin" in Chinese is "pǔtōnghuà."

A: "四川话" 是 什么 意思?
A: "Sìchuānhuà" shì shénme yìsi?

What is the meaning of "Sichuanhua?"

B: "四川话" 的意思是
B: "Sìchuānhuà" de yìsi shì
"Sichuan dialect"。
"Sichuan dialect."

"Sichuanhua" means "Sichuan dialect."

A: 谢谢。
Xièxie.

Thank you.

B: 不客气。
Bú kèqi.

You're welcome.

A: 请问, 中国　银行　在 哪儿?
Qǐngwèn, Zhōngguó yínháng zài nǎr?

Excuse me, where is Bank of China?

B: 对不起, 我不 懂 你的话, 请 再 说 一遍。
Duìbuqǐ, wǒ bù dǒng nǐde huà, qǐng zài shuō yíbiàn.

Sorry. I don't understand what you said. Could you please say it again?

A: 你知道 中国　银行　在 哪儿吗?
Nǐ zhīdao Zhōngguó yínháng zài nǎr ma?

Do you know where Bank of China is?

B: 知道。中国　银行　在 中国城。
Zhīdao. Zhōngguó yínháng zài Zhōngguóchéng.

Yes, Bank of China is in Chinatown.

A: 谢谢。
Xièxie.

Thank you.

B: 不谢。
Bú xiè.

Don't mention it.

A: 请问,　男厕所 在哪儿?
Qǐngwèn, náncèsuǒ zài nǎr?

Excuse me, where is the men's room?

B: 在 五楼。
Zài wǔ lóu.

On the fifth floor.

A: 谢谢。
Xièxie.

Thank you.

B: 不客气。
Bú kèqi.

You're welcome.

A: 香港人　　说　什么　话　　　What dialect do people in
Xiānggǎngrén shuō shénme huà?　　Hong Kong speak?

B: 香港人　　说　广东话　　　People in Hong Kong speak
Xiānggǎngrén shuō Guǎngdōnghuà.　Cantonese.

A: 你会　不会说　广东话?　　Do you speak Cantonese?
Nǐ huì bu huì shuō Guǎngdōnghuà?

B: 我　懂　广东话,　　　　I understand Cantonese,
Wǒ dǒng Guǎngdōnghuà ,　　but I don't speak it.
但是　我不　会　说。
dànshì wǒ bú huì shuō.

WORDS AND EXPRESSIONS

Nouns

国	guó	country
英语	Yīngyǔ	English language
英国	Yīngguó	U.K.
法国	Fǎguó	France
德国	Déguó	Germany
法语	Fǎyǔ	French language
西班牙语	Xībānyáyǔ	Spanish language
广州	Guǎngzhōu	Canton (the city)
广东	Guǎngdōng	Canton (the province)
四川	Sìchuān	Sichuan (province)
香港	Xiānggǎng	Hong Kong
语言	yǔyán	language
普通话	pǔtōnghuà	Mandarin
国语	guóyǔ	Mandarin
意思	yìsi	meaning
话	huà	speech, dialect
楼	lóu	floor, building
一遍	yíbiàn	one time
一点儿	yìdiǎnr	a little

Verbs

会	huì	know how to, to be able to
说	shuō	speak, say
用	yòng	use
懂	dǒng	understand

Adverbs

慢	màn	slowly
再	zài	again
只	zhǐ	only

Presposition

从	cóng	from

Classifiers

种	zhǒng	kind, type

Interrogatives

怎么	zěnme	how

SUPPLEMENTARY WORDS AND EXPRESSIONS

Nouns

外国	wàiguó	foreign country
外国人	wàiguórén	foreigner
外语	wàiyǔ	foreign language
日语	Rìyǔ	Japanese language
俄语	Éyǔ	Russian language
德语	Déyǔ	German language
韩国	Hánguó	Korea
阿拉伯语	Ālābóyǔ	Arabic language
字	zì	Chinese character
报纸	bàozhǐ	newspaper
杂志	zázhì	magazine
新闻	xīnwén	news
电视	diànshì	television
课文	kèwén	text
会话	huìhuà	conversation
生词	shēngcí	new word
语法	yǔfǎ	grammar
句子	jùzǐ	sentence
练习	liànxí	exercise
书法	shūfǎ	calligraphy
词典	cídiǎn	dictionary

Verbs

教	jiāo	teach
写	xiě	write
听	tīng	listen
翻译	fānyì	translate
回答	huídá	answer

LANGUAGE POINTS

1. Nationality terms

It is easy to form nationality terms in Chinese. All you need to do is to add the word 人 (rén) after the name of the country, such as:

美国 (Měiguó, *America*)   美国人 (Měiguórén, *American*)
中国 (Zhōngguó, *China*)   中国人 (Zhōngguórén, *Chinese*)
英国 (Yīngguó, *Britain*)   英国人 (Yīngguórén, *British*)
法国 (Fǎguó, *France*)   法国人 (Fǎguórén, *French*)
德国 (Déguó, *Germany*)   德国人 (Déguórén, *German*)
韩国 (Hánguó, *Korea*)   韩国人 (Hánguórén, *Korean*)

国 (guó) in all these expressions simply means *country*.

If the name of a country consists of more than one syllable, the word 国 (guó) is usually not used. For example:

加拿大 (Jiānádà, *Canada*)   加拿大人 (Jiānádàrén, *Canadian*)

日本 (Rìběn, *Japan*)   日本人 (Rìběnrén, *Japanese*)
意大利 (Yìdàlì, *Italy*)   意大利人 (Yìdàlìrén, *Italian*)
越南 (Yuènán, *Vietnam*)   越南人 (Yuènánrén, *Vietnamese*)
西班牙 (Xībānyá, *Spain*)   西班牙人 (Xībānyárén, *Spanish*)

The word 人 (rén) can also be used after the name of a specific location within a country to mean a native of that place. For example:

北京 (Běijīng, *Beijing*)   北京人 (Běijīngrén, *Beijing native*)

上海 (Shànghǎi, *Shanghai*)   上海人 (Shànghǎirén, *Shanghai native*)

纽约 (Niǔyuē, *New York*)   纽约人 (Niǔyuērén, *New Yorker*)

香港 (Xiānggǎng, *Hong Kong*)

台湾 (Táiwān, *Taiwan*)

香港人 (Xiānggǎngrén, *Hong Kong native*)

台湾人 (Táiwānrén, *Taiwanese*)

To ask where someone is from, we use 你是哪国人 (nǐ shì nǎ guó rén), which literally means *which country person are you*. The interrogative word 哪 (nǎ, *which*) is used because we are asking the other person to choose from a range of possible answers.

It is to be noted that to the Chinese, 中国人 (Zhōngguórén), 英国人 (Yīngguórén), 日本人 (Rìběnrén) and so on refer to a person's ethnic background, having nothing to do with his or her own citizenship. Thus a person of Chinese descent is always 中国人 (Zhōngguórén), even though he or she may have been born in a foreign country or become a citizen of a foreign country through immigration.

2. 你是哪儿人 (nǐ shì nǎr rén)?

This expression, meaning literally *you are what place person*, is used when you know a person's nationality and you want to know what part of the country the person is from. The response takes such forms as: 我是纽约人 (wǒ shì Niǔyuērén, *I'm a New Yorker*), 我是加州人 (wǒ shì Jiāzhōurén, *I am a Californian*), and 我是杭州人 (wǒ shì Hángzhōurén, *I am from Hangzhou*).

3. 你会说中文吗 (nǐ huì shuō Zhōngwén ma)?

会 (huì) is not necessary in English when you ask somebody if he can speak a certain language, but it is usually used in Chinese. It means *know how to* and is used for things and skills that are acquired through learning such as language, driving, swimming, and cooking.

4. "Mandarin" 用中文怎么说 ("Mandarin" yòng Zhōngwén zěnme shuō)?

This is a useful expression used when you want to ask someone how to say something in Chinese. In the expression, the verb 说 (shuō) is modified by two adverbials 用中文 (yòng Zhōngwén, *using Chi-*

nese) and 怎么 (zěnme, *how*). As such, they are placed before the verb. 用 (yòng) in 用中文 (yòng Zhōngwén) means *to use*. You may want to take the phrase to mean *using Chinese* or *in Chinese*. The item of interest—Mandarin—is placed first as is often in Chinese, although it is the object of the verb 说 (shuō). The subject is not present in the sentence because it is generic. It would be *you*, *I* or *one*. The response pattern for this question is "Mandarin"用中文说是普通话 ("Mandarin" yòng Zhōngwén shuō shì pǔtōnghuà).

5. "四川话" 是什么意思 (Sìchuānhuà shì shénme yìsi)?

This is the other side of the above question, used when you heard a Chinese expression, but did not know what it meant. The answer to this question is "四川话" 的意思是 Sichuan dialect ("Sìchuānhuà" de yìsi shì Sichuan dialect). Literally, it is *Sichuanhua's meaning is Sichuan dialect*.

EXERCISES

I. Answer the following questions:

1. 你是 哪国 人?
   Nǐ shì nǎ guó rén?

   _____

2. 你是 哪儿人?
   Nǐ shì nǎr rén?

   _____

3. 你会 说 什么 语言?
   Nǐ huì shuō shénme yǔyán?

   _____

4. 你会 说 西班牙语吗?
   Nǐ huì shuō Xībānyáyǔ ma

   _____

5. 你妈妈 会说 几种 语言?
   Nǐ māma huì shuō jǐ zhǒng yǔyán?

   _____

6. 你的中文 老师 会 说 英语 吗?
   Nǐde Zhōngwén lǎoshī huì shuō Yīngyǔ ma?

   _____

7. 德国人 说 什么 语言?
   Déguórén shuō shénme yǔyán?

   _____

8. 香港人　　说　什么　话?
   Xiānggǎngrén shuō shénme huà?

_____

9. "Doctor" 用　中文　　怎么　说?
   "Doctor" yòng Zhōngwén zěnme shuō?

_____

10. "Cānguǎn" 是什么　　意思?
    "Cānguǎn" shì shénme yìsi?

_____

II. 用中文怎么说 (yòng zhōngwén zěnme shuō):

1. bank   _____
2. friend   _____
3. house   _____
4. bathroom   _____
5. noon   _____
6. birthday   _____
7. lunch   _____
8. college   _____
9. high school student _____
10. doctor   _____

III.它们是什么意思 (tāmen shì shénme yìsi)?

1. 西班牙语   _____
   Xībānyáyǔ
2. 国语   _____
   guóyǔ
3. 普通话   _____
   pǔtōnghuà
4. 亚洲   _____
   Yàzhōu

5. 非洲   _____
  Fēizhōu

6. 商店   _____
  shāngdiàn

7. 南京话   _____
  Nánjīnghuà

8. 餐馆   _____
  cānguǎn

9. 懂   _____
  dǒng

10. 法语   _____
  Fǎyǔ

IV. Fill in the blanks with appropriate words:

1. 你会 说 法语_____?
  Nǐ huì shuō Fǎyǔ _____?

2. 你姐姐会 说 几 _____ 语言?
  Nǐ jiějie huì shuō jǐ _____ yǔyán?

3. 你的朋友 _____ 哪儿来?
  Nǐde péngyou _____ nǎr lái?

4. 他会 说 _____ 西班牙语。
  Tā huì shuō _____ Xībānyáyǔ.

5. 对不起, 我 不懂 你的 _____。
  Duìbuqǐ, wǒ bù dǒng nǐde _____.

6. 请 慢 _____ 说。
  Qǐng màn _____ shuō.

7. 她从　上海　＿＿＿＿＿＿。她是　上海人。
   Tā cóng Shànghǎi ＿＿＿＿＿＿. Tā shì Shànghǎirén.

8. 南京人　说　＿＿＿＿＿＿　话?
   Nánjīngrén shuō ＿＿＿＿＿＿ huà?

9. 你懂　不＿＿＿＿＿＿我的话?
   Nǐ dǒng bu ＿＿＿＿＿ wǒde huà?

10. 你妈妈　＿＿＿＿＿＿　说　日语　吗?
    Nǐ māma ＿＿＿＿＿＿ shuō Rìyǔ ma?

V. Translate the following into Chinese:

1. Excuse me, do you know how to say "speaking slowly" in Chinese?

   _____

2. Excuse me, what does "汽车" (qìchē) mean?

   _____

3. "汽车" (qìchē) means "car."

   _____

4. My Chinese teacher doesn't speak English.

   _____

5. He came from Germany, but he doesn't speak German.

   _____

6. She speaks a little Spanish.

   _____

7. People in Hong Kong speak Cantonese.

_____

8. Who speaks English?

_____

9. She is from Shanghai, but she doesn't speak Shanghai dialect.

_____

10. How do you write this character?

_____

VI. Translate the following into English:

1. 我 是 英国人， 我 太太是 法国人。
   Wǒ shì Yīngguórén, wǒ tàitai shì Fǎguórén.

_____

2. 上海人　 不 懂 广东话。
   Shànghǎirén bù dǒng Guǎngdōnghuà.

_____

3. 我的 男朋友　 会 说 四种　 语言, 我 只会 说
   Wǒde nánpéngyou huì shuō sì zhǒng yǔyán, wǒ zhǐ huì shuō
   英语。
   Yīngyǔ.

_____

_____

4. 你说　 什么? 我 不 懂。请　 再 说　 一遍。
   Nǐ shuō shénme? Wǒ bù dǒng. Qǐng zài shuō yíbiàn.

_____

5. 我 懂 台湾话，可是不会 说。
Wǒ dǒng Táiwānhuà, kěshì bú huì shuō.

---

6. 他的 广东话   很 好, 但是 国语 不太好。
Tāde Guǎngdōnghuà hěn hǎo, dànshì guóyǔ bú tài hǎo.

---

7. 请问，   谁 会 说 英语?
Qǐngwèn, shéi huì shuō Yīngyǔ?

---

8. 你知道 不 知道 "公园"   是 什么   意思?
Nǐ zhīdao bu zhīdao "gōngyuán" shì shénme yìsi?

---

9. 她的话，我只 懂   一点儿。
Tāde huà, wǒ zhǐ dǒng yìdiǎnr.

---

10. 对不起, 我不会 说   四川话。
Duìbuqǐ,   wǒ bú huì shuō Sìchuānhuà.

VII. Each sentence below contains a mistake. Find and correct it:

1. 你有 几中文   书?
Nǐ yǒu jǐ Zhōngwén shū?

---

2. 你认识 不 认识 那医生?
Nǐ rènshi bu rènshi nà yīshēng?

---

3. 他每 天 上班　 在 八 点。
   Tā měi tiān shàngbān zài bā diǎn.

---

4. 你是 不是学生　 吗?
   Nǐ shì bu shì xuésheng ma?

---

5. 他有 姐姐, 不有 哥哥。
   Tā yǒu jiějie, bù yǒu gēge.

---

6. 我 有 二个中国　 朋友。
   Wǒ yǒu èr ge Zhōngguó péngyou.

---

7. 请问,　 中国城　　 是 哪儿?
   Qǐngwèn, Zhōngguóchéng shì nǎr?

---

8. 他工作　 在 餐馆。
   Tā gōngzuò zài cānguǎn.

---

9. 王　 太太不去银行　 今天。
   Wáng Tàitai bú qù yínháng jīntiān.

10.你们 学校　 的 图书馆 有 几本 书?
   Nǐmen xuéxiào de túshūguǎn yǒu jǐ běn shū?

VIII. Recognize and practice writing the following characters:

ér　儿儿儿

| 儿 | 儿 | 儿 | 儿 | | | | | | |

cóng　从从从从从

| 从 | 从 | 从 | 从 | | | | | | |

dōng　东东东东东东

| 东 | 东 | 东 | 东 | | | | | | |

zhǐ　只只只只只只

| 只 | 只 | 只 | 只 | | | | | | |

sì　四四四四四四

| 四 | 四 | 四 | 四 | | | | | | |

yòng　用用用用用用

| 用 | 用 | 用 | 用 | | | | | | |

huì　会会会会会会会

| 会 | 会 | 会 | 会 | | | | | | |

zài　再再再再再再再

| 再 | 再 | 再 | 再 | | | | | | |

yán　言言言言言言言言

| 言 | 言 | 言 | 言 | | | | | | |

zěn　怎怎怎怎怎怎怎怎怎

| 怎 | 怎 | 怎 | 怎 | | | | | | |

CULTURAL INSIGHTS

As with any other language, Chinese is an abstract amalgam. It is realized in a variety of representations called 方言 (fāngyán, *regional speech or dialect*). Unlike many other languages, dialects of Chinese can be so drastically different that they are not mutually intelligible. There are places in China where people do not understand each other even though they only live a few miles apart. Since association and banding had never been encouraged in traditional China because they tended to breed the seeds of discontent or rebellion, the difficulty with which people had in communicating with each other had been a godsend opportunity for emperors to exercise effective social control over the population, much like the "confusion of tongues" described in the biblical story of the Tower of Babel. Due to mutual unintelligibility, different dialect groups in China are often conceived by scholars outside China as being different languages, but Chinese scholars have vehemently denied this claim.

There are seven major dialect groups in China, which are distributed over different geographic areas of the country. Each of these dialect groups has its own variations and local subdialects. The most widely used dialect of Chinese is Mandarin. It is spoken by 70% of the population in northern and parts of southern China that account for three quarters of the country. Mandarin itself has a number of subvarieties. The standard form of Mandarin is based on the northern Mandarin, with the Beijing phonological system as its norm. This standard form is used on television, radio and other official and administrative occasions. It is the dialect that children throughout the country go to school learning. As such, it is understood by 94% of the population. Other dialects include Wu (spoken by 8% of the population), Gan (2%), Hakka (4%), Xiang (5%), Min/Fukienese (4%) and Yue/Catonese (5%). Of these seven major dialects, only Mandarin is indigenous and homogenous, i.e. it evolved locally in northern China over thousands of years. The other six dialects are spoken primarily in central and southeastern China. They are the result of southward migration of population since the very beginning of Chinese history.

The mutual unintelligibility of dialects had much to do with the segregation of the population in traditional China. Due to an elaborate system of administration, local governors and generals were often given unbridled power, which enabled them to exercise tight control of the people in their jurisdictions. Such tight control resulted in a practical segregation: there was little mobility and interaction between people who belonged to different political and administrative entities. Consequently, the differences in their speech became more and more divergent.

Another reason that contributed to the divergence of dialects was the preference of agriculture and suppression of trade and commerce by the government in traditional China. Under such a government policy, people were tied down to their land and dreaded venturing out unless there was a war or some other natural calamity.

Natural barriers such as rivers and mountains further restricted the interaction between people. These boundaries often mark the boundaries of dialect groups, particularly when they coincide with the boundaries of the units of political administration.

Although Mandarin has become the official dialect, the use of local dialects is not entirely discouraged by the government. In fact, with its countenance, dialects in some places are actually thriving. Shanghai is a typical example. It is one of the few places that still maintain radio and television programs in the local dialects. The prestige of the dialect is closely related to the sense of superiority felt by Shanghai natives to people elsewhere. It used to be the case that if you didn't speak the Shanghai dialect, you would get indifferent service while visiting there. To overcome this, outsiders had to learn the Shanghai dialect, at least a few phrases for the occasion before they ventured into the city. Mobility has vastly increased following the reform efforts in recent years in Shanghai and other places. A recent survey showed that currently there is an annual influx of 3 million migrant workers in Shanghai seeking short-term work and taking up temporary residence. To accommodate such a large population and serve as the major center of trade and finance, Mandarin has inevitably emerged as the *lingua franca*. This trend is observed not only in Shanghai, but throughout China.

Visit unclp.org/countrynames.htm
for a complete list of the names of countries
with English, characters and pinyin.

LESSON 7

MONEY & SHOPPING

SENTENCE PATTERNS

你要 买 什么?
Nǐ yào mǎi shénme?

What would you like to buy?

这 件 衣服多少 钱?
Zhè jiàn yīfu duōshao qián?

How much is this piece of clothing?

你们 收 不 收 美元?
Nǐmen shōu bu shōu měiyuán?

Do you accept U.S. dollars?

这 件 毛衣 怎么样?
Zhè jiàn máoyī zěnmeyàng?

What do you think of this sweater?

我 觉得很 好。
Wǒ juéde hěn hǎo.

I think it's very good.

第一百货公司 的东西
Dìyī bǎihuògōngsī de dōngxi
最 多。
zuì duō.

The First Department Store has the most stuff.

你能 告诉 我在 哪儿能
Nǐ néng gàosu wǒ zài nǎr néng
换 美元 吗?
huàn měiyuán ma?

Can you tell me where I can change U.S. dollars?

一美元 换 多少 人民币?
Yì měiyuán huàn duōshao rénmínbì?

How much does one U.S. dollar convert to Renminbi?

请 等 一下儿。
Qǐng děng yíxiàr.

Just a minute.

我 能 看 看 吗?
Wǒ néng kàn kan ma?

Can I take a look?

太 贵了。
Tài guì le.

It's too expensive.

听说   上海   的东西
Tīngshuō Shànghǎi de dōngxi
很 贵。
hěn guì.

I heard that things in Shanghai are very expensive.

要 看 什么   店。
Yào kàn shénme diàn.

It depends on what store.

有的 店 东西 贵, 有的
Yǒude diàn dōngxi guì, yǒude
店 东西 很 便宜。
diàn dōngxi hěn piányi.

Some stores are expensive, other stores are very cheap.

多少   钱 一 张?
Duōshao qián yì zhāng?

How much is a piece?

CONVERSATIONS

A: 你去哪儿?
Nǐ qù nǎr?

Where are you going?

B: 我 去买 东西。
Wǒ qù mǎi dōngxi.

I'm going shopping.

A: 你去哪儿买 东西?
Nǐ qù nǎr mǎi dōngxi?

Where are you going shopping?

B: 我 去百货公司 买 东西。
Wǒ qù bǎihuògōngsī mǎi dōngxi.

I'm going shopping at the department store.

A: 你要 买 什么?
Nǐ yào mǎi shénme?

What are you going to buy?

B: 我 要 买 衣服。
Wǒ yào mǎi yīfu.

I'm going to buy clothes.

你知道 哪个百货公司
Nǐ zhīdao nǎ ge bǎihuògōngsī
的东西 最多?
de dōngxi zuì duō?

Do you know which department store has the most stuff?

A: 第一百货公司 的东西
Dìyī bǎihuògōngsī de dōngxi
最 多。
zuì duō.

The First Department Store has the most stuff.

A: 你们 收 不 收 美元?
Nǐmen shōu bu shōu měiyuán?

Do you accept U.S. dollars?

B: 对不起, 我们 不收 美元。
Duìbuqǐ, wǒmen bù shōu měiyuán.
我们 只收 人民币。
Wǒmen zhǐ shōu rénmínbì.

Sorry, we don't accept U.S. dollars.
We only accept Renminbi.

A: 你能　告诉我　在哪儿能　　　　Can you tell me where I can
Nǐ néng gàosu wǒ zài nǎr　néng　　change U.S. dollars?
换　美元　吗?
huàn měiyuán ma?

B: 你可以在　银行　换，　　　　You can change them at the
Nǐ kěyǐ　zài　yínháng huàn,　　　bank or at the hotel.
也可以在　饭店　换。
yě kěyǐ　zài fàndiàn huàn.

A: 谢谢。　　　　　　　　　　Thank you.
Xièxie.

B: 不客气。　　　　　　　　　You're welcome.
Bú kèqi.

A: 这儿能　换　美元　吗?　　Can I exchange U.S. dollars
Zhèr　néng huàn měiyuán ma?　　here?

B: 能。你要　换　多少?　　　Yes, how much do you want
Néng. Nǐ yào huàn　duōshao?　　to exchange?

A: 一美元　今天　能　换　　How much Renminbi can one
Yì měiyuán jīntiān néng　huàn　　U.S. dollar convert to today?
多少　人民币?
duōshao rénmínbì?

B: 一美元　今天　能　换　　One U.S. dollar converts to 7
Yì měiyuán jīntiān néng　huàn　　*kuai* Renminbi today.
七块　人民币。
qī kuài rénmínbì.

A: 我　换　三百　美元。　　I want to change $300.
Wǒ huàn sān bǎi měiyuán.

B: 好，请　等　一下儿。　　OK. Just a minute.
Hǎo, qǐng　děng yíxiàr.
这　是　两　千　一百块　This is 2,100 *kuai* Renminbi.
Zhè shì liǎng qiān　yì bǎi kuài
人民币。
rénmínbì.

A: 谢谢。 Thank you.
Xièxie.

A: 你买 什么? What would you like to buy?
Nǐ mǎi shénme?

B: 这 件 大衣多少 钱? How much is this coat?
Zhè jiàn dàyī duōshao qián?

A: 两 百 五十 块。 250 *kuai*.
Liǎng bǎi wǔshí kuài.

B: 我 能 不能 看看? Can I take a look?
Wǒ néng bu néng kànkan?

A: 当然 可以。 Sure.
Dāngrán kěyǐ.

B: 我 能 试试 吗? Can I try it on?
Wǒ néng shìshi ma?

A: 没问题。 No problem.
Méi wèntí.

A: 请问, 那条 裤子 Excuse me, how much is that
Qǐngwèn, nà tiáo kùzi pair of pants?
多少 钱?
duōshao qián?

B: 一百 块。 100 *kuai*.
Yì bǎi kuài.

A: 太 贵了。有 没 有 Too expensive. Do you have
Tài guì le. Yǒu méi yǒu anything cheaper?
便宜 一点儿的?
piányi yìdiǎnr de?

B: 有,你看看 这 条。 Yes, take a look at this pair.
Yǒu, nǐ kànkan zhè tiáo.

A: 谢谢。 Thank you.
Xièxie.

A: 听说　　上海　　的东西　　I heard that things in Shanghai
Tīngshuō Shànghǎi de dōngxi　　are very expensive.
很　贵。
hěn guì.

B: 不 一定, 要看　什么 店。　Not necessarily. It depends
Bù yídìng, yào kàn shénme diàn.　on the store.
有的 店 东西 贵,　　Some stores are expensive,
Yǒude diàn dōngxi guì,　　others are very cheap.
有的 店 东西 很 便宜。
yǒude diàn dōngxi hěn piányi.

A: 什么　店 东西　　贵,　　What stores are expensive
Shénme diàn dōngxi guì,　　and what stores are cheap?
什么　店 东西 便宜?
shénme diàn dōngxi piányi?

B: 大 店 的东西 贵,　　Big stores are expensive,
Dà diàn de dōngxi guì,　　small ones are not.
小 店　的 东西 不太 贵。
xiǎo diàn de dōngxi bú tài guì.

A: 你们 卖 不卖　邮票?　Do you sell stamps?
Nǐmen mài bu mài yóupiào?

B: 卖。你要 几张?　Yes. How many do you want?
Mài. Nǐ yào jǐ zhāng?

A: 多少　钱 一张?　How much is one?
Duōshao qián yì zhāng?

B: 两　毛 一张。　20 cents each.
Liǎng máo yì zhāng.

A: 我 要 十五 张。　I want 15.
Wǒ yào shíwǔ zhāng.
一共　多少　钱?　How much altogether?
Yígòng duōshao qián?

B: 一共　三块。　3 *kuai* altogether.
Yígòng sān kuài.

A: 这 件 毛衣 怎么样?
Zhè jiàn máoyī zěnmeyàng?

What do you think of this sweater?

B: 很　好看。
Hěn hǎokàn.

Looks very good.

A: 长　　不长?
Cháng bu cháng?

Is it too long?

B: 我 觉得不长。
Wǒ juéde bù cháng.

I don't think it's too long.

A: 颜色　怎么样?
Yánsè zěnmeyàng?

What do you think of its color?

B: 颜色 也不错。多少　钱?
Yánsè yě bú cuò. Duōshao qián?

The color is also good. How much is it?

A: 一百　二十块。
Yì bǎi èrshí kuài.

120 *kuai*.

B: 我 觉得不太贵, 你看　呢?
Wǒ juéde bú tài guì, nǐ kàn ne?

I don't think it's too expensive. What do you think?

A: 我 看　也很　好。
Wǒ kàn yě hěn hǎo.

I also think it's good.

WORDS AND EXPRESSIONS

Nouns

钱	qián	money
东西	dōngxi	things, stuff
百货公司	bǎihuògōngsī	department store
衣服	yīfu	clothes, clothing
毛衣	máoyī	sweater
大衣	dàyī	coat
裤子	kùzi	pants
颜色	yánsè	color
邮票	yóupiào	stamp
美元	měiyuán	U.S. dollar
人民币	rénmínbì	*Renminbi*
块	kuài	*monetary unit*
毛	máo	*monetary unit*
分	fēn	*monetary unit*

Verbs

买	mǎi	buy
卖	mài	sell
要	yào	want
收	shōu	accept
能	néng	can
可以	kěyǐ	may
换	huàn	change, exchange
试	shì	try
告诉	gàosu	tell
等	děng	wait
觉得	juéde	feel, think

Adjectives

多	duō	many, much
贵	guì	expensive
便宜	piányi	cheap
长	cháng	long

Adverbs

最	zuì	most
一共	yígòng	altogether, in total

Prefix

第	dì	*ordinal number indicator*

Classifiers

张	zhāng
条	tiáo
件	jiàn

Expressions

当然	dāngrán	of course
听说	tīngshuō	it is said
有的	yǒude	some ... others ...
有的	yǒude	
要看	yàokàn	it depends
不一定	bù yídìng	not necessarily

SUPPLEMENTARY WORDS AND EXPRESSIONS

Nouns

售货员	shòuhuòyuán	sales clerk
顾客	gùkè	customer
市场	shìchǎng	market
鞋子	xiézi	shoes
帽子	màozi	hat

袜子	wàzǐ	socks
衬衫	chènshān	shirt, blouse
咖啡	kāfēi	coffee
服装店	fúzhuāngdiàn	clothing store
鞋店	xiédiàn	shoe store
书店	shūdiàn	bookstore
纪念品	jìniànpǐn	souvenir
工艺品	gōngyìpǐn	handicraft product
价格	jiàgé	price
信用卡	xìnyòngkǎ	credit card
支票	zhīpiào	check
日元	rìyuán	Japanese yen
欧元	ōuyuán	Euro

Verbs

付	fù	pay
穿	chuān	wear, put on
开门	kāimén	open (for business)
关门	guānmén	close (for business)

Adjectives

合适	héshì	suitable
短	duǎn	short
肥	féi	loose
瘦	shòu	tight
少	shǎo	few or little

Classifiers

| 双 | shuāng | pair |
| 杯 | bēi | cup |

LANGUAGE POINTS

1. 东西 (dōngxi)
东西 (dōngxi), a combination of two opposite words 东 (dōng, *east*) and 西 (xī, *west*), is used in the sense of *things* or *stuff*. It always refers to physical and tangible objects, often used after certain verbs to avoid making specific references. Here are some examples:

买 东西
mǎi dōngxi
buy things

卖 东西
mài dōngxi
sell things

吃 东西
chī dōngxi
eat something

喝 东西
hē dōngxi
drink something

写 东西
xiě dōngxi
do some writing

听 东西
tīng dōngxi
listen to something

洗东西
xǐ dōngxi
do some washing

看 东西
kàn dōngxi
read something

2. 要 (yào)
Used in conjunction with another verb, 要 (yào) functions as a modal verb with the meaning of *to be going to*, *would like*, or *want*. For example:

他星期五 要 去中国。   He is going to China on Friday.
Tā xīngqīwǔ yào qù Zhōngguó.

你要 买 什么?   What would you like to buy?
Nǐ yào mǎi shénme?

你要 换 多少 钱?   How much money do you
Nǐ yào huàn duōshao qián?   want to change?

3. 第一百货公司 (dìyī bǎihuògōngsī)

As compared with English, ordinal numbers (such as first, second, and third) are much easier to form from cardinal numbers (such as one, two, and three) in Chinese. We simply prefix the cardinal number with 第 (dì). Keep in mind that like cardinal numbers, ordinal numbers also require the use of classifiers when used with nouns. See for example:

第一个人   the first person
dìyī   ge rén

第五本 书   the fifth book
dìwǔ běn shū

第十件 大衣   the tenth coat
dìshí jiàn dàyī

4. 第一百货公司的东西最多 (dìyī bǎihuògōngsī de dōngxi zuì duō)

多 (duō, *many* or *much*) and 少 (shǎo, *few* or *little*) are seldom used as predicatives in English. That's why we don't often hear people say *my money is little* and *his money is much*; or *people in that city are many* and *people in this city are few*. The more familiar forms in English are *I have little money, he has a lot of money*; *there are many people in that city*, and *there are few people in this city*. In Chinese, however, it is commonplace to use 多 (duō) and 少 (shǎo) as predicatives such as:

我的 钱 很 少，她的钱 很 多。
Wǒde qián hěn shǎo, tāde qián hěn duō.
I have little money; she has a lot of money.

这 个学校 的 学生 很 多, 那个学校 的
Zhè ge xuéxiào de xuésheng hěn duō, nà ge xuéxiào de
学生 很 少。
xuésheng hěn shǎo.
There are many students in this school, but very few students
in that school.

5. Formation of superlatives

It is very simple to form superlative adjectives in Chinese: prefix
the word 最 (zuì) to the adjectives. Here are some more examples:

最 好 zuì hǎo	best	最 高兴 zuì gāoxìng	happiest
最 忙 zuì máng	busiest	最 累 zuì lèi	the most tired
最 少 zuì shǎo	least	最 慢 zuì màn	slowest

6. 能 (néng) and 可以 (kěyǐ)

能 (néng) and 可以 (kěyǐ) are modal verbs in Chinese similar to *can*
and *may* in English. They should be used in conjunction with another verb. 能 (néng) is usually used in questions and 可以 (kěyǐ)
in answers. For example:

A: 你能 告诉 我 在 哪儿   Can you tell me where I can
  Nǐ néng gàosu wǒ zài nǎr   change U.S. dollars?
能 换 美元 吗?
néng huàn měiyuán ma?

B: 你可以在 银行 换,　　You can change them at the
　Nǐ kěyǐ zài yínháng huàn,　bank or at the hotel.
　也可以在饭店 换。
　yě kěyǐ zài fàndiàn huàn.

A: 我 能 不 能 看看?　Can I take a look?
　Wǒ néng bu néng kànkan?

B: 当然 可以。　　Of course you can.
　Dāngrán kěyǐ.

7. Monetary units in Chinese

There are three monetary units in the Chinese currency 人民币 (rén-mínbì), abbreviated as RMB: 元 (yuán) /块 (kuài), 角 (jiǎo)/毛 (máo) and 分 (fēn). The difference between 元 (yuán) and 块 (kuài) and between 角 (jiǎo) and 毛 (máo) is that 元 (yuán) and 角 (jiǎo) are formal and written expressions, whereas 块 (kuài) and 毛 (máo) are spoken and everyday forms. One 元 (yuán)/块 (kuài) consists of 10 角 (jiǎo)/ 毛 (máo) and one 角 (jiǎo)/ 毛 (máo) consists of 10 分 (fēn) in turn. Comparison should be made with the American monetary system where there are only two formal units: dollar and cent. We may say 99 cents in English, but we can never say 99 分 (fēn) in Chinese simply because there is an additional unit for 10 cents in Chinese. The correct form of 99 cents in Chinese is 9 毛 (máo) 9 分 (fēn).

8. 件 (jiàn) and 条 (tiáo)

It was mentioned in Lesson 4 that 件 (jiàn) and 条 (tiáo) are classifiers for clothing. The interesting difference between them is that 件 (jiàn) is used for clothing that we wear on the upper part of our body such as *shirt, blouse, coat* and *jacket* and 条 (tiáo) is used for clothing that we wear on the lower part of our body such as *pants, shorts, skirt,* and *underwear.* Besides clothing, 条 (tiáo) is also used for things that are narrow and long such as *river, belt, scarf, tie, street, banner* and *fish.*

9. 等一下儿 (děng yíxiàr)

一下儿 (yíxiàr) in 等一下儿 (děng yíxiàr) indicates that the action expressed by the verb is informal, brief or tentative. For example:

你来一下儿。 Nǐ lái yíxiàr.	Come over for a minute.
我 看 一下儿。 Wǒ kàn yíxiàr.	Let me take a look.
请 坐 一下儿。 Qǐng zuò yíxiàr.	Please have a seat.

The idea can also be expressed by the following two alternative patterns: 1) duplication of the verb, and 2) duplication of the verb while inserting 一 (yi) in between. Compare:

我 看 一下儿。 Wǒ kàn yíxiàr.	Let me take a look.
我 看看。 Wǒ kànkan.	Let me take a look.
我 看 一看。 Wǒ kàn yi kàn.	Let me take a look.

一 (yi) is pronounced in the neutral tone in the pattern.

Motion verbs such as 来 (lái) and 去 (qù) usually can only use the form with 一下儿 (yíxiàr).

10. 这件衣服多少钱 (zhè jiàn yīfu duōshao qián)?

This sentence illustrates the standard form of asking price, where the item of interest (clothing or anything else) is placed first followed by 多少钱 (duōshao qián). If the item of interest is not defined by a demonstrative pronoun such as 这 (zhè) or 那 (nà), a number with a classifier can be attached at the end of the question to indicate the unit. For example:

鞋子多少 钱 一双?   How much is a pair of shoes?
Xiézi duōshao qián yì shuāng?

咖啡多少 钱 一杯?   How much is a cup of coffee?
Kāfēi duōshao qián yì bēi?

邮票 多少 钱 一张?   How much is a stamp?
Yóupiào duōshao qián yì zhāng?

11. 太贵了 (tài guì le)

Particle 了 (le) is often used in conjunction with 太 (tài) after an adjective to soften the tone if the adjective conveys a negative meaning such as 贵 (guì). In addition, *too*, which is the seeming equivalent of 太 (tài) in Chinese, usually carries a negative tone, meaning *excessively* such as *too good (to be true)* and *too fast (to be safe)*, whereas 太 (tài) in Chinese is not always so. See for example:

太 好 了。   It's great.
Tài hǎo le.

我 太高兴 了。   I'm elated.
Wǒ tài gāoxìng le.

12. 听说上海的东西很贵 (tīngshuō Shànghǎi de dōngxi hěn guì)

听说 (tīngshuō) is equivalent to *I heard, I learned, it is said* or *they say* in English. If the subject is the first person pronoun 我 (wǒ), it is often left out:

听说   他会说 中文。   I heard that he can speak
Tīngshuō tā huì shuō Zhōngwén.   Chinese.

听说　　他在纽约　住。　I heard that he lives in New
Tīngshuō tā zài Niǔyuē zhù.　　York.

听说　　香港　　的　　They say things in Hong
Tīngshuō Xiānggǎng de　　Kong are very cheap.
东西 很 便宜。
dōngxi hěn piányi.

13. 要看什么店 (yào kàn shénme diàn)

"要看 (yào kàn) ...... " is used in the sense of *it depends on* ... The
subject is usually absent. See for example:

A: 你明天　　去不去　　Are you going to the park
Nǐ míngtiān qù bu qù　　tomorrow?
公园?
gōngyuán?

B: 要 看 天气 怎么样。 It depends on the weather.
Yào kàn tiānqì zěnmeyàng.

A: 你喜欢 不喜欢 看　Do to you like to watch TV?
Nǐ xǐhuan bu xǐhuān kàn
电视?
diànshì?

B: 要 看 是 什么 电视。 It depends on what is on TV.
Yào kàn shì shénme diànshì.

14. 这件毛衣怎么样 (zhè jiàn máoyī zěnmeyàng)?

"Something + 怎么样 (zěnmeyàng)" is a very useful expression
used to solicit opinions or suggestions, meaning "How is ...?" or
"What do you think of ...?" It is always placed at the end of a sentence such as:

你的中文　　老师　　How is your Chinese teacher?
Nǐde Zhōngwén lǎoshī
怎么样?
zěnmeyàng?

昨天　的电影　怎么样?　How was the movie yesterday?
Zuótiān de diànyǐng zěnmeyàng?

我们　去中国城,　　Let's go to Chinatown,
Wǒmen qù Zhōngguóchéng,　shall we?
怎么样?
zěnmeyàng?

...... 怎么样 (zěnmeyàng) is very often used interchangeably with the expression 好不好 (hǎo bu hǎo).

EXERCISES

I. Answer the following questions:

1. 你的中文　　书 多少　钱?
   Nǐde Zhōngwén shū duōshao qián?

   _____

2. 你有 中国　　钱 吗?
   Nǐ yǒu Zhōngguó qián ma?

   _____

3. 你知道 一美元　能　换　多少　人民币 吗?
   Nǐ zhīdao yì měiyuán néng huàn duōshao rénmínbì ma?

   _____

4. 在 美国　能　用 日元 吗?
   Zài Měiguó néng yòng rìyuán ma?

   _____

5. 英国人　用　什么　钱?
   Yīngguórén yòng shénme qián?

   _____

6. 旧金山 (San Francisco) 的东西 贵 不 贵?
   Jiùjīnshān　　　　　　 de dōngxi guì bu guì?

   _____

7. 纽约　哪个百货公司　最大?
   Niǔyuē nǎ ge bǎihuògōngsī zuì dà?

   _____

8. 你今天 去不去百货公司？ 你去买 什么？
   Nǐ jīntiān qù bu qù bǎihuògōngsī? Nǐ qù mǎi shénme?

   _____

9. 你一般在 哪儿买 衣服？
   Nǐ yībān zài nǎr mǎi yīfu?

   _____

10. 你们 那儿有 没 有 中文   书店？
    Nǐmen nàr   yǒu méi yǒu Zhōngwén shūdiàn?

    _____

II. Fill in the blanks with appropriate words:

1. 这 _____ 毛衣 多少 钱？
   Zhè _____ máoyī duōshao qián?

2. 你们 _____ 不收 日元？
   Nǐmen _____ bu shōu rìyuán?

3. _____ 有 美国 银行？
   _____ yǒu Měiguó yínxíng?

4. 这 个 店 的东西 不贵, 很 _____ 。
   Zhè ge diàn de dōngxi bú guì, hěn _____.

5. 你要 换 _____ 美元？
   Nǐ yào huàn _____ měiyuán?

III. How do you say the following sums in Chinese?

1. ¥10 _____
2. ¥1.20 _____
3. ¥5.64 _____

4. ¥7.08 _____
5. ¥33.94 _____
6. ¥580 _____
7. ¥99.99 _____
8. ¥6,832.81 _____
9. ¥40.60 _____
10. ¥2,080.01 _____

IV. Translate the following into Chinese:

1. Please come (here) for a minute.

   _____

2. How much is this dictionary?

   _____

3. Sorry. We only accept U.S. dollars. We don't accept Renminbi.

   _____

4. Could you tell me where I can find a shoe store?

   _____

5. Some stores accept credit cards and others don't.

   _____

6. Which department store is the largest in Beijing?

   _____

7. It depends on how much it is.

   _____

8. You can't change money in the stores.

   _____

9. Can I try on this pair of shoes?

_____

10. I heard that things in Chinatown are very cheap.

_____

V. Translate the following into English:

1. 我 没 有 美元， 我 只有 日元。
   Wǒ méi yǒu měiyuán , wǒ zhǐ yǒu rìyuán.

_____

2. 昨天 一美元 能 换 六块 人民币。
   Zuótiān yì měiyuán néng huàn liù kuài rénmínbì.

_____

3. 那个 书店 的英语 书 最 多。
   Nà ge shūdiàn de Yīngyǔ shū zuì duō.

_____

4. 很 多 人 喜欢 去上海 买 东西。
   Hěn duō rén xǐhuan qù Shànghǎi mǎi dōngxi.

_____

5. 美国 的商店 卖 很 多 中国 的东西。
   Měiguó de shāngdiàn mài hěn duō Zhōngguó de dōngxi.

_____

6. 这 条 裤子太长 了, 有 没 有 短 一点儿的?
   Zhè tiáo kùzi tài cháng le , yǒu méi yǒu duǎn yìdiǎnr de?

_____

7. 这 件 大衣多少 钱?
   Zhè jiàn dàyī duōshao qián?

_____

8. 听说　　日本 东西 很 贵。
   Tīngshuō Rìběn dōngxi hěn guì.

9. 能　不 能 去中国　　要 看 我 有 没 有 钱。
   Néng bu néng qù Zhōngguó yào kàn wǒ yǒu méi yǒu qián.

10. 便宜 的东西 不 一定不好。
    Piányi de dōngxi bú yídìng bù hǎo.

VI. Recognize and practice writing the following characters:

bǎi   百 百 百 百 百 百 百

| 百 | 百 | 百 | 百 | | | | | | |

yī   衣 衣 衣 衣 衣 衣 衣

| 衣 | 衣 | 衣 | 衣 | | | | | | |

kuài   块 块 块 块 块 块 块

| 块 | 块 | 块 | 块 | | | | | | |

mài   卖 卖 卖 卖 卖 卖 卖 卖 卖

| 卖 | 卖 | 卖 | 卖 | | | | | | |

CULTURAL INSIGHTS

The debate about the causal relationship between language and thought has been of perennial interest among linguists, anthropologists, psychologists and philosophers. No consensus has been reached due to the circular nature of evidencing. Thought is not empirically observable except through language and the effect of language is manifested again in language. However the correlation between aspects of language and thought is indisputable. The absence of a linguistic mechanism is often accompanied by an absence of a conceptual scheme. Comparison between English and Chinese in terms of the way in which questions about ordinal numbers are formed illustrates a good case in point.

Unlike English where ordinal numbers can be morphologically very different from cardinal numbers, ordinal numbers in Chinese bear close formal resemblance to cardinal numbers in a consistent way. They are formed by prefixing the word 第 (dì) before the cardinal numbers such as 第一 (dìyī, *first*), 第二 (dì'èr, *second*), 第三 (dìsān, *third*), etc. 第 (dì) serves a function similar to *-th* at the end of cardinal numbers in English. However, the similarity quickly ends when we ask questions about ordinal numbers in Chinese and English.

It is extremely difficult in English to form a question that elicits an unambiguous answer in the form of an ordinal number. Try to formulate a natural question to the following sentence that elicits the answer "the 40th":

Ronald Reagan was the 40th President of the United States.

Native speakers of English would find the task impossible to accomplish other than to express it in a two-step process such as *George Washington was the first President of the United States, what about Reagan?* Some of the attempts resulted in awkward questions like *Which President was Reagan?* (the answer is not necessarily *the 40th*, it could very well be *he was the one with an actor's background*).

Questions about ordinal numbers, however, do not present any problem in Chinese. To ask a question about an ordinal number in Chinese, all you need to do is to use 几 (jǐ), the question word about numbers, after the ordinal number indicator 第 (dì) such as 第几个人 (dì jǐ ge rén) and 第几本书 (dì jǐ běn shū) (no translation is attempted since it is impossible to translate).

What should interest us is not why it is difficult in English to ask questions about ordinal numbers, but rather why it is that it never bothers English speakers to ask such questions. Does it mean that order and sequence are important to the Chinese, but not to the speakers of English? It is true that order and sequence in the form of seniority, seating arrangement and so on are of consequence to the Chinese who are a number-conscious people, but no one would accept the claim that they are not important to speakers of English. The reason that English speakers never agonize about how to ask such questions is simply that it never occurs to them to ask such questions. Language is the tool through which thinking is conducted. A linguistic gap necessarily creates a conceptual gap. To explore gaps such as this in linguistic mechanism in relation to conceptual schemes in various languages would be a worthwhile pursuit.

Language is often thought of as being a mirror that reflects the external reality. Nothing, in fact, could be further from the truth. Language is a mirror, but it is a "fun house" mirror distorting our perception of the external reality. The external reality is cut up and classified differently in different languages. The classic example is the color system. While some languages have up to 20 terms for primary colors, others have only two. Units of numbers in Chinese, as compared with those in English provide another example, where they often do not correspond to each other:

billion			million			thousand		hundreds	tens	ones	*English*
亿				万			千	百	十	个	*Chinese*
yì				wàn			qiān	bǎi	shí	gè	
3	2	1	9	8	7	6	5	4	3	2	1

The above number is read in Chinese as 三千二百一十九亿八千七百六十五万四千三百二十一 (sānqiān èrbǎi yī shíjiǔ yì bāqiān qībǎi liùshí wǔwàn sìqiān sānbǎi èrshí yī). The chart also shows that large numbers in English are grouped by increments of 1,000, whereas in Chinese they are grouped by increments of 10,000.

Go to www.mandarintools.com/numbers.html, where you can enter an Arabic number and get the Chinese number, or the other way around. This is not only a utility tool, but also a good learning tool. The site also provides a description of the Chinese numerical system.

LESSON 8
FOOD & EATING

SENTENCE PATTERNS

月宫　　好像　不　错。
Yuègōng hǎoxiàng bú　cuò.

The Moon Palace seems very good.

月宫　　的什么　菜　有名?
Yuègōng　de shénme cài yǒumíng?

What are the specialty dishes at the Moon Palace?

你们　要　米饭还是　要
Nǐmen yào mǐfàn háishi yào
面条?
miàntiáo?

Do you want rice or noodles?

我　都　不要。
Wǒ dōu bú yào.

I want neither.

你吃　过　北京　烤鸭　吗?
Nǐ chī guo Běijīng kǎoyā ma?

Have you had Beijing Duck?

你有　没有　　喝过　青岛
Nǐ yǒu méiyou　hē guo Qīngdǎo
啤酒?
píjiǔ?

Have you ever had Qingdao beer?

CONVERSATIONS

A: 你们 饿不饿?
Nǐmen è bu è?

Are you hungry?

B: 我 有点儿饿。
Wǒ yǒudiǎnr è.

I'm a little hungry.

C: 我 很饿。
Wǒ hěn è.

I'm very hungry.

A: 我们 去吃中国 菜,
Wǒmen qù chī Zhōngguó cài,
怎么样?
zěnmeyàng?

Let's go to have Chinese food, shall we?

B: 当然 好! 我们 去
Dāngrán hǎo! Wǒmen qù
哪儿吃?
nǎr chī?

Great idea! Where shall we go?

A: 去中国城, 好不 好?
Qù Zhōngguóchéng, hǎo bu hǎo?

Let's go to Chinatown, shall we?

B: 好。你知道 中国城
Hǎo. Nǐ zhīdao Zhōngguóchéng
哪家餐馆 好 吗?
nǎ jiā cānguǎn hǎo ma?

Sure. Do you know which restaurant in Chinatown is good?

A: 月宫 好像 不错。
Yuègōng hǎoxiàng bú cuò.

The Moon Palace seems very good.

B: 月宫 的什么 菜有名?
Yuègōng de shénme cài yǒumíng?

What are the specialty dishes at the Moon Palace?

A: 月宫 的烤鸭 和 海鲜
Yuègōng de kǎoyā hé hǎixiān
最 有名。
zuì yǒumíng.

The roast duck and seafood there are the most famous.

A: 几位?   How many people?
   Jǐ wèi?

B: 三位。   Three.
   Sān wèi.

A: 请这儿　坐。   Please come sit here.
   Qǐng zhèr zuò.

   这　是　菜单。   This is the menu.
   Zhè shì càidān.

B: 谢谢。   Thank you.
   Xièxie.

A: 你们　要　什么　菜?   What dishes would you like
   Nǐmen yào shénme cài?   to order?

B: 我们　　要　一个酸辣汤,   We want a sweet and sour
   Wǒmen yào yí ge suānlàtāng,   soup, a sautéed beef with
   一个西兰花牛肉　和一   broccoli and a roast duck.
   yí ge xīlánhuā niúròu hé yí
   个烤鸭。
   ge kǎoyā.

A: 还　要　什么?   What else would you like to
   Hái yào shénme?   have?

B: 我们　还　要一个素菜。   We would also like to have a
   Wǒmen hái yào yí ge sùcài.   vegetable dish.

A: 你们　要　喝点儿什么?   What would you like to drink?
   Nǐmen yào hē diǎnr shénme?

B: 你们　有　什么?   What do you have?
   Nǐmen yǒu shénme?

A: 我们　有　白酒, 红酒   We have liquor, wine, and
   Wǒmen yǒu báijiǔ, hóngjiǔ   beer.
   和　啤酒。
   hé píjiǔ.

B: 你们　有　没　有　青岛　啤酒? Do you have Qingdao beer?
   Nǐmen yǒu méi yǒu Qīngdǎo píjiǔ?

A: 有，要几瓶?
Yǒu, yào jǐ píng?

Yes, how many bottles?

B: 我们 要 五 瓶。
Wǒmen yào wǔ píng.

We'd like to have five.

A: 你们 要 米饭还是 要
Nǐmen yào mǐfàn háishi yào
面条?
miàntiáo?

Do you want rice or noodles?

B: 我 要 米饭。
Wǒ yào mǐfàn.

I want rice.

C: 我 要 面条。
Wǒ yào miàntiáo.

I want noodles.

D: 我 都 不要。
Wǒ dōu bú yào.

I want neither.

能 不能 给我 面包?
Néng bù néng gěi wǒ miànbāo?

Can you give me bread?

A: 当然 可以。
Dāngrán kěyǐ.

Certainly.

A: 你吃 过 北京 烤鸭 吗?
Nǐ chī guo Běijīng kǎoyā ma?

Have you had Beijing Duck
before?

B: 没有。这 是第一次。
Méiyou. Zhè shì dìyī cì.

No, this is the first time.

A: 味道 怎么样?
Wèidao zěnmeyàng?

How does it taste?

B: 味道 好 极了。
Wèidao hǎo jí le.

It tastes great.

A: 你有 没有 喝过
Nǐ yǒu méiyou hē guo
青岛 啤酒?
Qīngdǎo píjiǔ?

Have you had Qingdao beer
before?

B: 喝 过。
Hē guo.

Yes.

A: 你觉得怎么样?
Nǐ juéde zěnmeyàng?

What do you think of it?

B: 青岛　啤酒很　好喝。
Qīngdǎo píjiǔ hěn hǎohē.

Qingdao beer tastes very good.

A: 你最　喜欢　吃　中国
Nǐ zuì xǐhuan chī Zhōngguó
的什么　菜?
de shénme cài?

What Chinese dish do you like to eat the most?

B: 我　最　喜欢　吃　四川　菜。
Wǒ zuì xǐhuan chī Sìchuān cài.

I like to eat the Sichuan (Sezchuan) dish the most.

A: 听说　四川　菜很　辣。
Tīngshuō Sìchuān cài hěn là.

I heard that the Sichuan (Sezchuan) dishes are very spicy.

B: 对，但是很　好吃。
Duì, dànshì hěn hàochī.

Right, but they are delicious.

A: 我们的　菜　怎么样?
Wǒmende cài zěnmeyàng?

How is our food?

B: 很　好吃。
Hěn hàochī.

Delicious.

A: 谢谢。这　是帐单。
Xièxie. Zhè shì zhàngdān.

Thank you. Here is the check.

B: 一共　多少　钱?
Yígòng duōshao qián?

How much altogether?

A: 一共　四十五块。
Yígòng sìshí wǔ kuài.

45 dollars altogether.

B: 这　是　四十五　块。
Zhè shì sìshí wǔ kuài.

This is 45 dollars.

这　是　小费。
Zhè shì xiǎofèi.

This is the tip.

A: 谢谢。欢迎　再来。
Xièxie. Huānyíng zài lái.

Thank you. Come again.

WORDS AND EXPRESSIONS

Nouns

米饭	mǐfàn	(cooked) rice
面包	miànbāo	bread
菜	cài	dishes
烤鸭	kǎoyā	roast duck
海鲜	hǎixiān	seafood
菜单	càidān	menu
汤	tāng	soup
西兰花	xīlánhuā	broccoli
牛肉	niúròu	beef
素菜	sùcài	vegetable dish
白酒	báijiǔ	liquor
红酒	hóngjiǔ	wine
啤酒	píjiǔ	beer
瓶	píng	bottle
肉	ròu	meat
帐单	zhàngdān	check, bill
小费	xiǎofèi	tip
味道	wèidào	taste
次	cì	time (occurance)
月宫	Yuègōng	Moon Palace
青岛	Qīngdǎo	Qingdao

Verbs

好像	hǎoxiàng	seem
喝	hē	drink
坐	zuò	sit
给	gěi	give
欢迎	huānyíng	welcome

Adjectives

有名	yǒumíng	famous
酸	suān	sour
辣	là	spicy
对	duì	right, correct

Adverbs

还	hái	additionally, still
极了	jíle	extremely
一定	yídìng	certainly, definitely

Classifiers

位	wèi
家	jiā

Particles

过	guo

Expressions

有点儿	yǒudiǎnr	a little, somewhat

SUPPLEMENTARY WORDS AND EXPRESSIONS

Nouns

猪肉	zhūròu	pork
羊肉	yángròu	lamb
鸡	jī	chicken
鱼	yú	fish
茶	chá	tea
鸡蛋	jīdàn	egg
牛奶	niúnǎi	milk
饺子	jiǎozi	dumpling
包子	bāozi	steamed stuffed bun
水果	shuǐguǒ	fruit

甜点	tiándiǎn	dessert
碗	wǎn	bowl
盘子	pánzi	plate
筷子	kuàizi	chopsticks
刀	dāo	knife
叉	chā	fork
餐巾	cānjīn	napkin
糖	táng	sugar
盐	yán	salt
电影	diànyǐng	movie

Verbs

炒	chǎo	fry
炸	zhá	deep fry
做饭	zuòfàn	cook
请...... 吃饭	qǐng ...... chīfàn	invite sb. to a meal

Adjectives

红	hóng	red
绿	lǜ	green
咸	xián	salty
甜	tián	sweet

LANGUAGE POINTS

1. 家 (jiā)

家 (jiā), as a classifier, is used with such words as *hospital, bank, company, factory, movie theater, store,* and *restaurant*. What is common among these words is that they are all home-like (the original meaning of 家 jiā) buildings and structures.

2. 几位 (jǐ wèi)?

几位 (jǐ wèi) is an abbreviated form for 你们是几位客人 (nǐmen shì jǐ wèi kèrén), where 位 (wèi) is a polite classifier for people, usually used for words like *guest, teacher, customer, friend, gentleman,* and *lady*. In informal and familiar speech, 个 (ge) is used instead.

3. 你们要喝点儿什么 (nǐmen yào hē diǎnr shénme)?

点儿 (diǎnr) is short for 一点儿 (yìdiǎnr). When the number is one, we often leave it out. For example:

我 有 个 问题。
Wǒ yǒu ge wèntí.

I have a question.

她要 买 件 大衣。
Tā yào mǎi jiàn dàyī.

She is going to to buy a coat.

4. 你们要米饭还是要面条 (nǐmen yào mǐfàn háishi yào miàntiáo)?

This is an alternative question involving a choice. The question is indicated by 还是 (háishi), which is placed between the two choices. Please note that 还是 (háishi) used in the sense of *or* is an interrogative expression. As such, it can only be used in questions. In other words, 还是 (háishi) can never be used in affirmative sentences in the sense of *or*. The Chinese word for *or* in affirmative sentences like *he is coming either today or tomorrow* is 或 (huò) or 或者 (huòzhě).

There are three possible answers to an alternative question: 1) making one choice, 2) accepting both choices, and 3) rejecting both choices. See the following illustrations:

你喜欢 法国 电影　还是 美国　电影?

Nǐ xǐhuan Fǎguó diànyǐng háishi Měiguó diànyǐng?

Do you like French movies or American movies?

我 喜欢 美国　电影　*or*　我 喜欢 法国 电影。

Wǒ xǐhuan Měiguó diànyǐng.　　　Wǒ xǐhuan Fǎguó diànyǐng.

I like American movies.　　　　　I like French movies.

我 都 喜欢。　　　　　　I like both.

Wǒ dōu xǐhuan.

我 都 不喜欢。　　　　　I like neither.

Wǒ dōu bù xǐhuan.

In the second and third answers, 都 (dōu) is used to indicate inclusiveness, positive or negative. This is different from English, where *both* is used in affirmative responses whereas *neither* is used in negative responses. Note should also be taken of the peculiarity of 都 (dōu) such that the adverb can only refer back, not forward. For this reason, it is not correct to say:

我 都 喜欢 米饭和面条。

Wǒ dōu xǐhuan mǐfàn hé miàntiáo.

The correct form is:

米饭 和面条　我 都 喜欢。

Mǐfàn hé miàntiáo wǒ dōu xǐhuan.

5. 你吃过北京烤鸭吗 (nǐ chī guo Běijīng kǎoyā ma)?

The grammatical particle 过 (guo) is used after a verb to indicate an action that took place at an unspecified time in the past. The emphasis is on the experience rather than the result or completion of the action. It can often be translated into the perfect tense in English (such as *I have done ... before, he has been to ... before*, and *they have seen ... before*). See the following examples:

我 爸爸去过 北京。   My father has been to Beijing.
Wǒ bàba qù guo Běijīng.

他吃 过 法国 菜。   He has had French food.
Tā chī guo Fǎguó cài.

他们 学 过 中文。   They have studied Chinese.
Tāmen xué guo Zhōngwén.

The negative of the sentence is indicated by 没有 (méiyou) instead of 不 (bù), for example:

我 爸爸没有 去过   My father has not been to
Wǒ bàba méiyou qù guo   Beijing.
北京。
Běijīng.

他没有 吃过 法国 菜。 He has not had French food.
Tā méiyou chī guo Fǎguó cài.

他们 没有 学过 中文。 They have not studied Chinese.
Tāmen méiyou xué guo Zhōngwén.

Like sentences with a present or future reference, there are two yes/no forms for sentences using 过 (guo) to indicate past experience: attaching 吗 (ma) at the end of the sentence or using 有没有 (yǒu méiyou) before the verb. See for example:

Has your father been to Beijing?
你爸爸去过 北京 吗?
Nǐ bàba qù guo Běijīng ma?
你爸爸有 没有　去 过 北京?
Nǐ bàba yǒu méiyou qù guo Běijīng?

Has he ever had French food?
他吃 过 法国 菜吗?
Tā chī guo Fǎguó cài ma?
他有 没有　吃 过 法国 菜?
Tā yǒu méiyou chī guo Fǎguó cài?

Have they ever studied Chinese?
他们 学 过 中文　　吗?
Tāmen xué guo Zhōngwén ma?
他们 有 没有　学 过 中文?
Tāmen yǒu méiyou xué guo Zhōngwén?

To give a yes answer to the above questions, simply take the verb with 过 (guo). To give a no answer, use 没有 (méiyǒu) before the verb and 过 (guo). The following are yes/no answers to the above questions:

去 过 / 没有 去过
Qù guo / méiyou qù guo

吃 过 / 没有 吃 过
Chī guo / méiyou chī guo

学 过 / 没有 学 过
Xué guo / méiyou xué guo

6. 很好吃 (hěn hǎochī)

好 (hǎo) is often used with a verb to form an adjective, meaning *good to* ... For example:

好喝 (hǎohē)	good to drink
好听 (hǎotīng)	good to listen (used to describe music, voice, etc.)
好看 (hǎokàn)	good-looking, interesting (used to describe people, books, movies, etc.)
好玩 (hǎowán)	fun, interesting (used to describe places, toys, etc.)

EXERCISES

I. Answer the following questions:

1. 你喜欢 吃 中国 菜 还是日本 菜?
   Nǐ xǐhuan chī Zhōngguó cài háishi Rìběn cài?

   _____

2. 你喝过 青岛 啤酒吗?
   Nǐ hē guo Qīngdǎo píjiǔ ma?

   _____

3. 你吃 肉 吗? 你喜欢 吃 什么 肉?
   Nǐ chī ròu ma? Nǐ xǐhuan chī shénme ròu?

   _____

4. 你去 过 中国 吗?
   Nǐ qù guo Zhōngguó ma?

   _____

5. 你会 不会 做 菜? 你会 做 什么 菜?
   Nǐ huì bu huì zuò cài? Nǐ huì zuò shénme cài?

   _____

6. 你家谁 做 饭?
   Nǐ jiā shéi zuò fàn?

   _____

7. 你喝不喝酒? 你喝 什么 酒?
   Nǐ hē bu hē jiǔ? Nǐ hē shénme jiǔ?

   _____

8. 纽约　的什么　最 有名?
   Niǔyuē　de shénme zuì　yǒumíng?

   _____

9. 中国　　茶好喝 不好喝? 你喜欢 红茶　　还是
   Zhōngguó chá hǎohē bu hǎohē?　Nǐ xǐhuan hóngchá háishi
   绿茶?
   lǜchá?

   _____

10. 你在 学校　工作　还是 在公司 工作?
    Nǐ zài xuéxiào gōngzuò háishi　zài gōngsī gōngzuò?

    _____

II. Fill in the blanks with appropriate words:

1. 你是 中国人　　_____　美国人?
   Nǐ shì Zhōngguórén _____ Měiguórén?

2. 你喜欢　_____　喜欢 法国 菜?
   Nǐ xǐhuan _____ xǐhuan Fǎguó cài?

3. 他 没有　去 _____　英国。
   Tā méiyou qù _____ Yīngguó.

4. 日本 音乐 很 好 _____。
   Rìběn yīnyuè hěn hǎo _____.

5. 我 妈妈 吃 _____ 北京 烤鸭。
   Wǒ māma chī _____ Běijīng kǎoyā.

6. 你 _____ 没有 看 过 这 本 书?
   Nǐ _____ méiyou kàn guo zhè běn shū?

7. _____ 有 中国　餐馆?
_____ yǒu Zhōngguó cānguǎn?

8. 一共 _____ 钱?
Yígòng _____ qián?

9. 这 _____ 餐馆　的菜很 有名。
Zhè _____ cānguǎn de cài hěn yǒumíng.

10. 这 是 我 第二 _____ 喝青岛　啤酒。
Zhè shì wǒ dì'èr _____ hē Qīngdǎo píjiǔ.

III. First change the following sentences into yes/no questions and then change them into negative sentences:

1. 我 看 过 英国　电影。
Wǒ kàn guo Yīngguó diànyǐng.

_____

_____

2. 她的老师 学 过 德语。
Tāde lǎoshī xué guo Déyǔ.

_____

_____

3. 他去过 香港。
Tā qù guo Xiānggǎng.

_____

_____

4. 我的 中国　朋友　来 过我 家。
Wǒde Zhōngguó péngyou lái guo wǒ jiā.

_____

_____

5. 他们 吃 过 法国 菜。
Tāmen chī guo Fǎguó cài.

_____

_____

6. 她的男朋友　听 过 日本 音乐。
Tāde nánpéngyou tīng guo Rìběn yīnyuè.

_____

_____

7. 你爸爸在 中国　银行　工作　过。
Nǐ bàba zài Zhōngguó yínháng gōngzuò guo.

_____

_____

8. 他妈妈 在 中国　换 过 钱。
Tā māma zài Zhōngguó huàn guo qián.

_____

_____

9. 王　老师 在那个 商店　买 过 东西。
Wáng lǎoshī zài nà ge shāngdiàn mǎi guo dōngxi.

_____

_____

10. 你弟弟在 加州　住 过。
Nǐ dìdi zài Jiāzhōu zhù guo.

_____

_____

IV. Translate the following into Chinese:

1. I'm not too hungry.

   _____

2. Peking Duck is very famous.

   _____

3. Is the men's room on the second floor or third floor?

   _____

4. Would you like coffee or tea?

   _____

5. This restaurant's dishes are delicious.

   _____

6. Have you been to Chinatown in New York?

   _____

7. You look very tired.

   _____

8. This was my first time eating Japanese food. I found the taste
   was very good.

   _____

9. Restaurants in China don't accept tips.

   _____

10. What else would you like to eat?

   _____

V. Translate the following into English:

1. 你爸爸在 大学 工作 还是 在 中学 工作?
Nǐ bàba zài dàxué gōngzuò háishi zài zhōngxué gōngzuò?

_____

2. 绿茶 不好喝，我喜欢 红茶。
Lùchá bù hǎohē, wǒ xǐhuan hóngchá.

_____

3. 你的女朋友 是 中国人 还是 美国人?
Nǐde nǚpéngyou shì Zhōngguórén háishi Měiguórén?

_____

4. 我 先生 没有 看 过 中国 电影。
Wǒ xiānsheng méiyou kàn guo Zhōngguó diànyǐng.

_____

5. 广州 的什么 菜 有名?
Guǎngzhōu de shénme cài yǒumíng?

_____

6. 我 姐姐不能 喝白酒，能 喝 一点儿红酒。
Wǒ jiějie bù néng hē báijiǔ, néng hē yìdiǎnr hóngjiǔ.

_____

7. 米饭 和面条 我 都 不要，我 要 面包。
Mǐfàn hé miàntiáo wǒ dōu bú yào, wǒ yào miànbāo.

_____

8. 他家他太太做 饭，我 家我 做 饭。
Tā jiā tā tàitai zuò fàn, wǒ jiā wǒ zuò fàn.

_____

9. 你今天 晚上   在 家吃饭 还是在 餐馆   吃饭?
   Nǐ jīntiān wǎnshang zài jiā chīfàn háishi zài cānguǎn chīfàn?

10. 中国人   有时   只 吃 饭不 吃 菜，美国人
    Zhōngguórén yǒushí zhǐ chī fàn bù chī cài, Měiguórén
    有时 只 吃 菜不 吃饭。
    yǒushí zhǐ chī cài bù chī fàn.

VI. Recognize and practice writing the following characters:

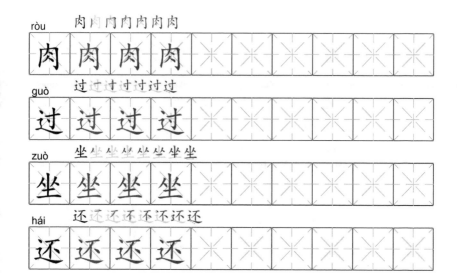

róu 肉 肉 肉 肉 肉 肉 肉

肉 肉 肉 肉

guò 过 过 过 过 过 过

过 过 过 过

zuò 坐 坐 坐 坐 坐 坐 坐

坐 坐 坐 坐

hái 还 还 还 还 还 还 还

还 还 还 还

CULTURAL INSIGHTS

Few people in the world have never had some culinary experience with Chinese food. To many people, the very term China or Chinese conjures up images of savory cuisine. It is indisputable that the Chinese people attach great importance to the preparation of their food, which can reach incredible levels of sophistication, elaboration, and variety. Dishes not only have to taste good, but also have to be aesthetically appealing. If you are invited by your friends in China to a meal, you can expect to see a lavish spread of food, which is the best way in Chinese culture to show hospitality to friends, particularly those coming from afar.

Meals are called 饭 (fàn) in Chinese. A typical Chinese meal consists of two parts: 饭 (fàn) and 菜 (cài). 饭 (fàn) is a grain or starch-based staple that includes rice, noodles, steamed bread, steamed buns, dumplings, and so on. It comes in a bowl and is served individually. 菜 (cài) refers to dishes that consists of two types—素菜 (sùcài) and 荤菜 (hūncài). 素菜 (sùcài) are vegetable dishes and 荤菜 (hūncài) are dishes with meat or fish. Dishes are usually served on a plate, which is shared. Of particular mention are the terms for the meat of various animals. In English, the term for the meat served on the table is often different from that used for the animal in the pen or the stable, a result of the Norman Conquest. In Chinese however, the terms for the meat of various animals are simply the combination of the word for the animal and the word 肉 (ròu) such as 猪肉 (zhūròu, *pig meat*, thus pork), 牛肉 (niúròu, *cow meat*, thus beef) and 羊肉 (yángròu, *sheep meat*, thus lamb). They may not sound as elegant as those Norman-French terms, but they are logical and easy to remember. You may have already noticed that the staple food and the meal, of which the staple food is a part, are both called 饭 (fàn). This is for a good reason. There is a rhetorical device in language called *synecdoche* whereby the part can be used to refer to the whole, such as *roof* for the *house* and *waves* for the *ocean*. 饭 (fàn) is a good case in point. Traditionally, and to a large extent still true today, 饭 (fàn) *the staple* is held more important than 菜 (cài) to the Chinese, providing about 75 percent of caloric intake for the population. For this reason, 饭 (fàn) is often called 主食 (zhǔshí, *main food*) in Chinese. 饭 (fàn) *the staple* is considered so important chiefly for an economic reason. It is easier to afford 饭 (fàn) *the staple* than 菜 (cài). In the West, 饭 (fàn) *the staple* only serves as side food and may be dispensed with altogether, whereas in China, sometimes people only eat 饭 (fàn) *the staple* without 菜 (cài). Since 饭 (fàn) *the staple* was taken so seriously, it came to be used to refer to the whole meal that includes 菜 (cài) as well. This explains why the Chinese do not think you have eaten even if you are full, eating a lot of dishes, but no rice or bread, because you have not eaten 饭 (fàn) *the staple*, a play upon words that can be interpreted as 饭 (fàn) *the meal*.

汤 (tāng, *soup*) is part of 菜 (cài), which can be of many varieties. Different from the practice in the West, 汤 (tāng) is served in China either with the meal or at the end of the meal, but never before the meal. On formal occasions, people do drink. The word used by the Chinese for drink is a generic one—酒 (jiǔ), which simply means alcoholic beverage, covering liquor, wine, and beer. At the meal, Chinese people like to urge their guests to drink more on the belief that if they do not let their guests drink to their hearts' content, they are mistreating them. Mistreatment of guests is definitely a sin. For this reason, the hosts will go out of their way to make their guests drink more by finding all sorts of justifications. It is customary in China for a guest to tell the host that he can only drink 30 percent when he can actually drink 100 percent just to leave enough room to maneuver with the host. Failing to do so, you may become the object of repeated toasts in a shower of hospitality.

Tea is an everyday drink for which there is a national taste. This native product is served on all occasions. Visitors to someone's house will be served tea without asking. Chinese teas fall into the following general types: green tea, black tea (which is actually called red tea in Chinese), jasmine tea, and *wulong* tea, each of which can be further divided. The classification is often based on the manner in which a particular kind of tea is produced. Green tea is unfermented, black tea is fermented, *wulong* tea is semi-fermented, and jasmine tea is made from a combination of black tea, green tea, *wulong* tea and some fragrant flowers. Although the taste for tea varies from individual to individual, generally people in southern China prefer green tea, whereas those in northern China prefer jasmine tea. *Wulong* tea is the favorite in areas of Guangdong and Fujian. This geographical preference may have to do with the climatic conditions. Green tea is popular in the warm south because it is soothing and jasmine tea is favored in the cold north because it adds heat to the body temperature.

One of the headaches for foreigners traveling to China is that they don't know how to order in a restaurant. The names of many Chinese dishes are so fancy and flowery that native speakers of Chinese often don't even know what they mean. However, you can find a list of Chinese dishes in English at bbs.chinanews.com.cn/thread-372202-1-1.html. The dishes are grouped into categories. Print it out and arm yourself with it when you go to a restaurant in China.

LESSON 9
TRAVEL

SENTENCE PATTERNS

你每 天 怎么 去上班?
Nǐ měi tiān zěnme qù shàngbān?

How do you go to work everyday?

我 每 天 坐 地铁去上班。
Wǒ měi tiān zuò dìtiě qù shàngbān.

I go to work by subway everyday.

从 南京 路 坐 地铁到
Cóng Nánjīng Lù zuò dìtiě dào
火车站 要 多少 时间?
huǒchēzhàn yào duōshao shíjiān?

How long does it take to go from Nanjing Road to the train station by subway?

你们 去华盛顿 做 什么?
Nǐmen qù Huáshèngdùn zuò shénme?

Why are you going to Washington?

我们 去玩。
Wǒmen qù wán.

We are going there for pleasure.

你家离学校 远 不 远?
Nǐ jiā lí xuéxiào yuǎn bu yuǎn?

Is your home far from the school?

我 有时骑自行车 去上学,
Wǒ yǒushí qí zìxíngchē qù shàngxué,
有时 走 去上学。
yǒushí zǒu qù shàngxué.

Sometimes I go to school by bike, sometimes I go there on foot.

你今年 在哪儿过 圣诞节?
Nǐ jīnnián zài nǎr guò Shèngdànjié?

Where are you going to spend your Christmas this year?

我 想 坐 飞机去。
Wǒ xiǎng zuò fēijī qù.

I'd like to go by plane.

你去洛杉矶　住　哪儿?
Nǐ qù Luòshānjī zhù nǎr?

Where are you going to stay in Los Angeles?

旅馆　好找　不好找?
Lǚguǎn hǎozhǎo bu hǎozhǎo?

Is it easy to find a hotel?

你一定　要　去玩玩。
Nǐ yídìng yào qù wánwan.

You must go there for a visit.

你去过　中国　几次?
Nǐ qù guo Zhōngguó jǐ cì?

How many times have you been to China?

你去过　中国　的什么
Nǐ qù guo Zhōngguó de shénme
地方?
dìfang?

Where in China have you been?

CONVERSATIONS

A: 你在哪儿工作?
Nǐ zài nǎr gōngzuò?

Where do you work?

B: 我 在中国   银行
Wǒ zài Zhōngguó yínháng
工作。
gōngzuò.

I work at Bank of China.

A: 你每 天 怎么 去上班?
Nǐ měi tiān zěnme qù shàngbān?

How do you go to work everyday?

B: 我 每 天 坐 地铁去
Wǒ měi tiān zuò dìtiě qù
上班。
shàngbān.

I go to work by subway everyday.

A: 你太太每 天 也坐 地铁
Nǐ tàitai měi tiān yě zuò dìtiě
去上班   吗?
qù shàngbān ma?

Does you wife also go to work by subway everyday?

B: 她不坐   地铁, 她坐 汽车。
Tā bú zuò dìtiě, tā zuò qìchē.

She does not take the subway, she takes the bus.

A: 上海   有 地铁吗?
Shànghǎi yǒu dìtiě ma?

Are there subways in Shanghai?

B: 有。
Yǒu.

Yes.

A: 从 南京   路坐 地铁到
Cóng Nánjīng Lù zuò dìtiě dào
火车站   要 多少 时间?
huǒchēzhàn yào duōshao shíjiān?

How long does it take to go from Nanjing Road to the train station by subway?

B: 差不多   五 分钟。
Chàbuduō wǔ fēnzhōng.

About five minutes.

A: 上海　　有 几路地铁?
Shànghǎi yǒu jǐ lù dìtiě?

How many subway lines are there in Shanghai?

B: 上海　　有 十五路地铁。
Shànghǎi yǒu shíwǔ lù dìtiě.

There are 15 subway lines in Shanghai.

A: 这 个周末　你去哪儿?
Zhè ge zhōumò nǐ qù nǎr?

Where are you going to go this weekend?

B: 我 和我太太去华盛顿。
Wǒ hé wǒ tàitai qù Huáshèngdùn.

My wife and I are going to Washington.

A: 你们 去华盛顿　　做
Nǐmen qù Huáshèngdùn zuò
什么?
shénme?

Why are you going there?

B: 我们　去玩。
Wǒmen qù wán.

We are going there for pleasure.

A: 你们 怎么 去?
Nǐmen zěnme qù?

How are you going?

B: 我们　开车 去。
Wǒmen kāichē qù.

We are driving there.

A: 从　纽约　开车 到
Cóng Niǔyuē kāichē dào
华盛顿　　要 几个小时?
Huáshèngdùn yào jǐ ge xiǎoshí?

How long does it take to drive from New York to Washington?

B: 差不多　要 四个小时。
Chàbuduō yào sì ge xiǎoshí.

It takes about four hours.

A: 你家离学校　远 不远?
Nǐ jiā lí xuéxiào yuǎn bu yuǎn?

Is your home far from the school?

B: 不 太远。坐　汽车只
Bú tài yuǎn. Zuò qìchē zhǐ
要 十分钟。
yào shí fēnzhōng.

Not too far. It only takes about ten minutes by bus.

A: 你每天怎么去上学?
Nǐ měi tiān zěnme qù shàngxué?

How do you go to school everyday?

B: 我有时骑自行车去,
Wǒ yǒushí qí zìxíngchē qù,
有时走去。
yǒushí zǒu qù.

Sometimes I go there by bike, sometimes on foot.

A: 你骑自行车要多少
Nǐ qí zìxíngchē yào duōshao
时间?
shíjiān?

How long does it take you to go by bike?

B: 骑自行车要十五分钟。
Qí zìxíngchē yào shíwǔ fēnzhōng.

It takes 15 minutes by bike.

A: 走呢?
Zǒu ne?

What about walking?

B: 走要三十分钟。
Zǒu yào sānshí fēnzhōng.

It takes 30 minutes.

A: 你今年在哪儿过
Nǐ jīnnián zài nǎr guò
圣诞节?
Shèngdànjié?

Where are you going to spend your Christmas this year?

B: 我去加州。
Wǒ qù Jiāzhōu.

I'm going to California.

A: 你去加州的什么地方?
Nǐ qù Jiāzhōu de shénme dìfang?

Where in California are you going?

B: 我去洛杉矶。
Wǒ qù Luòshānjī.

I'm going to Los Angeles.

A: 你怎么去?
Nǐ zěnme qù?

How are you going?

B: 我想坐飞机去,
Wǒ xiǎng zuò fēijī qù,
可是飞机票很贵,
kěshì fēijīpiào hěn guì,

I'd like to go by plane, but I may take the train, because the plane ticket is very expensive.

我 可能 坐 火车 去。
wǒ kěnéng zuò huǒchē qù.

A: 你去洛杉矶 住 哪儿?　　Where are you going to stay
Nǐ qù Luòshānjī zhù nǎr?　　　in Los Angeles?

B: 我 住 旅馆。　　　　　　I'm going to stay in a hotel.
Wǒ zhù lǚguǎn.

A: 旅馆 好找 不好找?　　　Is it easy to find a hotel?
Lǚguǎn hǎozhǎo bu hǎozhǎo?

B: 好找。 洛杉矶 有 很　　Yes, there are many hotels in
Hǎozhǎo. Luòshānjī yǒu hěn　　Los Angeles.
多 旅馆。
duō lǚguǎn.

A: 你去过 中国　　吗?　　Have you been to China?
Nǐ qù guo Zhōngguó ma?

B: 去过。　　　　　　　　Yes.
Qù guo.

A: 你去过 几次?　　　　　How many times have you
Nǐ qù guo jǐ cì?　　　　　　　been there?

B: 我 去过 两 次。　　　I've been there twice.
Wǒ qù guo liǎng cì.

A: 你去过 中国　 的什么　Where in China have you
Nǐ qù guo Zhōngguó de shénme　been to?
地方?
dìfang?

B: 我 去过 中国　 的　　I've been to Beijing, Shanghai
Wǒ qù guo Zhōngguó de　　　Shanghai, Suzhou and
北京, 上海,　 苏州 和　Hangzhou.
Běijīng, Shànghǎi, Sūzhōu hé
杭州。
Hángzhōu.

A: 你最 喜欢 什么 地方?　What places do you like the
Nǐ zuì xǐhuan shénme dìfang?　best?

B: 我 最喜欢 苏州 和
Wǒ zuì xǐhuan Sūzhōu hé
杭州。 你知道 吗?
Hángzhōu. Nǐ zhīdao ma?
中国人 常 说,
Zhōngguórén cháng shuō,
"上 有 天堂, 下 有
"shàng yǒu tiāntáng, xià yǒu
苏杭"。
Sū Háng."

I like Suzhou and Hangzhou the best. Do you know? Chinese people often say, "up above there is paradise, down below there is Suzhou and Hangzhou."

WORDS AND EXPRESSIONS

Nouns

车	chē	vehicle
路	lù	road, route
小时	xiǎoshí	hour
分钟	fēnzhōng	minute
年	nián	year
圣诞节	Shèngdànjié	Christmas
飞机	fēijī	airplane
地铁	dìtiě	subway
自行车	zìxíngchē	bicycle
旅馆	lǚguǎn	hotel
地方	dìfang	place
票	piào	ticket
天堂	tiāntáng	paradise
华盛顿	Huáshèngdùn	Washington
苏州	Sūzhōu	Suzhou
杭州	Hángzhōu	Hangzhou

Verbs

开	kāi	operate, drive
骑	qí	ride
走	zǒu	walk
玩	wán	play, have fun, go sightseeing
上学	shàngxué	go to school
想	xiǎng	would like
过	guò	celebrate, spend (a holiday)
找	zhǎo	look for, find
可能	kěnéng	maybe

Adverbs

差不多	chàbuduō	approximately, about
常	cháng	often
上	shàng	up
下	xià	down

Prepositions

从	cóng	from ... to ...
到	dào	
离	lí	away from

SUPPLEMENTARY WORDS AND EXPRESSIONS

Nouns

出租汽车	chūzūqìchē	taxi
电车	diànchē	trolley-bus
街	jiē	street
警察	jǐngchá	police, policeman
护照	hùzhào	passport
签证	qiānzhèng	visa
旅行	lǚxíng	travel
旅行社	lǚxíngshè	travel agency
行李	xíngli	luggage
船	chuán	boat, ship
海关	hǎiguān	customs
导游	dǎoyóu	guide
市中心	shìzhōngxīn	city center, downtown
亚洲	Yàzhōu	Asia
欧洲	Ōuzhōu	Europe
美洲	Měizhōu	America (continent)
非洲	Fēizhōu	Africa
澳州	Àozhōu	Australia

Adjectives

新	xīn	new
近	jìn	close, near

LANGUAGE POINTS

1. 你每天怎么去上班 (nǐ měitiān zěnme qù shàngbān)?

怎么 (zěnme, *how*) in the question serves as an adverbial of manner. As such, it is placed before the verb with 每天 (měi tiān, *everyday*), which is an adverbial of time. Similarly we can say:

你明天　怎么来? Nǐ míngtiān zěnme lái?	How are you coming tomorrow?
这 个字怎么 写? Zhè ge zì zěnme xiě?	How do you write this character?
"English" 用 中文 "English" yòng Zhōngwén 怎么 说? zěnme shuō?	How do you say "English" in Chinese?

2. 我每天坐地铁去上班 (wǒ měi tiān zuò dìtiě qù shàngbān)

To answer the question "你每天怎么去上班" (nǐ měi tiān zěnme qù shàngbān), all you need to do is to specify, where the question word is, the manner of traveling such as taking a bus, train, taxi, riding a bicycle or walking, for example:

我 每 天 坐 汽车去上班。(by bus)
Wǒ měi tiān zuò qìchē qù shàngbān.

我 每 天 坐 火车 去上班。(by train)
Wǒ měi tiān zuò huǒchē qù shàngbān.

我 每 天 坐 出租车 去上班。(by taxi)
Wǒ měi tiān zuò chūzūchē qù shàngbān.

我 每 天 骑自行车 去上班。(by bike)
Wǒ měi tiān qí zìxíngchē qù shàngbān.

我 每 天 走 去上班。(on foot)
Wǒ měi tiān zǒu qù shàngbān.

3. 从南京路坐地铁到火车站要多少时间 (cóng Nánjīng Lù zuò dìtiě dào huǒchēzhàn yào duōshao shíjiān)?
"从 ...... 到 ......" (cóng ...... dào ......) is equivalent to *from ... to ...* in English. For example:

从 早 到 晚   from morning till night
cóng zǎo dào wǎn

从 学校 到 家   from school to home
cóng xuéxiào dào jiā

从 中国 到 美国   from China to the United
cóng Zhōngguó dào Měiguó   States

Since Chinese strictly adheres to the principal of temporal sequence whereby what happens first is placed first, the temporal sequence in the question is 1) departing from Nanjing Road, 2) taking the subway, and 3) arriving at the train station. They thus follow each other. Sometimes however, "taking the subway" can be placed either before 1) or after 3) as in:

坐 地铁从 南京 路到 火车站 要 多少 时间?
Zuò dìtiě cóng Nánjīng Lù dào huǒchēzhàn yào duōshao shíjiān?

从 南京 路到 火车站 坐 地铁要 多少
Cóng Nánjīng Lù dào huǒchēzhàn zuò dìtiě yào duōshao
时间?
shíjiān?

The word 要 (yào) in Chinese has two basic meanings: 1) *want, need*, or *be going to*, and 2) *take* or *require* (time, etc.). 要 (yào) is used in the first sense when the subject is animate, be a person or personified object. 要 (yào) is used in the second sense when the subject is impersonal in the form of a process or an action. Compare:

她明天　要 去中国。 Tā míngtiān yào qù Zhōngguó.	She is going to China tomorrow.
去火车站　你要 坐 Qù huǒchēzhàn nǐ yào zuò 汽车。 qìchē.	You need to take the bus to go to the train station.
开车 去 要 两 天。 Kāichē qù yào liǎng tiān.	It takes two days to drive there.

4. 你们去华盛顿做什么 (nǐmen qù Huáshèngdùn zuò shénme)?

"去做什么" (qù zuò shénme) is a question frequently used to ask the purpose of going to a certain place. Although Mandarin does have a specific expression equivalent to *why* in English 为什么 (wèishénme), it is not as often used as this question form in this instance.

5. 我们去玩 (wǒmen qù wán)

玩 (wán) is a difficult word to translate into English. Although dictionaries often define it as *play*, it is widely used in Chinese to mean *enjoy, have fun, have a good time, hang out,* or *do something for pleasure*. It is basically opposed to work. The various meanings of 玩 (wán) are illustrated in the following examples:

你有 时间 请 来 Nǐ yǒu shíjiān qǐng lái 我 家玩。 wǒ jiā wán.	Please drop by my house when you have time.

北京 很 好玩。
Běijīng hěn hǎowán.

Beijing is a fun place.

这 个 周末 我 去
Zhè ge zhōumò wǒ qù
公园   玩。
gōngyuán wán.

I'm going to the park this
weekend (to relax).

6. 你家离学校远不远 (nǐ jiā lí xuéxiào yuǎn bu yuǎn)?

"A 离 (lí) B 远 (yuǎn)/近 (jìn)" is a pattern used to indicate the distance of one place relative to another place, equivalent to English *A is far from/close to B*. Since "离 (lí) B" (away from B or close to B) is an adverbial expression indicating a point of reference, it is placed before the verb, or the adjective as in this case.

Distinction should be made between 从 (cóng) and 离 (lí), which are often confused because both can be translated into English as *from*. Keep in mind that 从 (cóng) indicates a point of origin or departure, usually used with motion verbs such as 来 (lái, *come*) or 去 (qù, *go*). On the other hand, 离 (lí) marks a point of reference, usually used with a static verb or adjective. Compare:

他从   美国   来。
Tā cóng Měiguó lái.

He comes from the United
States.

我 家离 银行 很 近。
Wǒ jiā lí yínháng hěn jìn.

My home is close to the bank.

7. 你今年在哪儿过圣诞节 (nǐ jīnnián zài nǎr guò Shèngdànjié)?

过 (guò), meaning *spend, celebrate,* or *observe,* is often used in connection with holidays, festivals, birthdays, and other important occasions. Although it may be glossed as *spend,* it is never used with money to mean *spend money.* For example:

中国人　　过 不过　　　　Do people in China celebrate
Zhōngguórén guò bu guò　　Christmas?
圣诞节?
Shèngdànjié?

孩子们 最喜欢　过年。　Children like to celebrate
Háizǐmen zuì xǐhuan guò nián.　New Year's Day the most.

你太太的生日 怎么 过?　How do you celebrate your
Nǐ tàitai de shēngri zěnme guò?　wife's birthday?

8. 今年 **(jīnnián)**

The following are various ways to express days (today, yesterday, tomorrow), week, month and year (current, previous and next):

今天	今年	这 个 星期	这 个月
jīntiān	jīnnián	zhè ge xīngqī	zhè ge yuè
today	*this year*	*this week*	*this month*
昨天	去年	上　个星期	上　个月
zuótiān	qùnián	shàng ge xīngqī	shàng ge yuè
yesterday	*last year*	*last week*	*last month*
明天	明年	下个星期	下个 月
míngtiān	míngnián	xià ge xīngqī	xià ge yuè
tomorrow	*next year*	*next week*	*next month*

It is clear that 天 (tiān) and 年 (nián) share the same descriptive expressions except *last year*, which is not 昨年 (zuónián), but rather 去年 (qùnián), and 星期 (xīngqī) and 月 (yuè) share the same descriptive expressions.

9. 你去过中国的什么地方 (nǐ qù guo Zhōngguó de shénme dìfang)?

什么地方 (shénme dìfang) is a descriptive interrogative expression about place with the same meaning as 哪儿 (nǎr). 你去过中国的 什么地方 (nǐ qù guo Zhōngguó de shénme dìfang) means *where in China have you been to* (literally *you have been to China's what places*). Similarly we can say:

你去过　欧洲 的哪儿 / Where in Europe have you
Nǐ qù guo Ōuzhōu de nǎr /　been?
什么　地方?
shénme dìfang?

10. 我想坐飞机去 (wǒ xiǎng zuò fēijī qù)

想 (xiǎng) in the sentence is used as a modal verb, meaning *would like, wish,* or *want* (usually in the negative when used in the sense of *want*). It is to be followed by a lexical verb. For example:

你想　吃 什么?　　　What would you like to eat?
Nǐ xiǎng chī shénme?

你想　不　想　去看　　Would you like to go to the
Nǐ xiǎng bu xiǎng qù kàn　movies?
电影?
diànyǐng?

他不想　去学校。　　He doesn't want to go to school.
Tā bù xiǎng qù xuéxiào.

想 (xiǎng) can also be used as a lexical verb with the meaning *think, believe,* or *miss.* For example:

我 很 想 你。　　　I miss you very much.
Wǒ hěn xiǎng nǐ.

我 想 坐 火车 要
Wǒ xiǎng zuò huǒchē yào
六个 小时。
liù ge xiǎoshí.

I think it takes six hours by train.

你想 不想 家?
Nǐ xiǎng bu xiǎng jiā?

Do you miss home?

11. 你去洛杉矶住哪儿 (nǐ qù Luòshānjī zhù nǎr)?

The distinction in English between *to live* and *to stay* is not made in Chinese, where both are expressed by the word 住 (zhù). For example:

你们的 中文 老师
Nǐmende Zhōngwén lǎoshī
住 哪儿?
zhù nǎr?

Where does your Chinese teacher live?

你去北京 住 哪儿?
Nǐ qù Běijīng zhù nǎr?

Where are you going to stay when you go to Beijing?

You may have noticed that the adverbial of place is placed after, instead of before, the verb and the preposition 在 (zài) is not present. This is because with certain verbs (住 zhù is one of them), the adverbial can be placed either before or after the verb. For example, we can either say 你在哪儿住 (nǐ zài nǎr zhù) or 你住在哪儿 (nǐ zhù zài nǎr). However, the adverbial of place must follow the verb when it is used in conjunction with the motion verbs 来 (lái, *come*) and 去 (qù, *go*):

你来纽约 住哪儿?
Nǐ lái Niǔyuē zhù nǎr?

Where are you going to stay when you come to New York?

你去北京　住 什么　　　Which hotel are you going to
Nǐ qù Běijīng zhù shénme　　stay in when you go to
饭店?　　　　　　　　　　Beijing?
fàndiàn?

When the adverbial follows the verb, the preposition 在 (zài) is often left out.

12. 上有天堂，下有苏杭 (shàng yǒu tiāntáng, xià yǒu Sū Háng)

This is a saying in Chinese describing the unsurpassing beauty of Suzhou and Hangzhou. Literally it means "up above there is paradise, down below there is Suzhou and Hangzhou." Notice the rhyme and the grammatical symmetry of the two lines.

EXERCISES

I. Answer the following questions:

1. 你工作　　不工作？　你每 天 怎么 去上班？
Nǐ gōngzuò bu gōngzuò? Nǐ měi tiān zěnme qù shàngbān?

_____

2. 你是 学生　　吗？ 你每 天 怎么 去学校？
Nǐ shì xuésheng ma?　Nǐ měi tiān zěnme qù xuéxiào?

_____

3. 你家离银行　远　不远？
Nǐ jiā lí yínháng yuǎn bu yuǎn?

_____

4. 明年　　的中国　　新年　是几月几号？
Míngnián de Zhōngguó xīnnián shì jǐ yuè jǐ hào?
你过 不过？ 怎么　过？
Nǐ guò bu guò? Zěnme guò?

_____

_____

5. 你去过 英国　吗？ 你去过 英国　的什么　地方？
Nǐ qù guo Yīngguó ma?　Nǐ qù guo Yīngguó de shénme dìfāng?

_____

6. 你想　不 想 去中国？　　你想 什么　时候 去？
Nǐ xiǎng bu xiǎng qù Zhōngguó?　Nǐ xiǎng shénme shíhou qù?

_____

7. 从　纽约　坐飞机到 洛杉矶 要 几个小时?
Cóng Niǔyuē zuò fēijī dào Luòshānjī yào jǐ ge xiǎoshí?

_____

8. 你这 个 周末 做 什么?
Nǐ zhè ge zhōumò zuò shénme?

_____

9. 你去过 香港　　吗? 你去过 几次?
Nǐ qù guo Xiānggǎng ma? Nǐ qù guo jǐ cì?

_____

10. 你有 没有　开 过日本 车?
Nǐ yǒu méiyou kāi guo Rìběn chē?

_____

II. Fill in the blanks with appropriate words:

1. 你知道 _____ 写这 个字吗?
Nǐ zhīdao _____ xiě zhè ge zì ma?

2. 你爸爸去香港 _____ 什么?
Nǐ bàba qù Xiānggǎng _____ shénme?

3. 天安门 _____ 我们的 饭店 很 近, 坐
Tiānānmén _____ wǒmende fàndiàn hěn jìn, zuò
地铁 只 要 十 分钟。
dìtiě zhǐ yào shí fēnzhōng.

4. 明天　是你太太的生日, 你们 怎么 _____?
Míngtiān shì nǐ tàitai de shēngri, nǐmen zěnme _____?

5. 骑自行车 去你的学校 要 _____ 时间?
Qí zìxíngchē qù nǐde xuéxiào yào _____ shíjiān?

6. 他去 过 法国 _____ 什么 地方？
   Tā qù guo Fǎguó _____ shénme dìfang?

7. 杭州   很 好 _____。
   Hángzhōu hěn hǎo _____.

8. 我 去过 纽约 三 _____。
   Wǒ qù guo Niǔyuē sān _____.

9. _____ 火车站   去北京   大学要 坐 汽车。
   _____ huǒchēzhàn qù Běijīng dàxué yào zuò qìchē.

10. 你知道 地铁站 在 _____ 吗？
    Nǐ zhīdao ditiězhàn zài _____ ma?

III. Translate the following into Chinese:

1. Is it easy to find a hotel in San Francisco?

   _____

2. Xi'an is far from Guangzhou.

   _____

3. It takes about 10 hours to go from Beijing to Shanghai by train.

   _____

4. Are there subways in Nanjing?

   _____

5. Many Chinese go to work by bike.

   _____

6. How do you go to Guangzhou from Hong Kong?

   _____

7. She has been to Japan five times.

_____

8. I would like to go to China next year.

_____

9. My friend won't stay in a hotel. He will stay in my house.

_____

10. Many Chinese people are now celebrating Christmas.

_____

IV. Translate the following into English:

1. 这 个 周末 我 和我 太太去 公园 玩。
   Zhè ge zhōumò wǒ hé wǒ tàitai qù gōngyuán wán.

_____

2. 我 妈妈 去过 欧洲 的英国 和 法国。
   Wǒ māma qù guo Oūzhōu de Yīngguó hé Fǎguó.

_____

3. 火车票 很 便宜, 但是 火车 很 慢。
   Huǒchēpiào hěn piányi, dànshì huǒchē hěn màn.

_____

4. 现在 旅馆 不太好找。
   Xiànzài lǚguǎn bú tài hǎozhǎo.

_____

5. 我 家离公司 很 近, 我 走 去上班。
   Wǒ jiā lí gōngsī hěn jìn, wǒ zǒu qù shàngbān.

_____

6. 从 我 家开车 到 公司 要 三十 分钟。
Cóng wǒ jiā kāichē dào gōngsī yào sānshí fēnzhōng.

---

7. 我 想 苏州 一定 很 好玩。
Wǒ xiǎng Sūzhōu yídìng hěn hǎowán.

---

8. 她爸爸去过 中国 的 很 多 地方, 他最 喜欢
Tā bàba qù guo Zhōngguó de hěn duō dìfang, tā zuì xǐhuan
南京。
Nánjīng.

---

9. 你怎么 去火车站?
Nǐ zěnme qù huǒchēzhàn?

---

10. 我有时 在 家吃 中饭, 有时 在 学校 吃
Wǒ yǒushí zài jiā chī zhōngfàn, yǒushí zài xuéxiào chī
中饭。
zhōngfàn.

V. Recognize and practice writing the following characters:

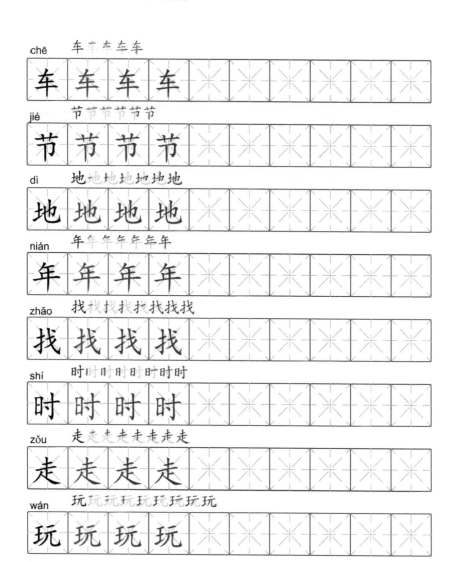

chē 车车车车车
车 车 车 车

jié 节节节节节节
节 节 节 节

dì 地地地地地地地
地 地 地 地

nián 年年年年年年年
年 年 年 年

zhǎo 找找找找找找找
找 找 找 找

shí 时时时时时时时
时 时 时 时

zǒu 走走走走走走走走
走 走 走 走

wán 玩玩玩玩玩玩玩玩玩
玩 玩 玩 玩

CULTURAL INSIGHTS

Earthshaking changes have taken place in China in the last two decades. In the words of a *Newsweek* commentator, "In two decades China has experienced the same degree of industrialization, urbanization and social transformation as Europe did in two centuries." If we use one word to describe China's transformation, most experts would probably pick "ambitious." The most impressive manifestation of the country's ambitiousness is its manic drive to build its infrastructure, which has basically brought a new look to China. Traveling used to be difficult in China, but not anymore, with the expansion of bridges, roads, high-speed rail networks, and far-reaching airline routes. To travel from Beijing to Shanghai by train used to take up to 20 hours. Now the train ride has been shortened to half of the time. By 2012, a new high-speed train will further shorten the trip to 4 hours. The high-speed train from Wuhan to Guangzhou that went into operation at the end of 2009 has become the world's fastest train, cutting the normal travel time from 10 hours to 3.

With all these developments, it is no wonder that China is a major travel destination. As commented by the travel guru Arthur Frommer, "China is a country that every American needs to see, to glimpse the role that China will play as the 21st century unfolds." According to the United Nations World Tourism Organization, by 2010 China will exceed Spain to become the world's second most popular travel country, and by 2020 it will become the largest travel destination in the world. If you are interested in taking a trip to China, there is no lack of places of interest for you to see. For people who are going to China for the first time and have about 10 to 14 days to spend, I would recommend the following cities, either in this order or in the reverse order: Hong Kong, Guilin via Guangzhou, Xi'an, Beijing and Shanghai as they represent a cross-section of the country. A gateway to China served by almost every top airline in the world, Hong Kong is a fascinating blend of East and West, scenic wonders, sublime modern architecture, great food and shopping paradise. Guilin is hailed by many as the most picturesque and serene place in China with its shapely-rising limestone hills and crystal-clear waters. Offering 30 miles of breathtaking scenery, a boat ride on the Li River presents one of the finest excursions on your tour of China. Xi'an is a city steeped in history, being the starting point of the famed "Silk Road" and the capital of 11 dynasties from the 11th century BC to the early 10th century AD. It is a continual source of new archaeological discoveries, the most famous being the extraordinary terracotta army of the first emperor of China. Beijing is undoubtedly China's imperial jewel in the crown, having served as the capital of China for over 500 years and is home to such imposing sights as the Forbidden City, Summer Palace and the Great Wall. The largest city in China, Shanghai beams an atmosphere of vitality and a dynamic that rivals any city in the world in terms of ultra-modernity. It is a cosmopolitan city where the East meets the West and the past meets the present and a place where you can sense, feel and experience the pulsating development of modern China.

To plan your visit, check out the website of China National Tourist Office at www.cnto.org, where you can see profiles of cities in China and suggested travel routes and packages. On its homepage, it states:

China is forever linked to its ancient civilization, friendly people, and many of the world's most revered treasures, such as The Great Wall, Terra-Cotta Warriors & Horses and the Yangtze River. Today, one can also find spectacular architecture and towering skylines in Shanghai and Beijing (site of the 2008 Summer Olympics), a wealth of luxury accommodations – and as always – exquisite cuisine. Come and see why China is drawing millions of visitors from all over the world. And, why each and every one of them returns home smiling.

One of the most popular websites for finding domestic airfares, hotel rates and travel information in China is http://english.ctrip.com.

LESSON 10
WEATHER

SENTENCE PATTERNS

今天 多少 度?
Jīntiān duōshao dù?

What is the temperature today?

明天 没 有 雨。
Míngtiān méi yǒu yǔ.

There is no rain tomorrow.

你们 那儿昨天 下雨了吗?
Nǐmen nàr zuótiān xiàyǔ le ma?

Did it rain in your place yesterday?

下 了。
Xià le.

Yes, it did.

昨天 有 没有 下雪?
Zuótiān yǒu méiyou xiàxuě?

Did it snow yesterday?

北京 冬天 的天气
Běijīng dōngtiān de tiānqì
怎么样?
zěnmeyàng?

What's the weather like in Beijing in winter?

美国人 夏天 一般做
Měiguórén xiàtiān yībān zuò
什么?
shénme?

What do American people usually do in summer?

今天 比昨天 冷。
Jīntiān bǐ zuótiān lěng.

It is colder today than yesterday.

南京 夏天 有 多 热?
Nánjīng xiàtiān yǒu duō rè?

How hot is it in Nanjing in summer?

CONVERSATIONS

A: 今天 天气怎么样?
Jīntiān tiānqì zěnmeyàng?

How is the weather today?

B: 今天 是 晴天, 但是
Jīntiān shì qíngtiān, dànshì
很 冷。
hěn lěng.

It is sunny today, but it is very cold.

A: 今天 多少 度?
Jīntiān duōshao dù?

What is the temperature today?

B: 今天 28 度。
Jīntiān 28 dù.

It is 28 degrees today.

A: 你知道 明天 天气
Nǐ zhīdao míngtiān tiānqì
怎么样 吗?
zěnmeyàng ma?

Do you know what the weather will be like tomorrow?

B: 听说 有 雨。
Tīngshuō yǒu yǔ.

I heard that it will rain.

A: 大雨 还是小 雨?
Dà yǔ háishi xiǎo yǔ?

Is the rain going to be heavy?

B: 可能 是大雨, 你最好
Kěnéng shì dà yǔ, nǐ zuìhǎo
带伞。
dài sǎn.

It's probably going to be heavy. You'd better take your umbrella.

A: 谢谢。
Xièxie.

Thank you.

A: 你们 那儿昨天 下雨
Nǐmen nàr   zuótiān xiàyǔ
了吗?
le ma?

Did it rain in your place yesterday?

B: 下 了。
Xià le.

Yes, it did.

A: 昨天   的雨大不大?
Zuótiān de yǔ dà bu dà?

Was the rain yesterday heavy?

B: 不太大。
Bú tài dà.

Not too bad.

A: 昨天 有 没有 下雪?
Zuótiān yǒu méiyou xiàxuě?

Did it snow yesterday?

B: 没有。
Méiyou.

No, it didn't.

A: 北京 冬天 的天气
Běijīng dōngtiān de tiānqì
怎么样?
zěnmeyàng?

What's the weather like in Beijing in winter?

B: 北京 冬天 很 冷,
Běijīng dōngtiān hěn lěng,
常常   有 大风。
chángcháng yǒu dà fēng.

It's very cold and windy in Beijing in winter.

A: 北京 冬天 常常
Běijīng dōngtiān chángcháng
下雪 吗?
xiàxuě ma?

Does it often snow in Beijing in winter?

B: 对, 常常   下雪。
Duì, chángcháng xiàxuě.

Yes, it often does.

A: 北京 什么 季节最 好?
Běijīng shénme jìjié   zuì hǎo?

What's the best season in Beijing?

B: 北京　秋天　最好，
Běijīng qiūtiān zuì hǎo,
不冷　也　不热。
bù lěng yě bú rè.

Fall is the best in Beijing,
it is neither cold nor hot.

A: 广州　　夏天　热不热?
Guǎngzhōu xiàtiān rè bu rè?

Is it hot in Guangzhou in
summer?

B: 广州　　夏天　非常　热。
Guǎngzhōu xiàtiān fēicháng rè.

It's very hot in Guangzhou in
summer.

A: 有　多　热?
Yǒu duō rè?

How hot is it?

B: 广州　　夏天　常常
Guǎngzhōu xiàtiān chángcháng
有　40度。
yǒu 40 dù.

It often reaches 40 degrees in
Guangzhou in summer.

A: 美国人　夏天　一般做
Měiguórén xiàtiān yībān zuò
什么?
shénme?

What do American people
usually do in summer?

B: 美国人　夏天　常常
Měiguórén xiàtiān chángcháng
去度假。
qù dùjià.

They often go on vacation in
the summer.

A: 他们　一般　去哪儿度假?
Tāmen yībān qù nǎr dùjià?

Where do they usually go for
vacation?

B: 有的　人　出国　旅行，
Yǒude rén chūguó lǚxíng,
有的　人去海滩。
yǒude rén qù hǎitān.

Some travel abroad and some
go to the beach.

A: 今天 冷 还是 昨天 冷?
Jīntiān lěng háishi zuótiān lěng?

Which day is colder, today or yesterday?

B: 今天 比昨天 冷。
Jīntiān bǐ zuótiān lěng.

It's colder today than yesterday.

A: 今天 的风 大还是
Jīntiān de fēng dà háishi
昨天 的 风 大?
zuótiān de fēng dà?

Which day is windier, today or yesterday?

B: 昨天 的风 大。
Zuótiān de fēng dà.

Yesterday was windier.

A: 你喜欢 热天 还是
Nǐ xǐhuan rè tiān háishi
冷 天?
lěng tiān?

Do you like hot weather or cold weather?

B: 我 喜欢 冷 天。
Wǒ xǐhuan lěng tiān.

I like cold weather.

A: 为什么?
Wèishénme?

Why?

B: 冷 天 可以去滑雪,
Lěng tiān kěyǐ qù huáxuě,
还 可以去溜冰。
hái kěyǐ qù liūbīng.

We can go skiing or ice skating in cold weather.

WORDS AND EXPRESSIONS

Nouns

天气	tiānqì	weather
雨	yǔ	rain
雪	xuě	snow
风	fēng	wind
季节	jìjié	season
冬天	dōngtiān	winter
夏天	xiàtiān	summer
秋天	qiūtiān	fall
春天	chūntiān	spring
度	dù	degree
伞	sǎn	umbrella
海滩	hǎitān	beach

Verbs

带	dài	carry
度假	dùjià	go on vacation
出	chū	go out
滑雪	huáxuě	ski
溜冰	liūbīng	ice skate

Adjectives

冷	lěng	cold
热	rè	hot
晴	qíng	sunny
阴	yīn	cloudy
大	dà	big
小	xiǎo	small

Adverbs

常常	chángcháng	often

Interrogatives

为什么	wèishénme	why

Prepositions

比	bǐ	than

Expressions

最好	zuìhǎo	best, it's better that

SUPPLEMENTARY WORDS AND EXPRESSIONS

Nouns

暖气	nuǎnqì	heat, heating
空调	kōngtiáo	air conditioning
云	yún	cloud
雾	wù	fog
雷	léi	thunder
闪电	shǎndiàn	lightning
台风	táifēng	typhoon
冰	bīng	ice
雨衣	yǔyī	raincoat
预报	yùbào	forecast
摄氏	shèshì	Centigrade, Celsius
华氏	huáshì	Fahrenheit
东	dōng	east
南	nán	south
西	xī	west
北	běi	north

Adjectives

暖	nuǎn	warm
凉	liáng	cool

LANGUAGE POINTS

1. 今天多少度 (jīntiān duōshao dù)?

The equivalent in Chinese to *temperature* is 温度 (wēndù). When referring to various types of temperatures, we usually use a specifying modifier with the word 温 (wēn) as in 体温 (tǐwēn, *body temperature*) and 气温 (qìwēn, *atmospheric temperature*). 度 (dù) in Chinese actually means *degree*. To ask about temperature, we would use 今天多少度 (jīntiān duōshao dù), since we are dealing with a number.

2. 了 (le) as an aspect marker

Chinese indicates a completed action with the particle 了 (le) after the verb. Compare:

我 吃 早饭。 Wǒ chī zǎofàn.	I eat breakfast.
我 吃了早饭。 Wǒ chī le zǎofàn.	I ate breakfast.
我 妈妈 今天下午 Wǒ māma jīntiān xiàwǔ 去银行。 qù yínháng.	My mother is going to the bank this afternoon.
我 妈妈 昨天下午 Wǒ māma zuótiān xiàwǔ 去了银行。 qù le yínháng.	My mother went to the bank yesterday afternoon.

It is important to keep in mind that the negative form of a verb with 了 (le) is not 不 (bù), but rather 没有 (méiyou). Once 没有 (méiyou) is used, 了 (le) has to be dropped from the sentence. This is because 了 (le) indicates the completion of an action. Since the action is not completed, 了 (le) naturally cannot be used. Compare the use of 不 (bù) and 没有 (méiyou) in the following sentences:

我 不吃 早饭。   I don't eat breakfast.
Wǒ bù chī zǎofàn.

我 没有 吃早饭。   I didn't eat breakfast.
Wǒ méiyou chī zǎofàn.

我 妈妈 今天下午 不   My mother is not going to the
Wǒ māma jīntiān xiàwǔ bú   bank this afternoon.
去银行。
qù yínháng.

我 妈妈 昨天 下午   My mother didn't go to the
Wǒ māma zuótiān xiàwǔ   bank yesterday afternoon.
没有 去银行。
méiyou qù yínháng.

For the same reason that 了 (le) is used to indicate the completion of an action, it is not to be used with cognitive verbs such as 认识 (rènshi, *know*), 知道 (zhīdao, *know*), 会 (huì, *know how to*), 喜欢 (xǐhuan, *like*) and so on because there is no completion to speak of. When these cognitive verbs are negated, we still use 不 (bù), rather than 没有 (méiyou) even though these verbs may have a past reference. Thus, depending on the context, 我不认识他 (wǒ bú rènshi tā) can be interpreted as either *I don't know him* or *I didn't know him*. Similarly, adjectives and prepositions can only be used with 不 (bù), since they do not indicate actions. Here are a few more examples:

他现在 不在 家。   He is not home now.
Tā xiànzài bú zài jiā.

他昨天 晚上 不在 家。 He was not home last night.
Tā zuótiān wǎnshang bú zài jiā.

我 今天 不忙。   I'm not busy today.
Wǒ jīntiān bù máng.

我 昨天 不忙。   I was not busy yesterday.
Wǒ zuótiān bù máng.

我的 女朋友 不会   My girlfriend can't speak
Wǒde nǚpéngyou bú huì   English.
说 英语。
shuō Yīngyǔ.

我的 女朋友 去年 不   My girlfriend couldn't speak
Wǒde nǚpéngyou qùnián bú English last year.
会 说 英语。
huì shuō Yīngyǔ.

Yes/no questions involving a completed action are formed in one of two ways:

1) Using the sentence-particle 吗 (ma):

你买 了衣服吗?   Did you buy the clothes?
Nǐ mǎi le yīfu ma?

他去了中国 吗?   Has he gone to China?
Tā qù le Zhōngguó ma?

2) Using the affirmative + negative form 有没有 (yǒu méiyou):

你今天 有 没有   Did you go to work today?
Nǐ jīntiān yǒu méiyou
上班?
shàngbān?

你有 没有　吃中饭?　　　Have you had lunch?
Nǐ yǒu méiyou chī zhōngfàn?

你有 没有　去看 电影?　Did you go to see the movie?
Nǐ yǒu méiyou qù kàn diànyǐng?

In this connection, it may be necessary to compare the use of 了 (le) with that of 过 (guo) discussed in Lesson 8. Although both of them are used to indicate a completed action, there is an important difference between them. While 了 (le) is used for an action that is completed at a specified time, 过 (guo) is usually used for an action completed at an unspecified time in the past. 了 (le) emphasizes the action, whereas 过 (guo) emphasizes the experience and the result. Compare:

他吃了中国　　菜。　　　He ate Chinese food.
Tā chī le Zhōngguó cài.　　*(just now or not long ago)*

他吃 过 中国菜。　　　　He has had Chinese food.
Tā chī guo Zhōngguócài.　　*(sometime in the past)*

我 昨天 看 了这本 书。　I read this book yesterday.
Wǒ zuótiān kàn le zhè běn shū.

我 看 过 这 本 书。　　I have read this book.
Wǒ kàn guo zhè běn shū.　　*(sometime in the past)*

我 爸爸来了美国。　　　My father has come to the
Wǒ bàba lái le Měiguó.　　United States.
　　　　　　　　　　　　　(he is still here)

我 爸爸来 过 美国。　　My father has been to the
Wǒ bàba lái guo Měiguó.　　United States.
　　　　　　　　　　　　　(he is not here unless there is some qualification)

It was mentioned in the introductory chapter on Chinese that verbs in Chinese are marked by specific particles for aspect (manner in which an action takes place), but not for time (past, present or future). What 了 (le) indicates is simply the completion of an action, which can take place in the future as well as the past, although completed actions are usually associated with the past. The following is an example of 了 (le) used to indicate a completed action in the future as projected from the present time:

我 吃了饭 去 看 电影。   After I've finished eating, I'll
Wǒ chī le fàn qù kàn diànyǐng.   go to see a movie.

5. 大雨 (dà yǔ) and 小雨 (xiǎo yǔ)

To describe the severity of a weather condition such as rain, snow or wind, Chinese uses the adjectives 大 (dà, *big*) and 小 (xiǎo, *small*). For example:

大雨 (dà yǔ, *heavy rain*)
小雨 (xiǎo yǔ, *drizzle*)

大雪 (dà xuě, *heavy snow*)
小雪 (xiǎo xuě, *light snow*)

大风 (dà fēng, *strong wind*)
小风 (xiǎo fēng, *breeze*)

Words like *rain* and *snow* can be used as verbs as well as nouns in English, but they are always nouns in Chinese. To indicate *to rain* and *to snow*, we usually use the verb 下 (xià, *fall*) as in 下雨 (xiàyǔ, *to rain*) and 下雪 (xiàxuě, *to snow*).

6. 广州夏天有多热 (Guǎngzhōu xiàtiān yǒu duō rè)?

To ask about the specific measure of certain conditions such as *how long*, *how cold*, etc., Chinese uses the pattern: Subject + 有多 (yǒu duō) + Adjective. For example:

纽约　的　冬天　有
Niǔyuē de　dōngtiān yǒu
多　冷?
duō lěng?

How cold is it in New York in winter?

长江　　有　多　长?
Chángjiāng yǒu duō cháng?

How long is the Yangtze River?

她的房子　有　多　大?
Tāde fángzi yǒu duō　dà?

How big is her house?

你有　多　高?
Nǐ yǒu duō gāo?

How tall are you/what's your height?

7. 今天比昨天冷 (jīntiān bǐ zuótiān lěng)

To indicate a comparison between two items, we use the pattern "A 比 (bǐ) B + Adjective," where A is the subject and the 比 (bǐ)-phrase is the adverbial of reference. As such, it is placed before the verb-like adjective. Other examples are:

纽约　比华盛顿　　大。
Niǔyuē bǐ Huáshèngdùn dà.

New York is larger than Washington.

上海　　的人比北京
Shànghǎi de rén bǐ Běijīng
的人　多。
de rén duō.

There are more people in Shanghai than in Beijing.

这　件　大衣比那件
Zhè jiàn dàyī bǐ nà jiàn
大衣贵。
dàyī guì.

This coat is more expensive than that coat.

中国　　菜比日本 菜
Zhōngguó cài bǐ Rìběn cài
好吃。
hàochī.

Chinese food tastes better
than Japanese food.

In all these sentences, there is no need for a *more* in Chinese. If there is specific measurement in the sentence indicating how much the two items being compared differs from each other, it should be placed last in the sentence. For example:

这 件 毛衣 比那件 毛衣 贵20 美元。
Zhè jiàn máoyī bǐ nà jiàn máoyī guì 20 měiyuán.
This sweater is $20 more expensive than that sweater.

今天 的温度 比昨天 的温度 高 三 度。
Jīntiān de wēndù bǐ zuótiān de wēndù gāo sān dù.
The temperature today is 3 degrees higher than yesterday.

他们的 公司 比我们的 公司 多 100个 人。
Tāmende gōngsī bǐ wǒmende gōngsī duō 100 ge rén.
Their company has 100 more people than ours.

EXERCISES

I. Answer the following questions:

1. 今天 天气 怎么样？ 昨天 呢？
Jīntiān tiānqì zěnmeyàng? Zuótiān ne?

_____

2. 明天 有 没 有 雨？
Míngtiān yǒu méi yǒu yǔ?

_____

3. 今天 多少 度？
Jīntiān duōshao dù?

_____

4. 今天 有 没 有 风？ 风 大不 大？
Jīntiān yǒu méi yǒu fēng? Fēng dà bu dà?

_____

5. 你们 那儿什么 季节天气 最 好？
Nǐmen nàr shénme jìjié tiānqì zuì hǎo?

_____

6. 你们 那儿夏天 热不热？ 有 多 热？
Nǐmen nàr xiàtiān rè bu rè? Yǒu duō rè?

_____

7. 你们 那儿冬天 有 没 有 雪？ 雪 大不 大？
Nǐmen nàr dōngtiān yǒu méi yǒu xuě? Xuě dà bu dà?

_____

8. 你喜欢 冷　天 还是 热天? 为什么?
Nǐ xǐhuan lěng tiān háishi rè tiān? Wèishénme?

_____

9. 你秋天 喜欢　做 什么?
Nǐ qiūtiān xǐhuan zuò shénme?

_____

10. 你今年 夏天 去不 去 度假? 去 哪儿度假?
Nǐ jīnnián xiàtiān qù bu qù dùjià? Qù nǎr dùjià?

_____

11. 你上　星期天 晚上　做 了什么?
Nǐ shàng xīngqītiān wǎnshang zuò le shénme?

_____

12. 你今天 有 没有　吃 中饭?
Nǐ jīntiān yǒu méiyou chī zhōngfàn?

_____

13. 你昨天　晚上　看 了电视 吗?
Nǐ zuótiān wǎnshang kàn le diànshì ma?

_____

14. 你有 没有　学 过 法语?
Nǐ yǒu méiyou xué guo Fǎyǔ?

_____

15. 你去过 欧洲　吗?
Nǐ qù guo Oūzhōu ma?

_____

II. Change the following sentences into yes/no questions, using two alternative forms:

1. 我 太太去了商店。
   Wǒ tàitai qù le shāngdiàn.

   _____

   _____

2. 我们的　中文　　老师 来了。
   Wǒmende Zhōngwén lǎoshī lái le.

   _____

   _____

3. 下雨了。
   Xiàyǔ le.

   _____

   _____

4. 纽约　今年 冬天　下 了很 多 雪。
   Niǔyuē jīnnián dōngtiān xià le hěn duō xuě.

   _____

   _____

5. 他们 下班 了。
   Tāmen xiàbān le.

   _____

   _____

III. Change the following into negative sentences:

1. 我 爸爸妈妈 昨天 都 来了。

   Wǒ bàba māma zuótiān dōu lái le.

   _____

2. 星期六 晚上 我 看 了电视。

   Xīngqīliù wǎnshang wǒ kàn le diànshì.

   _____

3. 银行 关门 了。

   Yínháng guānmén le.

   _____

4. 她用 了我的 汽车。

   Tā yòng le wǒde qìchē.

   _____

5. 我 先生 起床 了。

   Wǒ xiānsheng qǐchuáng le.

   _____

IV. Write five things that you did today. Pay attention to the indication of complete actions.

_____

_____

_____

_____

_____

V. Correct the error contained in each of the following sentences:

1. 我 昨天 不 吃早饭。
   Wǒ zuótiān bù chī zǎofàn.

   _____

2. 她妈妈 今天 早上   在了家。
   Tā māma jīntiān zǎoshang zài le jiā.

   _____

3. 你上   星期天 有 没有 去 教堂 (church) 吗?
   Nǐ shàng xīngqītiān yǒu méiyou qù jiàotáng   ma?

   _____

4. 他们 没有   来了中国。
   Tāmen méiyou lái le Zhōngguó.

   _____

5. 我 去年 没有 认识 她。
   Wǒ qùnián méiyou rènshi tā.

   _____

VI. Translate the following into Chinese:

1. What is the weather like in Shanghai in the fall?

   _____

2. Does it often rain in the summer in New York?

   _____

3. It's going to be a sunny day tomorrow.

   _____

4. Is there snow in Hangzhou?
   Sometimes there is, sometimes there is not.

   _____

   _____

5. In winter it is very windy where we live.

   _____

6. What was the temperature yesterday?
   It was 53 degrees.

   _____

   _____

7. I heard that there had been a lot of snow in France this year.

   _____

8. The weather is the best in Guangzhou in the spring.

   _____

9. How heavy was the rain yesterday?

   _____

10. It sometimes snows in Nanjing in the spring.

    _____

11. My mother went to the store.

    _____

12. He didn't eat breakfast this morning.

    _____

13. Have you ever driven a Chinese car?

    _____

14. I studied ten Chinese characters last night.

_____

15. They exchanged $500 at Bank of China today.

_____

VII. Translate the following into English:

1. 今天 是 阴天, 很 冷, 风 很 大。
   Jīntiān shì yīntiān, hěn lěng, fēng hěn dà.

_____

2. 今年 冬天 纽约 的雪 大不大?
   Jīnnián dōngtiān Niǔyuē de xuě dà bu dà?

_____

3. 中国人 夏天 喜欢 做 什么?
   Zhōngguórén xiàtiān xǐhuan zuò shénme?

_____

4. 很 多 美国人 冬天 喜欢 去滑雪。
   Hěn duō Měiguórén dōngtiān xǐhuan qù huáxuě.

_____

5. 去年 的冬天 不太 冷, 夏天 不太热。
   Qùnián de dōngtiān bú tài lěng, xiàtiān bú tài rè.

_____

6. 我 不喜欢 北京 的春天, 风 太 大。
   Wǒ bù xǐhuan Běijīng de chūntiān, fēng tài dà.

_____

7. 昨天 的雨大还是 今天 的 雨大?
   Zuótiān de yǔ dà háishi jīntiān de yǔ dà?

_____

8. 北京　大学　的学生　　比南京　大学　的
Běijīng dàxué de xuésheng bǐ Nánjīng dàxué de
学生　　多。
xuésheng duō.

9. 我　家离公司　比他家离公司　远。
Wǒ jiā lí gōngsī bǐ tā jiā lí gōngsī yuǎn.

10. 这　本　书　比那本　书　便宜　三块　　钱。
Zhè běn shū bǐ nà běn shū piányi sān kuài qián.

VIII. Describe today's weather conditions.

IX. Write a comparative sentence for the following sentences:

1. 今天　的雪　大。昨天　的　雪　不大。
Jīntiān de xuě dà.　Zuótiān de xuě bù dà.

2. 她的中文　　好。我的　中文　　不　好。
Tāde Zhōngwén hǎo.　Wǒde Zhōngwén bù hǎo.

3. 红酒　　好喝。白酒　不好喝。
Hóngjiǔ hǎohē.　Báijiǔ bù hǎohē.

4. 飞机快。火车　不快。
Fēijī kuài. Huǒchē bú kuài.

---

5. 北京　好玩。上海　　不好玩。
Běijīng hǎowán. Shànghǎi bù hǎowán.

---

6. 这 本 书 20块　钱。那本 书 10块　钱。
Zhè běn shū 20 kuài qián. Nà běn shū 10 kuài qián.

---

7. 我 爸爸忙。我 妈妈 不忙。
Wǒ bàba máng. Wǒ māma bù máng.

---

8. 纽约　的旅馆 好找。　洛杉矶 的 旅馆 不
Niǔyuē de lǚguǎn hǎozhǎo. Luòshānjī de lǚguǎn bù
好找。
hǎozhǎo.

---

9. 今天 50 度。昨天 40 度。
Jīntiān 50 dù. Zuótiān 40 dù.

---

10. 我们 学校　有600 个学生。　他们 学校　有
Wǒmen xuéxiào yǒu 600 ge xuésheng. Tāmen xuéxiào yǒu
400 个学生。
400　ge xuésheng.

X. Recognize and practice writing the following characters:

wèi 为 为 为 为 为

为	为	为	为						

bǐ 比 比 比 比 比

比	比	比	比						

qì 气 气 气 气 气

气	气	气	气						

dōng 冬 冬 冬 冬 冬 冬

冬	冬	冬	冬						

chū 出 出 出 出 出

出	出	出	出						

yīn 阴 阴 阴 阴 阴 阴 阴 阴

阴	阴	阴	阴						

lěng 冷 冷 冷 冷 冷 冷 冷 冷

冷	冷	冷	冷						

jì 季 季 季 季 季 季 季 季 季

季	季	季	季						

chūn 春 春 春 春 春 春 春 春 春

春	春	春	春						

qiū 秋 秋 秋 秋 秋 秋 秋 秋 秋

秋	秋	秋	秋						

CULTURAL INSIGHTS

After Russia and Canada, China is the third largest country in the world. Lying in East Asia, China shares borders with a host of countries, with Mongolia to the north, Russia to the northeast, Korea to the east, Myanmar (formerly Burma), Laos and Vietnam to the south, Afghanistan, Pakistan, India, Nepal, and Bhutan to the west and southwest, Kazakhstan, Kyrgyzstan and Tajikistan to the northwest.

The administrative divisions consist of a three-tier hierarchy: 1) Central Government, 2) provinces/autonomous regions/municipalities directly under the Central Government, and 3) cities. Counties, whose jurisdiction lies in the rural area, used to be directly under the province together with cities, but now they are for the most part under the administration of cities.

Under the Central Government, there are twenty-three provinces, five autonomous regions and four centrally administered municipalities. These divisions are all equal in status. Autonomous regions are so called because they enjoy some degree of independence in terms of public policy, as they are the areas with large settlements of ethnic minorities. The four centrally administered municipalities are Beijing, Shanghai, Tianjin and Chongqing. Outside the mainland, Hong Kong and Macao were reverted to China by Britain and Portugal respectively in the 1990s, ending their status as colonies. Taiwan, which is regarded by Mainland China as a renegade province, is still controlled by the Nationalist government.

Provinces are divided into cities. In recent years, cities have been given additional administrative power as counties have been brought under their jurisdiction. In the urban area, cities are subdivided into two levels: districts and wards. In the rural area, they are subdivided into counties and townships. In the cities, housing is generally provided by the *danwei* in designated apartment buildings. Neighborhoods thus formed are not stratified by occupation or income and most importantly, they are closely knit face-to-face communities, which contribute to residential stability and a low level of crime.

Of particular mention are the approximately 900,000 villages in the countryside, where most Chinese live. They are usually clustered around a market town that coincides in most cases with the seat of the township. The market town further links the farmers to a larger network of economy and society. But due to the restrictions imposed by the household registration system, farmers are confined to their villages and prevented from seeking opportunities elsewhere. With the recent reform, a substantial number of rural people are venturing out of their villages and expanding their social horizons to work and engage in social life in the cities, but still they cannot be formally employed by the government or state-owned businesses or set up residence there.

The Communist Party, with a 50-million membership, exercises the ultimate and unchallenged leadership and authority over the Chinese people. Its organization and supervision penetrate all the levels of government and are present in all the institutions, organizations and state-owned businesses. A *danwei* (work unit) usually has a dual system of supervision by a Party secretary and an administrator. In some units, the Party secretary and the administrator are one and the same person. In theory, the Party secretary oversees the implementation of the Party policies and guidelines and the administrators/managers are responsible for the day-to-day-operation of their *danwei*, but in reality, many of the administrative and managerial decisions have to be cleared with, or even made by, the Party secretary. The authority of the Party is omnipresent and unchallenged.

China uses Celsius for temperature measurement. You can convert it to Fahrenheit or the other way round at:
www.wbuf.noaa.gov/tempfc.htm

GLOSSARY

SC = simplified characters
TC = traditional characters (if different)
L = lesson #

SC	TC	Pinyin	English	L
A				
阿拉伯语	阿拉伯語	Àlābóyǔ	Arabic language	
澳州		Àozhōu	Australia	9
B				
八		bā	eight	4
八月		bāyuè	August	5
爸爸		bàba	father	1
百		bǎi	hundred	4
百货公司	百貨公司	bǎihuògōngsī	department store	7
白酒		báijiǔ	liquor	8
半		bàn	half	5
办公室	辦公室	bàngōngshì	office	3
包子		bāozi	steamed stuffed bun	8
报纸	報紙	bàozhǐ	newspaper	6
杯		bēi	cup	7
北		běi	north	10
北京		Běijīng	Beijing	3
本		běn	*classifier*	4
比		bǐ	than	10
冰		bīng	ice	10
博物馆		bówùguǎn	museum	3
不		bù	not	1
不一定		bù yīdìng	not necessarily	7

C

菜		cài	dishes	8
菜单	菜單	càidān	menu	8
餐馆	餐館	cānguǎn	restaurant	2
餐巾		cānjīn	napkin	8
厕所	廁所	cèsuǒ	restroom	3
叉		chā	fork	8
茶		chá	tea	8
常		cháng	often	9
常常		chángcháng	often	10
长	長	cháng	long	7
炒		chǎo	fry	8
车	車	chē	vehicle	9
城		chéng	town, city	3
衬衫	襯衫	chènshān	shirt, blouse	7
吃		chī	eat	8
出		chū	go out	10
穿		chuān	wear, put on	7
船		chuán	boat, ship	9
春天		chūntiān	spring	10
出租汽车	出租汽車	chūzūqìchē	taxi	9
次		cì	time (occurrence)	8
从	從	cóng	from	6
从 …… 到 ……	從 …… 到 ……	cóng …… dào ……	from ... to ...	9
错	錯	cuò	wrong, bad	1

D

带		dài	carry	10
当然	當然	dāngrán	of course	7
但是		dànshì	but	6
单位	單位	dānwèi	workplace	3
刀		dāo	knife	8
导游	導游	dǎoyóu	guide	9
大学	大學	dàxué	university	3
大学生	大學生	dàxuéshēng	college student	4
大衣		dàyī	coat	7

的		de	*possessive marker*	2
德国	德國	Déguó	Germany	6
德语	德語	Déyǔ	German language	6
等		děng	wait	7
第		dì	*ordinal number indicator*	7
点	點	diǎn	o'clock	5
电车	電車	diànchē	trolley-bus	9
电话	電話	diànhuà	telephone	3
电视	電視	diànshì	television	6
电影	電影	diànyǐng	movie	8
电影院	電影院	diànyǐngyuàn	movie theater	3
弟弟		dìdi	younger brother	1
地方		dìfāng	place	9
地铁	地鐵	dìtiě	subway	9
懂		dǒng	understand	6
东	東	dōng	east	10
冬天		dōngtiān	winter	10
东西	東西	dōngxi	things, stuff	7
都		dōu	both, all	2
度		dù	degree	10
度假		dùjià	go on vacation	10
大		dà	big	10
短		duǎn	short	7
对	對	duì	right, correct	8
对不起	對不起	duìbùqǐ	sorry	5
多		duō	many, much	7
多少		duōshao	*question word about numbers*	4

E

俄语	俄語	Éyǔ	Russian language	6
二		èr	two	4
二月		èryuè	February	5
儿子	兒子	érzi	son	2

F

饭店	飯店	fàndiàn	hotel	3
翻译	翻譯	fānyì	translate	6
法国	法國	Fǎguó	France	6
法语	法語	Fǎyǔ	French language	6
肥		féi	loose	7
飞机	飛機	fēijī	airplane	9
飞机场	飛機場	fēijīchǎng	airport	3
非洲	非洲	Fēizhōu	Africa	9
分		fēn	minute	5
分		fēn	monetary unit	7
风	風	fēng	wind	10
分钟	分鐘	fēnzhōng	minute	9
付		fù	pay	7
服装店		fúzhuāngdiàn	clothing store	7

G

告诉	告訴	gàosu	tell	7
高兴	高興	gāoxìng	happy	1
个	個	ge	*classifier*	4
哥哥		gēge	older brother	1
给	給	gěi	give	8
公安局		gōngānjú	police station	3
工人		gōngrén	factory worker	2
公司		gōngsī	company	2
工艺品	工藝品	gōngyìpǐn	handicraft product	7
公园	公園	gōngyuán	park	3
工作		gōngzuò	work	3
广东	廣東	guǎngdōng	Canton (province)	6
广州	廣州	guǎngzhōu	Canton (city)	6
关门	關門	guānmén	close (for business)	7
贵	貴	guì	distinguished	2
贵	貴	guì	expensive	7
顾客	顧客	gùkè	customer	7
过	過	guo	*aspect marker*	8
过	過	guò	celebrate	9

国	國	guó	country	6
国语	國語	Guóyǔ	Mandarin	6

H

海关	海關	hǎiguān	customs	9
海滩	海灘	hǎitān	beach	10
海鲜	海鮮	hǎixiān	seafood	8
韩国	韓國	Hánguó	Korea	6
杭州		Hángzhōu	Hangzhou	9
号	號	hào	number	5
好		hǎo	good	1
好像		hǎoxiàng	seem	8
和		hé	and	4
喝		hē	drink	8
很		hěn	very	1
合适	合適	héshì	suitable	7
红	紅	hóng	red	8
红酒	紅酒	hóngjiǔ	wine	8
话	話	huàn	speech, dialect	6
换		huàn	change, exchange	7
滑雪	滑雪	huáxuě	ski	10
欢迎	歡迎	huānyíng	welcome	8
华盛顿	華盛頓	huáshèngdùn	Washington	9
华氏	華氏	huáshì	Fahrenheit	10
会	會	huì	know how to	6
回答		huídá	answer	6
会话	會話	huìhuà	conversation	6
火车站	火車站	huǒchēzhàn	train station	3
护照	護照	hùzhào	passport	9

J

几	幾	jǐ	*question word about numbers*	4
鸡	雞	jī	chicken	8
鸡蛋	雞蛋	jīdàn	egg	8
家		jiā	home, family	3

价格	價格	jiàgé	price	7
件		jiàn	*classifier*	7
叫		jiào	call	2
教		jiāo	teach	6
教堂		jiàotáng	church	3
饺子	餃子	jiǎozi	dumpling	8
加州		Jiāzhōu	California	3
街		jiē	street	9
姐姐		jiějie	older sister	1
结束	結束	jiéshù	end	5
季节	季節	jìjié	season	10
极了	極了	jíle	extremely	8
纪念品	紀念品	jìniànpǐn	souvenir	7
近		jìn	close	9
警察		jǐngchá	police, policeman	9
经理	經理	jīnglǐ	manager	2
今年		jīnnián	this year	5
今天		jīntiān	today	5
九		jiǔ	nine	4
九月		jiǔyuè	September	5
旧金山	舊金山	Jiùjīnshān	San Francisco	3
觉得	覺得	juéde	feel, think	7
句子		jùzǐ	sentence	6

K

咖啡		kāfēi	coffee	7
开	開	kāi	operate, drive	9
开门	開門	kāimén	open (for business)	7
开始	開始	kāishǐ	begin	5
看		kàn	read, look	2
看书	看書	kànshū	read	5
烤鸭	烤鴨	kǎoyā	roast duck	8
课	課	kè	class, lesson	5
可能		kěnéng	maybe	9
客气	客氣	kèqi	be polite, be formal	2
课文	課文	kèwén	text	6

可以		kěyǐ	may	7
空调	空調	kōngtiáo	air conditioning	10
口		kǒu	*classifier*	4
块	塊	kuài	*monetary unit*	7
筷子		kuàizi	chopsticks	8
裤子	褲子	kùzi	pants	7

L

辣		là	spicy	8
来	來	lái	come	1
老板		lǎobǎn	boss	2
老师	老師	lǎoshī	teacher	1
累		lèi	tired	1
雷		léi	thunder	10
冷		lěng	cold	10
离	離	lí	away from	9
凉	涼	liáng	cool	10
练习	練習	liànxí	exercise, practice	6
零		líng	zero	4
历史	歷史	lìshǐ	history	4
六		liù	six	4
六月		liùyuè	June	5
溜冰		liūbīng	ice skate	10
楼	樓	lóu	floor, building	6
路		lù	road, route	9
绿	綠	lǜ	green	8
旅馆	旅館	lǚguǎn	hotel	9
洛杉矶	洛杉磯	Luòshānjī	Los Angeles	3
律师	律師	lǜshī	lawyer	1
旅行		lǚxíng	travel	9
旅行社		lǚxíngshè	travel agency	9

M

吗	嗎	ma	*particle*	1
买	買	mǎi	buy	7
卖	賣	mài	sell	7

妈妈	媽媽	māma	mother	1
马马虎虎	馬馬虎虎	mǎmahūhu	so-so	1
慢		màn	slowly	6
曼哈顿	曼哈頓	Mànhādùn	Manhattan	3
忙		máng	busy	1
毛		máo	*monetary unit*	7
毛衣		máoyī	sweater	7
帽子		màozi	hat	7
每		měi	every, each	5
没		méi	not	2
没关系	沒關系	méi guānxi	That's all right.	5
美国	美國	Měiguó	United States	1
妹妹		mèimei	younger sister	1
美元		měiyuán	U.S. dollars	7
美洲		Měizhōu	the Americas	9
们	們	men	*plural suffix*	2
面包		miànbāo	bread	8
面条	面條	miàntiáo	noodle	2
米饭	米飯	mǐfàn	cooked rice	8
明年		míngnián	next year	5
明天		míngtiān	tomorrow	5
名字		míngzi	name	2

N

那		nà	that	5
咸		xián	male	8
哪儿	哪兒	nǎr	what place	3
那儿	那兒	nàr	there	3
奶奶		nǎinai	paternal grandmother	4
男		nán	male	2
男孩		nánhái	boy	4
男朋友		nánpéngyou	boyfriend	2
南京		Nánjīng	Nanjing	3
哪		nǎ	which	4
南		nán	south	10
呢		ne	*particle*	1

能		néng	can	7
你		nǐ	you	1
年		nián	year	9
您		nín	you (polite form)	2
牛奶		niúnǎi	milk	8
牛肉		niúròu	beef	8
纽约	紐約	Niǔyuē	New York	3
暖		nuǎn	warm	10
暖气	暖氣	nuǎnqì	heat, heating	10
女		nǚ	female	2
女朋友		nǚpéngyǒu	girlfriend	2
女儿	女兒	nǚ'ér	daughter	2
女孩		nǚhái	girl	4

O

欧洲	歐洲	Oūzhōu	Europe	9

P

盘子	盤子	pánzi	plate	8
朋友		péngyou	friend	2
便宜		piányi	cheap	7
票		piào	ticket	9
啤酒		píjiǔ	beer	8
瓶		píng	bottle	8
普通话	普通話	pǔtōnghuà	Mandarin	6

Q

七		qī	seven	4
七月		qīyuè	July	5
骑	騎	qí	ride	9
千		qiān	thousand	4
钱	錢	qián	money	7
签证	簽證	qiānzhèng	visa	9
汽车站	汽車站	qìchēzhàn	bus stop	3
起床		qǐchuáng	get up	5
晴		qíng	sunny	10

请...吃饭	請...吃飯	qǐng ... chīfàn	treat sb. to a meal	8
青岛	青島	Qīngdǎo	Qingdao	8
请问	請問	qǐngwèn	May I ask ...	3
秋天		qiūtiān	fall	10
去		qù	go	1
去年		qùnián	last year	5

R

热	熱	rè	hot	10
人		rén	person, people	2
人民币	人民幣	rénmínbì	*Renminbi*	7
认识	認識	rènshi	know	1
日本		Rìběn	Japan	1
日语	日語	Rìyǔ	Japanese language	5
肉	肉	ròu	meat	8

S

三		sān	three	4
三月		sānyuè	March	5
伞	傘	sǎn	umbrella	10
闪电	閃電	shǎndiàn	lightening	10
上		shàng	up	9
上班		shàngbān	go to work	5
商店		shāngdiàn	store	3
上海		Shànghǎi	Shanghai	3
上午		shàngwǔ	morning	5
上学	上學	shàngxué	go to school	9
生词	生詞	shēngcí	new word	6
圣诞节	圣誕節	shèngdànjié	Christmas	9
生日		shēngri	birthday	5
什么	什麼	shénme	what	2
摄氏	攝氏	shèshì	Centigrade	10
十		shí	ten	4
十二月		shí'èryuè	December	5
十一月		shíyīyuè	November	5
十月		shíyuè	October	5

是		shì	be	1
试	試	shì	try	7
市场	市場	shìchǎng	market	7
时候	時候	shíhou	time	5
时间	時間	shíjiān	time	5
市长	市長	shìzhǎng	mayor	2
市中心		shìzhōngxīn	city center, downtown	9
瘦		shòu	tight	7
收		shōu	accept	7
手表		shǒubiǎo	watch	5
售票员	售票員	shòupiàoyuán	sales clerk	7
双	雙	shuāng	pair	7
书	書	shū	book	2
书店	書店	shūdiàn	bookstore	7
书法	書法	shūfǎ	calligraphy	6
谁	誰	shéi; shuí	who	4
水果		shuǐguǒ	fruit	8
睡觉	睡覺	shuìjiào	sleep	5
说	說	shuō	speak, say	6
四		sì	four	4
四月		sìyuè	April	5
四川		Sìchuān	Sichuan	6
酸		suān	sour	8
素菜		sùcài	vegetable dish	8
苏州	蘇州	Sūzhōu	Suzhou	9

T

他		tā	he	1
她		tā	she	1
太		tài	too, very	3
台风	臺風	táifēng	typhoon	10
糖		táng	sugar	8
汤	湯	tāng	soup	8
天		tiān	day, weather	5
甜		tián	sweet	8

甜点	甜點	tiándiǎn	dessert	8
天气	天氣	tiānqì	weather	10
天堂		tiāntáng	paradise	9
听	聽	tīng	listen	6
听说	聽說	tīngshuō	it is said	7
条	條	tiáo	*classifier*	7
同事		tóngshì	colleague	2
图书馆	圖書館	túshūguǎn	library	3

W

外公		wàigōng	maternal grandfather	4
外国	外國	wàiguó	foreign country	6
外国人	外國人	wàiguórén	foreigner	6
外婆	外婆	wàipó	maternal grandmother	4
外语	外語	wàiyǔ	foreign language	6
碗		wǎn	bowl	8
玩		wán	play	9
万	萬	wàn	ten thousand	4
晚饭	晚飯	wǎnfàn	dinner	5
晚上		wǎnshang	evening	5
袜子	襪子	wàzi	socks	7
位		wèi	*classifier*	8
味道		wèidao	taste	8
为什么	為什麼	wèishénme	why	10
问题	問題	wèntí	question	2
我		wǒ	I	1
五		wǔ	five	4
五月		wǔyuè	May	5
雾	霧	wù	fog	10

X

西		xī	west	10
下		xià	down, fall	9
下班		xiàbān	get off work	5
咸		xián	salty	8
想		xiǎng	would like, think	9

香港		Xiānggǎng	Hong Kong	6
先生		xiānsheng	Mr., husband	1
现在	現在	xiànzài	now	5
小		xiǎo	small	10
小费		xiǎofèi	tip	8
小姐		xiǎojie	Miss	1
小时	小時	xiǎoshí	hour	9
小学生	小學生	xiǎoxuéshēng	elementary school student	4
校长	校長	xiàozhǎng	school principal/ president	2
夏天		xiàtiān	summer	10
下午		xiàwǔ	afternoon	5
西班牙语	西班牙語	Xībānyáyǔ	Spanish language	6
写	寫	xiě	write	6
鞋店		xiédiàn	shoe store	7
谢谢	謝謝	xièxie	thank (you)	
鞋子		xiézi	shoes	7
喜欢	喜歡	xǐhuan	like	1
新		xīn	new	9
姓		xìng	family name	2
行李		xíngli	luggage	9
星期		xīngqī	week	5
星期二		xīngqī'èr	Tuesday	5
星期六		xīngqīliù	Saturday	5
星期三		xīngqīsān	Wednesday	5
星期四		xīngqīsì	Thursday	5
星期天		xīngqītiān	Sunday	5
星期五		xīngqīwǔ	Friday	5
星期一		xīngqīyī	Monday	5
新闻	新聞	xīnwén	news	6
信用卡		xìnyòngkǎ	credit card	7
雪		xuě	snow	10
学	學	xué	study	3
学生	學生	xuésheng	student	1
学习	學習	xuéxí	study	4
学校	學校	xuéxiào	school	2

Y

盐	鹽	yán	salt	8
羊肉		yángròu	lamb	8
颜色		yánsè	color	7
要		yào	want, take (time, etc)	7
要看		yào kàn	It depends	7
亚洲	亞洲	Yàzhōu	Asia	9
也		yě	also	1
夜里		yèlǐ	night	5
爷爷	爺爺	yéye	paternal grandfather	4
一		yī	one	4
一般		yībān	generally, usually	5
一遍		yíbiàn	once	6
一点儿	一點兒	yìdiǎnr	a little	6
一定		yídìng	certainly, definitely	8
一月		yīyuè	January	5
衣服		yīfu	clothes	7
一共		yígòng	altogether	7
阴	陰	yīn	cloudy	10
英国	英國	Yīngguó	United Kingdom	6
英语	英語	Yīngyǔ	English language	6
银行	銀行	yínháng	bank	2
医生	醫生	yīshēng	doctor	1
意思		yìsi	meaning	6
医院	醫院	yīyuàn	hospital	3
用		yòng	use	6
有		yǒu	have, there is/are	2
有的..... 有的		yǒude ... yǒude	some…, others …	7
有点儿	有點兒	yǒudiǎnr	a little, somewhat	8
邮票	郵票	yóupiào	post office	3
有名		yǒumíng	famous	8
邮票	郵票	yóupiào	stamps	7

有时......
  有时
	有時......
	  有時
		yǒushí ......
		  yǒushí
			sometimes …,
			  sometimes …
				5

鱼	魚	yú	fish	8
雨		yǔ	rain	10

远	遠	yuǎn	far	3
预报	預報	yùbào	forecast	10
月		yuè	month	5
语法	語法	yǔfǎ	grammar	6
云	雲	yún	cloud	10
语言	語言	yǔyán	language	6
雨衣		yǔyī	raincoat	10

Z

杂志	雜志	zázhì	magazine	6
在		zài	in, at	3
再		zài	again	6
再见	再見	zàijiàn	good-bye	2
早饭	早飯	zǎofàn	breakfast	5
早上		zǎoshang	early morning	5
怎么	怎麼	zěnme	how	6
怎么样	怎麼樣	zěnmeyàng	how is ...?	1
炸		zhá	deep fry	8
张	張	zhāng	*classifier*	7
帐单	帳單	zhàngdān	check, bill	8
找		zhǎo	look for, find	9
这	這	zhè	this	1
这儿	這兒	zhèr	here	3
只		zhǐ	only	6
知道		zhīdao	know	2
支票		zhīpiào	check	7
种	種	zhǒng	kind, variety	6
中饭	中飯	zhōngfàn	lunch	5
中国	中國	Zhōngguó	China	1
中文		Zhōngwén	Chinese language	2
中午		zhōngwǔ	noon	5
中学生	中學生	zhōngxuéshēng	secondary school student	4
周末		zhōumò	weekend	5
住		zhù	live	3
猪肉	豬肉	zhūròu	pork	8

字		zì	Chinese character	6
字典		zìdiǎn	dictionary	6
自行车	自行車	zìxíngchē	bicycle	9
走		zǒu	walk	9
最		zuì	most	7
最好		zuìhǎo	best, had better	10
作		zuò	do	4
坐		zuò	sit, take (the bus, etc)	8
做饭	做飯	zuòfàn	cook	8
昨天		zuótiān	yesterday	5

KEY TO THE EXERCISES

LESSON 1

II

1.
A: Zhao Xiānsheng, nǐ hǎo!
B: Huáng Xiǎojiě, nǐ hǎo!
A: Nǐ máng ma?
B: Bù máng, nǐ ne?
A: Wǒ hěn máng.

2.
A: Nǐ bàba qù Zhōngguó ma?
B: Qù.
A: Nǐ māma ne?
B: Tā yě qù.

3.
A :Nǐ gēge shì lǎoshī ma?
B: Shì.
A: Nǐ mèimei yě shì lǎoshī ma?
B: Bú shì, tā shì xuésheng.

4.
A: Zhè shì Huá Xiānsheng. Zhè shì Wáng Xiǎojiě.
B: Rènshi nǐ hěn gāoxìng.
C: Rènshi nǐ wǒ yě hěn gāoxìng.

III.
1. Nǐ lèi ma?
2. Hú Xiānsheng bú shì yīshēng. Tā shì lǜshī.
3. Wǒ bàba hěn máng. Wǒ māma bù máng.
4. Wǒ bú rènshi tā.
5. Tā dìdi hěn gāoxìng.

6. Zhè shì wǒ bàba.
7. Wǒ māma bú qù Zhōngguó. Tā qù Rìběn.
8. Lǐ Xiānsheng shì lǜshī. Lǐ Tàitài yě shì lǜshī.
9. Tā bàba māma lái Měiguó.
10. Nǐ gēge xǐhuan wǒ mèimei ma?

IV.

1. Nǐ mèimei lái Zhōngguó ma?   Lái./Bù lái.
2. Shěn Xiǎojiě shì lǎoshī ma?   Shì./Bú shì.
3. Tā rènshi wǒ bàba ma?   Rènshi./Bú rènshi.
4. Nǐ māma yě shì yīshēng ma?   Yě shì./Bú shì.
5. Tā gēge hěn xǐhuan Zhōngguó ma?   Xǐhuan./Bù xǐhuān.
6. Tā shì Wáng Xiānsheng ma?   Shì./Bú shì.
7. Zhāng Xiǎojiě hěn gāoxìng ma?   Hěn gāoxìng./Bù
                                      gāoxìng.
8. Tā jiějie shì xuésheng ma?   Shì./Bú shì.
9. Nǐ bàba māma hěn máng ma?   Hěn máng./Bù máng.
10. Nǐ hěn lèi ma?   Hěn lèi./Bù lèi.

LESSON 2

II.

1. Nǐ zhīdao tā nǔpéngyou de míngzi ma?   Bù zhīdào.
2. Nǐ rènshi wǒde Zhōngwén lǎoshī ma?   Rènshi.
3. Nǐ xìng Wáng ma?   Bù, wǒ xìng Zhāng.
4. Nǐ rènshi tā ma?   Wǒ zhīdao tā, dànshì
                                             wǒ bú rènshi tā.
5. Nǐ shì Zhāng Xiānsheng de tàitài ma?   Shì.
6. Rènshi nǐ hěn gāoxìng.   Rènshi nǐ wǒ yě hěn
                                             gāoxìng.

III.

1. Zhè shì shénme?
2. Tā shì wǒ gēge de nǔpéngyou.
3. Wǒ zhīdao tā, dànshì wǒ bú rènshi tā.
4. Wǒ tàitài jiào Lìli.

5. Tā nǚ'ér méi yǒu Zhōngguó péngyou.

IV.
1. Tā méi yǒu nánpéngyou.
2. Wǒ bú jiào Dàwèi.
3. Wǒmende Zhōngwén lǎoshī bú xìng Wáng.
4. Wǒ māma bù gāoxìng.
5. Tā méi yǒu érzi.
6. Tā tàitai méi yǒu gēge.
7. Wǒ bú rènshi tā xiānsheng.
8. Tāmen méi yǒu Měiguó péngyou.
9. Wǒ bàba bù máng.
10. Wǒmen bú qù Zhōngguó.

V.
1. I have an older brother and also an older sister. My older brother's name is Xiaohua and my older sister's name is Xiaohong.
2. I'm very happy to know your mother.
3. Her boyfriend is David, not Martin.
4. What is the name of your Chinese friend?
5. The family names of both my parents are Huang.

LESSON 3

II.
1. Nǐ jiā zài nǎr?
2. Nǎr yǒu yīyuàn?
3. Zhèr yǒu Zhōngwén xuéxiào ma?
4. Nǐ zài nǎr xué Zhōngwén?
5. Nàr méi yǒu Rìběn cānguǎn.
6. Nǚcèsuǒ zài nàr.
7. Wǒde nǚpéngyou zài Shànghǎi zhù.
8. (Any place name) zài nǎr?
9. Nǎr yǒu yínháng?
10. Nǐ qù nǎr?

III.

1. Qǐngwèn, náncèsuǒ zài nǎr?
2. Qǐngwèn, Běijīng yǒu Měiguóchéng ma?
3. Wǒ tàitài zài xuéxiào gōngzuò.
4. Tā nǚpéngyou zài Nánjīng dàxué xuéxí.
5. Zhèr méi yǒu Zhōngguó cānguǎn.
6. Wǒ māma bú shì yīshēng. Tā shì lǎoshī.
7. Wǒmende Zhōngwén lǎoshī zhù zài Jiùjīnshān.
8. Wǒ māma bú zài jiā.
9. Nǐ bàba māma qù cānguǎn ma?
10. Yīyuàn bú zài nàr.

IV.

1. There is no American bank in Beijing.
2. I work at a school and so does my wife.
3. There is no Japan-town in New York, but there is one in Los Angeles.
4. Excuse me, where is the train station?
5. Excuse me, where can I find a store?
6. What is the name of your school?
7. Are there any Japanese restaurants in Chinatown in New York?
8. I don't know where the bathroom is, but he does.
9. Where are you going? -I'm going to the airport.
10. My parents live in California.

LESSON 4

II.

1. sānshí èr
2. bā bǎi wǔshí sì
3. sān qiān líng èrshí
4. wǔ qiān liù bǎi
5. sì qiān qī bǎi jiǔshí bā
6. jiǔ wàn bā qiān qī bǎi liùshí wǔ
7. yí wàn líng sān bǎi líng sì

III.
1. zhāng: objects with flat surface or sheet-like
2. tiáo: long and narrow objects
3. kuài: small dimensional or cubic-like objects
4. zhī: small, thin, narrow and long objects
5. zhī: animals

IV.
1. Nǐ shì bu shì Zhōngguórén?
2. Tā yǒu méi yǒu háizi?
3. Nǐ bàba māma qù bu qù yínháng?
4. Zhèr yǒu méi yǒu cèsuǒ?
5. Nǐ xìng bu xìng Wáng?
6. Tā zài bu zài jiā?
7. Tāmen xué bu xué Zhōngwén?
8. Nǐde Zhōngwén lǎoshī shì bu shì Zhōngguórén?
9. Zhè shì bu shì nǐde shū?
10. Nǐ jiějiě shì bu shì dàxuéshēng?

V.
1. Wǒ jiā yǒu sì kǒu rén. Tāmen shì wǒ tàitai, wǒ érzi, wǒ nǚ'ér hé wǒ.
2. Nǐde Zhōngwén lǎoshī yǒu duōshao Zhōngwén shū?
3. Shànghǎi yǒu duōshao rén?
4. Wǒ tàitai bú zài gōngsī gōngzuò. Tā shì xuéxiào lǎoshī.
5. Wǒ bú rènshi nà ge rén. Nǐ rènshi tā ma?
6. Wǒ jiějie bú shì zhōngxuéshēng. Tā shì dàxuéshēng.
7. Nǐ jiějie zài dàxué xué shénme?
8. Nǐ zài nǎ ge gōngsī gōngzuò?
9. Wǒmen xuéxiào yǒu yì qiān wǔ bǎi ge xuésheng.
10. Nǐ mèimei duō dà?

VI.
1. I study American history at Beijing University.
2. There are two Chinese teachers in their school.

3. Their company is very big. There are 1,000 people there.
4. How many Chinese friends do you have?
5. My boyfriend does not like to study history. He likes to study Chinese.
6. My mother works at home.
7. Do you know how many universities there are in Shanghai?
8. That person's older brother is our Chinese teacher.
9. There are eight people in my family. How about yours?
10. He is a student at the University of California.

LESSON 5

I.

7:05 qī diǎn wǔ fēn	12:30 shí'èr diǎn sānshí fēn
4:15 sì diǎn shíwǔ fēn	9:43 jiǔ diǎn sìshí sān fēn
10:59 shí diǎn wǔshí jiǔ fēn	3:28 sān diǎn èrshí bā fēn
6:32 liù diǎn sānshí èr fēn	1:30 yì diǎn sānshí fēn
8:04 bā diǎn líng sì fēn	11:16 shíyī diǎn shíliù fēn

III.
1. Jīntiān xīngqī jǐ?
2. Zuótiān jǐ yuè jǐ hào?
3. Tā shénme shíhou lái?
4. Nǐde Měiguó péngyou jīnnián bā yuè qù nǎr?
5. Jīntiān shì jǐ yuè jǐ hào, xīngqī jǐ?

IV.
1. Nǐ zuótiān wǎnshang zài nǎr?
2. Duìbuqǐ, wǒ méi yǒu biǎo. Wǒ bù zhīdào xiànzài jǐ diǎn.
3. Nǐ xīngqī jǐ yǒu Zhōngwén kè?
4. Nǐ jīntiān xiàwǔ jǐ diǎn xiàbān?
5. Wǒ xīngqīliù wǎnshang yìbān zài cānguǎn chīfàn.
6. Wǒ bàba měi tiān liù diǎn qǐchuáng.
7. Wǒ bù chī zǎofàn.
8. Bù chī zǎo fàn bù hǎo.
9. Nǐ míngtiān xiàwǔ zuò shénme?

10. Nǐ shénme shíhou qù Zhōngguó?
    Míngnián liù yuè.

V.
1. I don't usually eat breakfast.
2. Sometimes she eats lunch at work, sometimes at home.
3. Next Wednesday is my wife's birthday.
4. I'm going to the bank at 9:00 tomorrow morning.
5. What time do you go to bed every day?

LESSON 6

II.

1. yínháng	6. shēngri
2. péngyou	7. zhōngfàn
3. jiā	8. dàxué
4. cèsuǒ	9. zhōngxuéshēng
5. zhōngwǔ	10. yīshēng

III.

1. Spanish	6. store
2. Mandarin	7. Nanjing dialect
3. Mandarin	8. restaurant
4. Asia	9. understand
5. Africa	10. French

IV.
1. Nǐ huì shuō Fǎyǔ ma?
2. Nǐ jiějie huì shuō jǐ zhǒng yǔyán?
3. Nǐde péngyou cóng nǎr lái?
4. Tā huì shuō yìdiǎnr Xībānyáyǔ.
5. Duìbuqǐ, wǒ bù dǒng nǐde huà.
6. Qǐng màn yìdiǎnr shuō.
7. Tā cóng Shànghǎi lái. Tā shì Shànghǎirén.
8. Nánjīngrén shuō shénme huà?
9. Nǐ dǒng bu dǒng wǒde huà?

10. Nǐ māma huì shuō Rìyǔ ma?

V.

1. Qǐngwèn, nǐ zhīdao yòng Zhōngwén zěnme shuō "speak slowly" ma?
2. Qǐngwèn, "qìchē "shì shénme yìsi?
3. "Qìchē "de yìsi shì "car".
4. Wǒde Zhōngwén lǎoshī bú huì shuō Yīngyǔ.
5. Tā cóng Déguó lái, dànshì tā bú huì shuō Déyǔ.
6. Tā huì shuō yìdiǎnr Xībānyáyǔ.
7. Xiānggǎng rén shuō Guǎngdōnghuà.
8. Shéi huì shuō Yīngyǔ?
9. Tā shì Shànghǎirén, dànshì tā bù shuō Shànghǎihuà.
10. Nǐ zěnme xiě zhè ge hànzì?

VI.

1. I'm English and my wife is French.
2. People in Shanghai do not understand Cantonese.
3. My boyfriend speaks four languages, but I only speak English.
4. Pardon? I don't understand. Please say it again.
5. I understand the Taiwan dialect, but I don't speak it.
6. His Cantonese is very good, but his Mandarin is not.
7. Excuse me, who speaks English?
8. Do you know what "gōngyuán" means?
9. I can only understand a little of what she said.
10. Sorry, I do not speak the Sichuan dialect.

VII.

1. Nǐ yǒu jǐ běn Zhōngwén shū?
2. Nǐ rènshi bu rènshi nà ge yīshēng?
3. Tāmen měi tiān bā diǎn shàngbān.
4. Nǐ shì bu shì xuésheng?
5. Tā yǒu jiějie, méi yǒu gēge.
6. Wǒ yǒu liǎng ge Zhōngguó péngyou.
7. Qǐngwèn, Zhōngguóchéng zài nǎr?
8. Tā zài cānguǎn gōngzuò.

9. Wáng tàitai jīntiān bú qù yínháng.

10. Nǐmen xuéxiào de túshūguǎn yǒu duōshao (běn) shū?

LESSON 7

II.

1. Zhè jiàn máoyī duōshao qián?

2. Nǐmen shōu bu shōu rìyuán?

3. Nǎr yǒu Měiguó yínháng?

4. Zhè ge diàn de dōngxi bú guì, hěn piányi.

5. Nǐ yào huàn duōshao měiyuán?

III.

1. ¥10	shí kuài
2. ¥1.20	yí kuài liǎng máo
3. ¥5.64	wǔ kuài liù máo sì (fēn)
4. ¥7.08	qī kuài líng bā (fēn)
5. ¥33.94	sānshí sān kuài jiǔ máo sì (fēn)
6. ¥580	wǔ bǎi bāshí kuài
7. ¥99.99	jiǔshí jiǔ kuài jiǔ máo jiǔ (fēn)
8. ¥6,832.81	liù qiān bā bǎi sānshí èr kuài bā máo yī (fēn)
9. ¥40.60	sìshí kuài liù máo
10. ¥2,080.01	èr qiān líng bāshí kuài líng yī (fēn)

IV.

1. Qǐng lái yíxiàr.

2. Zhè běn cídiǎn duōshao qián?

3. Duìbuqǐ, wǒmen zhǐ shōu měiyuán. Wǒmen bù shōu Rénmínbì.

4. Nǐ néng gàosu wǒ nǎr yǒu xiédiàn ma?

5. Yǒude shāngdiàn shōu xìnyòngkǎ, yǒude shāngdiàn bù shōu.

6. Beijīng nǎ ge bǎihuògōngsī zuì dà?

7. Yào kàn jiàgé.

8. Nǐ bù néng zài shāngdiàn huàn qián.

9. Wǒ néng shì yíxiàr zhè shuāng xié ma?

10. Tīngshuō Zhōngguóchéng de dōngxi hěn piányi.

V.

1. I don't have U.S. dollars. I only have Japanese yen.
2. One U.S. dollar could convert to six Renminbi yesterday.
3. That bookstore has the most English books.
4. Many people like to go shopping in Shanghai.
5. Stores in the United States sell a lot of Chinese products.
6. This pair of pants is too long. Do you have anything shorter?
7. How much is this overcoat?
8. I heard that things in Japan are very expensive.
9. Whether or not I can go to China depends on whether I have money.
10. Cheap stuff may not necessarily be bad.

LESSON 8

II.

1. Nǐ shì Zhōngguórén háishi Měiguórén?
2. Nǐ xǐhuan bu xǐhuān Fǎguó cài?
3. Tā méi yǒu qù guo Yīngguó.
4. Rìběn yīnyuè hěn hǎotīng.
5. Wǒ māma chī guo Běijīng kǎoyā.
6. Nǐ yǒu méiyou kàn guo zhè běn shū?
7. Nǎr yǒu Zhōngguó cānguǎn?
8. Yígòng duōshao qián?
9. Zhè jiā cānguǎn de cài hěn yǒumíng.
10. Zhè shì wǒ dì'èr cì hē qīngdǎo píjiǔ.

III.

1. Nǐ yǒu méiyou kàn guo Yīngguó diànyǐng?/ Wǒ méiyou kàn guo Yīngguó diànyǐng.
2. Tāde lǎoshī yǒu méiyou xué guo Déyǔ?/ Tāde lǎoshī méiyou xué guo Déyǔ.
3. Tā yǒu méiyou qù guo Xiānggǎng?/ Tā méiyou qù guo Xiānggǎng.
4. Nǐde Zhōngguó péngyou yǒu méiyou lái guo nǐ jiā? / Wǒde Zhōngguó péngyou méiyou lái guo wǒ jiā.

5. Tāmen chī guo Fǎguó cài ma?/ Tāmen méiyou chī guo Fǎguó cài.
6. Tāde nánpéngyou tīng guo Rìběn yīnyuè ma?/ Tāde nánpéngyou méiyou tīng guo Rìběn yīnyuè.
7. Nǐ bàba yǒu méiyou zài Zhōngguó yínháng gōngzuò guo?/ Wǒ bàba méiyou zài Zhōngguó yínháng gōngzuò guo.
8. Tā māma yǒu méiyou zài Zhōngguó huàn guo qián?/ Tā māma méiyou zài Zhōngguó huàn guo qián.
9. Wáng lǎoshī yǒu méiyou zài nà ge shāngdiàn mǎi guo dōngxi?/ Wáng lǎoshī méiyou zài nà ge shāngdiàn mǎi guo dōngxi.
10. Nǐ dìdi yǒu méiyou zài Jiāzhōu zhù guo?/ Wǒ dìdi méiyou zài Jiāzhōu zhù guo.

IV.
1. Wǒ bú tài è.
2. Beijīng kǎoyā hěn yǒumíng.
3. Náncèsuǒ zài èr lóu háishi sān lóu?
4. Nǐ yào kāfēi háishi chá?
5. Zhè jiā cānguǎn de cài hěn hǎochī.
6. Nǐ qù guo Niǔyuē de Zhōngguóchéng ma?
7. Nǐ hǎoxiàng hěn lèi.
8. Zhè shì wǒ dìyī cì chī Rìběn cài. Wǒ juéde wèidào hěn hǎo.
9. Zhōngguó de cānguǎn bù shōu xiǎofèi.
10. Nǐ hái xiǎng chī shénme?

V.
1. Does your father work at a college or a middle school?
2. The green tea doesn't taste good, but the black tea does.
3. Is your girlfriend Chinese or American?
4. My husband has never seen a Chinese movie.
5. What dishes are famous in Guangzhou?
6. My older sister can't drink liquor, but she can drink a little wine.
7. I want neither rice nor noodles. I want bread.
8. In his house, his wife cooks, but in my house, I cook.
9. Are you going to eat at home or in a restaurant tonight?
10. Chinese people sometimes only eat rice, not dishes, whereas Americans sometimes only eat dishes, not rice.

LESSON 9

II.
1. Nǐ zhīdao zěnme xiě zhè ge zì ma?
2. Nǐ bàba qù Xiānggǎng zuò shénme?
3. Tiān'ānmén lí wǒmende lǚguǎn hěn jìn. Zuò dìtiě zhǐ yào shí fēnzhōng.
4. Míngtiān shì nǐ tàitai de shēngri. Nǐmen zěnme guò?
5. Qí zìxíngchē qù nǐde xuéxiào yào duōshao shíjiān?
6. Tā qù guo Fǎguó de shénme dìfang?
7. Hángzhōu hěn hǎowán.
8. Wǒ qù guo Niǔyuē sān cì.
9. Cóng huǒchēzhàn qù Běijīng dàxué yào zuò qìchē.
10. Nǐ zhīdao dìtiězhàn zài nǎr ma?

III.
1. Jiùjīnshān lǚguǎn hǎozhǎo bu hǎozhǎo?
2. Xī'ān lí Guǎngzhōu hěn yuǎn.
3. Cóng Běijīng zuò huǒchē dào Shànghǎi chàbuduō yào shí ge xiǎoshí.
4. Nánjīng yǒu méi yǒu dìtiě?
5. Hěn duō Zhōngguórén qí zìxíngchē shàngbān.
6. Nǐ cóng Xiānggǎng zěnme qù Guǎngzhōu?
7. Tā qù guo Rìběn wǔ cì.
8. Wǒ xiǎng míngnián qù Zhōngguó.
9. Wǒde péngyou bú zhù lǚguǎn. Tā zhù wǒ jiā.
10. Hěn duō Zhōngguórén xiànzài guò Shèngdànjié.

IV.
1. I'm going to the park with my wife this weekend.
2. My mother has been to England and France in Europe.
3. Train tickets are very cheap, but trains are very slow.
4. It is not easy to find a hotel now.
5. My house is very close to my company and I walk to work.
6. It takes 30 minutes to drive to my company from my house.
7. I think Suzhou must be very fun.

8. Her father has been to many places in China. He likes Nanjing the best.
9. How are you going to the train station?
10. I sometimes eat lunch at home, sometimes in school.

LESSON 10

II.
1. Nǐ tàitai qù le shāngdiàn ma?/ Nǐ tàitai yǒu méiyou qù shāngdiàn?
2. Nǐmende Zhōngwén lǎoshī lái le ma?/ Nǐmende Zhōngwén lǎoshī yǒu méiyou lái?
3. Xiàyǔ le ma?/ Yǒu méiyou xiàyǔ?
4. Niǔyuē jīnnián dōngtiān xià le hěn duō xuě ma?/ Niǔyuē jīnnián dōngtiān yǒu méiyou xià hěn duō xuě?
5. Tāmen xiàbān le ma?/ Tāmen yǒu méiyou xiàbān?

III.
1. Wǒ bàba māma zuótiān dōu méiyou lái.
2. Xīngqīliù wǎnshang wǒ méiyou kàn diànshì.
3. Yínháng méiyou guānmén.
4. Tā méiyou yòng wǒde qìchē.
5. Wǒ xiānsheng méiyou qǐchuáng.

V.
1. Wǒ zuótiān méiyou chī zǎofàn.
2. Tā māma jīntiān zǎoshàng zài jiā.
3. Nǐ shàng xīngqītiān yǒu méiyou qù jiàotáng? Or nǐ shàng xīngqītiān qù le jiàotáng ma?
4. Tāmen méiyou lái Zhōngguó.
5. Wǒ qùnián bú rènshi tā.

VI.
1. Shànghǎi qiūtiān de tiānqì zěnmeyàng?
2. Niǔyuē xiàtiān chángcháng xiàyǔ ma?
3. Míngtiān shì qíngtiān.
4. Hángzhōu xià bu xiàxuě? Yǒushí xià, yǒushí bú xià.

5. Wǒmen zhèr dōngtiān fēng hěn dà.
6. Zuótiān duōshao dù? Wǔshí sān dù.
7. Tīngshuō Fǎguó jīnnián dōngtiān xià le hěn duō xuě.
8. Guǎngzhōu chūntiān de tiānqì zuì hǎo.
9. Zuótiān de yǔ yǒu duō dà?
10. Nánjīng chūntiān yǒushí xiàxuě.
11. Wǒ māma qù le shāngdiàn.
12. Tā jīntiān zǎoshàng méiyou chī zǎofàn.
13. Nǐ yǒu méiyou kāi guo Zhōngguó chē?
14. Wǒ zuótiān wǎnshang xué le shí ge hànzì.
15. Tāmen jīntiān zài Zhōngguó yínháng huàn le wǔ bǎi měiyuán.

VII.

1. It's cloudy today. It's cold and windy.
2. Was the snow heavy in New York this winter?
3. What do Chinese people like to do in summer?
4. Many Americans like to go skiing in winter.
5. It was not too cold last winter and not too hot last summer.
6. I don't like Beijing's spring. It's too windy.
7. Which was heavier, the rain yesterday or the rain today?
8. There are more students at Beijing University than at Nanjing University.
9. My house is farther away from the company than his house.
10. This book is three dollars cheaper than that book.

IX.

1. Jīntiān de xuě bǐ zuótiān de xuě dà.
2. Tāde Zhōngwén bǐ wǒde Zhōngwén hǎo.
3. Hóngjiǔ bǐ báijiǔ hǎohē.
4. Fēijī bǐ qìchē kuài.
5. Beijīng bǐ Shànghǎi hǎowán.
6. Zhè běn shū bǐ nà běn shū guì shí kuài qián.
7. Wǒ bàba bǐ wǒ māma máng.
8. Niǔyuē de lǚguǎn bǐ Luòshānjī de lǚguǎn hǎozhǎo.
9. Jīntiān bǐ zuótiān gāo shí dù.
10. Wǒmen xuéxiào bǐ tāmen xuéxiào duō èr bǎi ge xuésheng.

PINYIN PRACTICE

Simple Vowels:

a   o   e   i   u   ü

Vowel Compounds:

ao   ai   an   ang

ou   ong

ei   en   eng

ia   ie   iu   iao   ian   in   iang   ing   iong

ua   uo   ui   uai   uan   uen   uang

üe   üan   ün

Consonants (ordered on the basis of shared sound properties such as *b* is paired with *p*, *d* paired with *t*, and *q* paired with *x*):

b p m f d t n l g k h j q x z c s zh ch sh r

B

bā, bá, bǎ, bà
bō, bó, bǒ, bò
bī, bí, bǐ, bì
bū, bú, bǔ, bù

bāi, bái, bǎi, bài
bāo, báo, bǎo, bào
bān, bán, bǎn, bàn
bāng, báng, bǎng, bàng

bēi, béi, běi, bèi
bēn, bén, běn, bèn
bēng, béng, běng, bèng

biāo, biáo, biǎo, biào
biē, bié, biě, biè
biān, bián, biǎn, biàn
bīn, bín, bǐn, bìn
bīng, bíng, bǐng, bìng

P

pā, pá, pǎ, pà
pō, pó, pǒ, pò
pī, pí, pǐ, pì
pū, pú, pǔ, pù

pāi, pái, pǎi, pài
pāo, páo, pǎo, pào
pān, pán, pǎn, pàn
pāng, páng, pǎng, pàng

pēi, péi, pěi, pèi
pēn, pén, pěn, pèn
pēng, péng, pěng, pèng

piāo, piáo, piǎo, piào
piē, pié, piě, piè
piān, pián, piǎn, piàn
pīn, pín, pǐn, pìn
pīng, píng, pǐng, pìng

M

mā, má, mǎ, mà
mō, mó, mǒ, mò
mē, mé, mě, mè
mī, mí, mǐ, mì
mū, mú, mǔ, mù

māi, mái, mǎi, mài
māo, máo, mǎo, mào
mān, mán, mǎn, màn
māng, máng, mǎng, màng

mēi, méi, měi, mèi
mēn, mén, měn, mèn
mēng, méng, měng, mèng

miāo, miáo, miǎo, miào
miē, mié, miě, miè
miū, miú, miǔ, miù
miān, mián, miǎn, miàn
mīn, mín, mǐn, mìn
mīng, míng, mǐng, mìng

mōu, móu, mǒu, mòu

F

fā, fá, fǎ, fà
fō, fó, fǒ, fò
fū, fú, fǔ, fù

fān, fán, fǎn, fàn
fāng, fáng, fǎng, fàng

fēi, féi, fěi, fèi
fēn, fén, fěn, fèn
fēng, féng, fěng, fèng

fōu, fóu, fǒu, fòu

D
dā, dá, dǎ, dà
dē, dé, dě, dè
dī, dí, dǐ, dì
dū, dú, dǔ, dù

dāi, dái, dǎi, dài
dāo, dáo, dǎo, dào
dān, dán, dǎn, dàn
dāng, dáng, dǎng, dàng

dōng, dóng, dǒng, dòng

dēi, déi, děi, dèi
dēn, dén, děn, dèn
dēng, déng, děng, dèng

diāo, diáo, diǎo, diào
diē, dié, diě, diè
diū, diú, diǔ, diù
diān, dián, diǎn, diàn
dīng, díng, dǐng, dìng

duō, duó, duǒ, duò
duī, duí, duǐ, duì
duān, duán, duǎn, duàn
dūn, dún, dǔn, dùn

T
tā, tá, tǎ, tà
tē, té, tě, tè
tī, tí, tǐ, tì
tū, tú, tǔ, tù

tāi, tái, tǎi, tài
tāo, táo, tǎo, tào
tān, tán, tǎn, tàn
tāng, táng, tǎng, tàng

tōng, tóng, tǒng, tòng

tēng, téng, těng, tèng

tiāo, tiáo, tiǎo, tiào
tiē, tié, tiě, tiè
tiān, tián, tiǎn, tiàn
tīng, tíng, tǐng, tìng

tuō, tuó, tuǒ, tuò
tuī, tuí, tuǐ, tuì
tuān, tuán, tuǎn, tuàn
tūn, tún, tǔn, tùn

N
nā, ná, nǎ, nà
nē, né, ně, nè
nī, ní, nǐ, nì
nū, nú, nǔ, nù
nǖ, nǘ, nǚ, nǜ

nāi, nái, nǎi, nài
nāo, náo, nǎo, nào
nān, nán, nǎn, nàn
nāng, náng, nǎng, nàng

nōng, nóng, nǒng, nòng

nēi, néi, něi, nèi
nēn, nén, něn, nèn
nēng, néng, něng, nèng

niāo, niáo, niǎo, niào
niān, nián, niǎn, niàn
niāng, niáng, niǎng, niàng
niē, nié, niě, niè
nīn, nín, nǐn, nìn
nīng, níng, nǐng, nìng
niū, niú, niǔ, niù

nuō, nuó, nuǒ, nuò
nuān, nuán, nuǎn, nuàn

nüē, nüé, nüě, nüè

L
lā, lá, lǎ, là
lē, lé, lě, lè
lī, lí, lǐ, lì
lū, lú, lǔ, lù
lǖ, lǘ, lǚ, lǜ

lāi, lái, lǎi, lài
lāo, láo, lǎo, lào
lān, lán, lǎn, làn
lāng, láng, lǎng, làng

lōng, lóng, lǒng, lòng

lēi, léi, lěi, lèi
lēng, léng, lěng, lèng

liā, liá, liǎ, già
liāo, liáo, liǎo, liào
liān, lián, liǎn, liàn
liāng, liáng, liǎng, liàng
liē, lié, liě, liè
līn, lín, lǐn, lìn
līng, líng, lǐng, lìng
liū, liú, liǔ, liù

luō, luó, luǒ, luò
lūn, lún, lǔn, lùn
luān, luán, luǎn, luàn

lüē, lüé, lüě, lüè

G
gā, gá, gǎ, gà
gē, gé, gě, gè
gū, gú, gǔ, gù

gāi, gái, gǎi, gài
gāo, gáo, gǎo, gào
gān, gán, gǎn, gàn
gāng, gáng, gǎng, gàng

gōng, góng, gǒng, gòng

gēi, géi, gěi, gèi
gēn, gén, gěn, gèn
gēng, géng, gěng, gèng

guā, guá, guǎ, guà
guāi, guái, guǎi, guài
guān, guán, guǎn, guàn
guāng, guáng, guǎng, guàng
guō, guó, guǒ, guò

gūi, gúi, gǔi, gùi
gūn, gún, gǔn, gùn

K
kā, ká, kǎ, kà
kē, ké, kě, kè
kū, kú, kǔ, kù

kāi, kái, kǎi, kài
kāo, káo, kǎo, kào
kān, kán, kǎn, kàn
kāng, káng, kǎng, kàng

kōng, kóng, kǒng, kòng

kēi, kéi, kěi, kèi
kēn, kén, kěn, kèn
kēng, kéng, kěng, kèng

kuā, kuá, kuǎ, kuà
kuāi, kuái, kuǎi, kuài
kuān, kuán, kuǎn, kuàn
kuāng, kuáng, kuǎng, kuàng
kuō, kuó, kuǒ, kuò
kūi, kúi, kǔi, kùi
kūn, kún, kǔn, kùn

H
hā, há, hǎ, hà
hē, hé, hě, hè
hū, hú, hǔ, hù

hāi, hái, hǎi, hài
hāo, háo, hǎo, hào
hān, hán, hǎn, hàn
hāng, háng, hǎng, hàng

hōng, hóng, hǒng, hòng

hēi, héi, hěi, hèi
hēn, hén, hěn, hèn
hēng, héng, hěng, hèng

huā, huá, huǎ, huà
huāi, huái, huǎi, huài
huān, huán, huǎn, huàn
huāng, huáng, huǎng, huàng
huō, huó, huǒ, huò
hūi, húi, hǔi, hùi
hūn, hún, hǔn, hùn

J
jī, jí, jǐ, jì
jū, jú, jǔ, jù

jiā, jiá, jiǎ, jià
jiāo, jiáo, jiǎo, jiào
jiān, jián, jiǎn, jiàn
jiāng, jiáng, jiǎng, jiàng
jiē, jié, jiě, jiè
jīn, jín, jǐn, jìn
jīng, jíng, jǐng, jìng
jiū, jiú, jiǔ, jiù
jiōng, jióng, jiǒng, jiòng

juē, jué, juě, juè,
juān, juán, juǎn, juàn
jūn, jún, jǔn, jùn

Q
qī, qí, qǐ, qì
qū, qú, qǔ, qù

qiā, qiá, qiǎ, qià
qiāo, qiáo, qiǎo, qiào
qiān, qián, qiǎn, qiàn
qiāng, qiáng, qiǎng, qiàng
qiē, qié, qiě, qiè
qīn, qín, qǐn, qìn
qīng, qíng, qǐng, qìng
qiū, qiú, qiǔ, qiù
qiōng, qióng, qiǒng, qiòng

quē, qué, quě, què,
quān, quán, quǎn, quàn
qūn, qún, qǔn, qùn

X
xī, xí, xǐ, xì
xū, xú, xǔ, xù

xiā, xiá, xiǎ, xià
xiāo, xiáo, xiǎo, xiào
xiān, xián, xiǎn, xiàn
xiāng, xiáng, xiǎng, xiàng
xiē, xié, xiě, xiè
xīn, xín, xǐn, xìn
xīng, xíng, xǐng, xìng
xiū, xiú, xiǔ, xiù
xiōng, xióng, xiǒng, xiòng

xuē, xué, xuě, xuè,
xuān, xuán, xuǎn, xuàn
xūn, xún, xǔn, xùn

Z
zā, zá, zǎ, zà
zē, zé, zě, zè
zī, zí, zǐ, zì

zū, zú, zǔ, zù

zāi, zái, zǎi, zài
zāo, záo, zǎo, zào
zān, zán, zǎn, zàn
zāng, záng, zǎng, zàng

zōng, zóng, zǒng, zòng

zēi, zéi, zěi, zèi
zēn, zén, zěn, zèn
zēng, zéng, zěng, zèng

zuō, zuó, zuǒ, zuò
zūi, zúi, zǔi, zùi
zūn, zún, zǔn, zùn
zuān, zuán, zuǎn, zuàn

C
cā, cá, cǎ, cà
cē, cé, cě, cè
cī, cí, cǐ, cì
cū, cú, cǔ, cù

cāi, cái, cǎi, cài
cāo, cáo, cǎo, cào
cān, cán, cǎn, càn
cāng, cáng, cǎng, càng

cōng, cóng, cǒng, còng

cēn, cén, cěn, cèn
cēng, céng, cěng, cèng

cuō, cuó, cuǒ, cuò
cūi, cúi, cǔi, cùi

cūn, cún, cǔn, cùn
cuān, cuán, cuǎn, cuàn

S

sā, sá, sǎ, sà
sē, sé, sě, sè
sī, sí, sǐ, sì
sū, sú, sǔ, sù

sāi, sái, sǎi, sài
sāo, sáo, sǎo, sào
sān, sán, sǎn, sàn
sāng, sáng, sǎng, sàng

sōng, sóng, sǒng, sòng

sēn, sén, sěn, sèn
sēng, séng, sěng, sèng

suō, suó, suǒ, suò
suī, suí, suǐ, suì
sūn, sún, sǔn, sùn
suān, suán, suǎn, suàn

Zh

zhā, zhá, zhǎ, zhà
zhē, zhé, zhě, zhè
zhī, zhí, zhǐ, zhì
zhū, zhú, zhǔ, zhù

zhāi, zhái, zhǎi, zhài
zhāo, zháo, zhǎo, zhào
zhān, zhán, zhǎn, zhàn
zhāng, zháng, zhǎng, zhàng

zhōng, zhóng, zhǒng, zhòng

zhēi, zhéi, zhěi, zhèi
zhēn, zhén, zhěn, zhèn
zhēng, zhéng, zhěng, zhèng

zhuā, zhuá, zhuǎ, zhuà
zhuāi, zhuái, zhuǎi, zhuài
zhuāng, zhuáng, zhuǎng,
zhuàng
zhuō, zhuó, zhuǒ, zhuò
zhūi, zhúi, zhǔi, zhùi
zhūn, zhún, zhǔn, zhùn
zhuān, zhuán, zhuǎn, zhuàn

Ch

chā, chá, chǎ, chà
chē, ché, chě, chè
chī, chí, chǐ, chì
chū, chú, chǔ, chù

chāi, chái, chǎi, chài
chāo, cháo, chǎo, chào
chān, chán, chǎn, chàn
chāng, cháng, chǎng, chàng

chōng, chóng, chǒng, chòng

chēn, chén, chěn, chèn
chēng, chéng, chěng, chèng

chuā, chuá, chuǎ, chuà
chuāi, chuái, chuǎi, chuài
chuāng, chuáng, chuǎng,
chuàng
chuō, chuó, chuǒ, chuò
chūi, chúi, chǔi, chùi
chūn, chún, chǔn, chùn

chuān, chuán, chuǎn, chuàn

Sh
shā, shá, shǎ, shà
shē, shé, shě, shè
shī, shí, shǐ, shì
shū, shú, shǔ, shù

shāi, shái, shǎi, shài
shāo, sháo, shǎo, shào
shān, shán, shǎn, shàn
shāng, sháng, shǎng, shàng

shēi, shéi, shěi, shèi
shēn, shén, shěn, shèn
shēng, shéng, shěng, shèng

shuā, shuá, shuǎ, shuà
shuāi, shuái, shuǎi, shuài
shuāng, shuáng, shuǎng, shuàng
shuō, shuó, shuǒ, shuò
shūi, shúi, shǔi, shùi
shūn, shún, shǔn, shùn
shuān, shuán, shuǎn, shuàn

R
rē, ré, rě, rè
rī, rí, rǐ, rì
rū, rú, rǔ, rù

rāo, ráo, rǎo, rào
rān, rán, rǎn, ràn
rāng, ráng, rǎng, ràng

rōng, róng, rǒng, ròng
rōu, róu, rǒu, ròu

rēn, rén, rěn, rèn
rēng, réng, rěng, rèng

ruō, ruó, ruǒ, ruò
rūi, rúi, rǔi, rùi
rūn, rún, rǔn, rùn
ruān, ruán, ruǎn, ruàn

COMPUTING IN CHINESE

The advancement of computer technology is a great boon for language learners, and particularly for students of Chinese in their dealing with Chinese characters. A complex character consisting of 20 to 30 strokes can be easily produced by tapping a couple of keys on the computer. It is so effective and fun at the same time that there are teachers of Chinese who are advocating a penless approach to writing characters using the computer.

For our purpose, computing in Chinese refers to two things: viewing or reading characters on the internet or emails, and producing characters using the computer.

Viewing Chinese

There are two ways to view characters. First, you need an add-on or a helper Chinese program that comes with a package of Chinese fonts. Such programs work in conjunction with regular word processors and internet browsers. When it comes to inputting (more on that later), most of them are resident in that they reside in the computer's memory and within whatever applications you use, but some are stand-alone. Popular Chinese programs include NJ Star (http://www.njstar.com) and Key (http://www.cjkware.com/). Mac users can use Chinese Language Kit for the Macintosh.

Second, most updated operating systems, such as Microsoft Windows XP and up, are now equipped with features which allow Chinese text to be displayed without the assistance of a helper program mentioned above. In order to make use of this built-in feature, you would need to change some computer configurations in your computer's "Control Panel". This is how if you use Windows XP:

From the Start button, select Settings and then the Control Panel.

From the options on the Control Panel select "Regional Options." The default selection under the General tab is English. Do not change it unless you want to work exclusively in the Chinese environment.

On the lower half of the window, select Simplified or Traditional Chinese. It is a good idea to select both because there are occasions when you may need to view both versions.

At this point, you will be asked to insert the Windows XP Install CD and copy over the files it needs. You will then need to reboot for the new settings to take effect. If you need a step-by-step guide on how to install the program, check this site:

http://californiadream.com/workshops/info/winXPLang/winX PlangInstallConfig.html

The latest version of two major browsers (Internet Explorer and Firefox) can also support Chinese without having to resort to any other add-on programs. Some Chinese web pages are so smart that it can trigger the browser for it to automatically apply Chinese fonts to display the characters. Web pages that do not have this feature, however, may not correctly display Chinese characters. When this happens, you need to adjust the settings under View in your browser. If you use Internet Explorer, select View, Encoding, and then simplified or traditional Chinese.

If your internet browser does not display Chinese correctly, the simplest thing for you to do is to upgrade your internet browser to a newer version or to install the free language support packs when you are prompted by your computer system. You can download the free Chinese language support package at the following website:

www.microsoft.com/windows/ie/downloads/recommended/ ime/install.asp

"Writing" Chinese

The software needed to write Chinese characters is basically the same as that for viewing Chinese characters. To do this, you use an add-on Chinese program or use the built-in input device that comes with certain operating systems.

Both popular add-on programs mentioned earlier (NJ Star and Key) can do the job very well. They come with a variety of input methods, but for students of Chinese, I suggest the *pinyin* method, which is not only easy, but also helpful in enhancing your awareness of *pinyin* and consequently the correct pronunciation of words. When you activate one of these add-on programs, a panel will appear on the screen. When you type *pinyin* for a particular character, word or even phrase, they will appear in the panel. Since Chinese is famous for the proliferation of homophones, you will get a list of characters that are pronounced the same when you type *pinyin* for a character. All the homophones are numbered. If the character you intend to produce happens to be the first choice, you can simply press the space bar and the character will go on the screen where the cursor is. If the intended character is not the first item on the list, you will then need to select it by pressing the corresponding number on the keyboard. Undoubtedly this is quite slow and time-consuming. The right way to input is to type by the word rather than individual characters. Since most words in Chinese today are dissyllabic, there are far fewer homophones for dissyllabic or polysyllabic words. For example, if you want to produce the word 中文 (zhongwen), which consists of two characters 中 (zhong) and 文 (wen), you can do it in one of the two ways. First, you can first type *zhong* and then *wen*. If you do that, you will get 17 characters for zhong and 15 characters for wen (on NJ Star). You will then need to pick the right character from the list. The second way is to enter the word in its entirety: *zhongwen*. When you do this, only one word appears on the panel because there is no other word in Chinese that is also pronounced *zhongwen*. Before long, you will find that you don't even have to type an entire *pinyin* before you can get a word of your choice. Some representations will suffice. For example, when you type *zhongw*, the characters for *zhongwen* already appear. If you become sufficiently familiar with the process, you will further find that you can get 中文 if you simply type *zhw*. It takes seven key strokes to type the word *Chinese* in English, but it only takes three strokes to produce the equivalent in Chinese. So it is not a myth that people can type Chinese characters as fast as they type English words, or even faster.

Alternatively, and more conveniently, you can use built-in input devices that come with certain operating systems. For PC users, the best input device is Google Pinyin. You can download it free at www.google.com/ime/pinyin. What makes it stand head and shoulders above the other input devices is that it is intelligent with its predictive technology. It uses Google Translate and its huge database of cache to predict the possible combination when a person is typing. The database is constantly updated so that the more you use the device, the more accurate its text prediction will be.

For Mac users, (OS X 10.3, 10.4, and 10.5), they can use the system's built-in multilingual support to input Chinese. These are the steps to set up the device:

Go to: System Preferences>International>Input Menu>
Scroll down to the bottom, and check off either the simplified
    Chinese or the original Chinese
Close System Preferences
Open Word or other applications
Click the US flag icon on the input menu bar and select Chinese.

For more detailed instructions on how to display and input Chinese for PC and Mac, please visit:
www.chinesehour.com/support/support_a_05/

RESOURCES FOR STUDENTS OF CHINESE

Bibliographic Resources

General

Davis, Temple Hope. 2009. *An Assault on My Senses: Living and Working in Central China*. College Station, TX: Virtualbookworm Publishing Inc.

Dernberger, Robert, et al. eds. 1991. *The Chinese: Adapting the Past, Facing the Future*. Center for Chinese Studies. Ann Arbor, MI: The University of Michigan.

Dillon, Mike. 2009. *Contemporary China: An Introduction*. New York: Routledge.

Ebrey, Patricia Buckley. 1993. *Chinese Civilization: A Source Book*. New York: Free Press.

Fairbank, John King. 1992. *China: A New History*. Cambridge, Mass.: Belknap Press of Harvard University Press.

Ho, Yong. 2000. *China: An Illustrated History*. New York: Hippocrene Books, Inc.

Hsu, Francis L.K. 1991. *Americans and Chinese: Passage to Differences*. Taipei: Bookman Books.

Hu, Wenzhong and Cornelius L. Grove. 1991. *Encountering the Chinese: A Guide for Americans*. Yarmouth, Maine: Intercultural Press, Inc.

Hutchings, Graham. 2001. *Modern China: A Guide to a Century of Change*. Cambridge, Mass.: Harvard University Press.

Jacques, Martin. 2009. *When China Rules the World: The End of the Western World and the Birth of a New Global Order*. Penguin Press.

Kristof, Nicholas D. and Sheryl WuDunn. 1994. *China Wakes: The Struggle for the Soul of a Rising Power*. New York: Times Books.

Naisbitt, John and Doris Naisbitt. 2010. *China's Megatrends: The 8 Pillars of a New Society.* New York: HarperCollins.

Ostrowski, Pierre and Gwen Penner. 2009. *It's All Chinese to Me: An Overview of Culture & Etiquette in China.* Manitoba, Canada: All Out Press.

Pye, Lucian W. and Mary W. Pye. 1991. *China: An Introduction.* New York: HarperCollins.

Schneiter, Fred. 1995. *The Joy of Getting Along with the Chinese.* Torrance, CA: Heian International Publishing Co.

Sly, Gord and Julie Sly. 2008. *China Unveiled: Living and Working Behind the Great Wall.* Bloomington:Trafford.

Spence, Jonathan D. 1990. *The Search for Modern China.* New York: W.W. Norton & Company, Inc.

Business

De Mente, Boye L. 2004. *Chinese Etiquette & Ethics in Business.* Lincolnwood, IL: NTC Business Books.

Genzberger, Christine and Edward Hinkleman, eds. 1994. *China Business: The Portable Encyclopaedia for Doing Business in China.* Petaluma, California: World Trade Press.

Huang, Quanyu, Richard S. Andrulis, & Tong Chen. 1994. *A Guide to Successful Business Relations with the Chinese: Opening the Great Wall's Gate.* New York: International Business Press.

Kenna, Peggy & Sondra Lacy. 1994. *Business China: A Practical Guide to Understanding Chinese Business Culture.* Lincolnwood, IL: NTC Business Books.

Plafker, Ted. 2007. *Doing Business In China: How to Profit in the World's Fastest Growing Market.* New York: Hachette Book Group USA.

Seligman, Scott D. 1999. *Chinese Business Etiquette: A Guide to Protocol, Manners, and Culture in the People's Republic of China* (A Revised and Updated Edition of "Dealing with the Chinese"). New York: Warner Books, Inc.

Shen, Michael. 2004. *How to Do Business in China.* Pittsburgh: Dorrance Publishing Co., Inc.

Stross, Randall E. 1993. *Bulls in the China Shop and Other Sino-American Business Encounters.* Honolulu: Univ. of Hawaii Press.

Tadla, Ernie. 2007. *How To Live & Do Business In China*. Victoria, Canada: Trafford Publishing.

Language

Bjorksten, Johan. 1994. *Learn to Write Chinese Characters*. New Haven: Yale University Press.

Choy, Rita Mei-Wah. 1981. *Read and Write Chinese: A Simplified Guide to the Chinese Characters*. San Francisco, Calif: China West Books.

_____1989. *Understanding Chinese: A Guide to the Usage of Chinese Characters*. San Francisco, Calif: China Books and Periodicals, Inc.

De Francis, John. 1986. *The Chinese Language: Fact and Fantasy*. Honolulu: University of Hawaii Press.

Fallows, Deborah. 2010. *Dreaming in Chinese And Discovering What Makes a Billion People Tick*. U.K. Short Books Ltd.

_____2010. *Dreaming in Chinese: Mandarin Lessons In Life, Love, And Language*. New York: Walker & Company.

Ho, Yong. 1993. *Aspects of Discourse Structure in Mandarin Chinese*. Lewiston, NY: Edwin Mellen.

_____ 2005. *Intermediate Chinese*. New York: Hippocrene Books, Inc.

Matthews, Laurence and Alison Matthews, 2007. *The First 100 Chinese Characters: Simplified Character Edition: The Quick and Easy Method to Learn the 100 Most Basic Chinese Characters*. Vermont: Tuttle Publishing.

Peng, Tan Huay. 2004. *Fun with Chinese Characters 1, 2, 3*. New York: Times International.

McCawley, James D. 2004. *The Eater's Guide to Chinese Characters*. Chicago: University of Chicago Press.

Norman, Jerry. 1988. *Chinese*. Cambridge: Cambridge University Press.

Ramsey, S. Robert. 1989. *The Languages of China*. Princeton: Princeton University Press.

Yin, John Jing-hua, 2006. *Fundamentals of Chinese Characters*. New Haven, CT: Yale University Press.

Dictionaries

Ho, Yong. 2001. *Chinese-English Frequency Dictionary: A Study Guide to Mandarin Chinese's 500 Most Frequently Used Words.* New York: Hippocrene Books, Inc.

_____ 2006. *Chinese-English/English-Chinese Dictionary & Phrasebook.* New York: Hippocrene Books, Inc.

_____ 2009. *Chinese-English/English-Chinese Practical Dictionary.* New York: Hippocrene Books, Inc.

Hornby, A.S. 2002. *Oxford Advanced Learners English Chinese Dictionary.* Oxford University Press.

Manser, Martin H. 1999. *The Concise English-Chinese, Chinese-English Dictionary.* Oxford University Press and the Commercial Press.

Wang, Huidi. 2005. *Cheng & Tsui Chinese Character Dictionary.* Boston: Cheng and Tsui Company.

Major Chinese Learning Material Suppliers and Distributors in the U.S.

Asia for Kids
www.afk.com/

Better Chinese
www.betterchinese.com/

Cheng and Tsui Company
www.cheng-tsui.com/

China Books and Periodicals
www.chinabooks.com/

ChinaSprout
www.chinasprout.com/

Nan Hai Books
www.nanhai.com/store/index.html

Internet Resources

Guides, Indexes & Portals

Chinese Home Page
www.uni.edu/becker/chinese.html
A complete reference to China/Chinese-related websites.

Chinese Language Webs
http://bubl.ac.uk/link/c/chineselanguage.htm
A catalog of internet resources.

Chinese Language & Linguistics
http://chinalinks.osu.edu/c-links3.htm
Annotated links compiled by Marjorie Chan to more than two hundred China and Chinese language- and linguistics-related websites.

Chinese Language & Writing
http://acc6.its.brooklyn.cuny.edu/~phalsall/texts/chinlng2.html
Includes the history of the Sino-Tibetan family of languages.

Confucius Institutes Online
www.confuciusinstitute.net
Comprehensive website with rich resources of Chinese learning and cultural information.

Teaching and Learning Chinese
http://topaz.kenyon.edu/projects/chinese/
A collection of resources for teaching and learning Chinese.

Chinese Characters

2500 Chinese Characters
www.shuifeng.net/pinyin.asp
Click on any of the 2500 characters alphabetically arranged according to pinyin to see its stroke order, radical, number of strokes and to hear its pronounciation.

A is for Love
www.chinapage.com/flash/love.html
This is a set of flash cards for learning Chinese. The face card shows a Chinese word. Clicking on the word will flip the card over, where the pronunciation and meaning are given.

Animated Chinese Characters
http://lost-theory.org/ocrat/chargif/
Click on any Chinese character to see how to write it.

Arch Chinese
www.archchinese.com/arch_stroke_order_rules.html
Online Chinese character learning tool designed for English speakers who have little or no knowledge of Mandarin Chinese. It offers a rich set of features that includes stroke order animation and dictionary.

Character Flashcards
www.mandarintools.com/flashcard.html
Database contains 1,000 most frequently used characters.

Chinese Character Annotator
http://lost-theory.org/ocrat/reaf/
Copy and paste Chinese text into the box and hit Search. The Chinese text will be marked up with pinyin and link to sound clips of the pronunciation.

Chinese Character Genealogy
www.zhongwen.com
An etymological Chinese-English dictionary.

Chinese Course
www.chinese-course.com
An audio flashcard system with multiple-choice tests.

eStroke
www.eon.com.hk/estroke
In addition to showing the stroke order of any Chinese character through animation, eStroke also creates extremely high quality stroke sequence that can be pasted into your documents. eStroke can also create worksheets, export to animated gif and flash video.

Flashcard Wizard
www.foolsworkshop.com/fw.html
Besides the ability to practice flashcards with 2 or 3 fields of information, these fields may include pictures and non-roman text for language study.

Hanlexon Chinese
www.hanlexon.org/
Amazing website that allows students to create and save worksheets of any Chinese characters. Worksheets of characters in this book were produced on this website.

Learn to Read and Write Chinese Characters
www.csulb.edu/~txie/character.htm
A list of resources.

List of Character Radicals
www.yellowbridge.com/chinese/radicals.php
See the list of 214 radicals in Chinese and their names in English.

Liwin Flash Card Practice
http://liwin.com/flashcards/index.php
Users can choose to review vocabulary from beginning textbooks like Conversational Mandarin Chinese Online, Integrated Chinese, and Practical Chinese Reader, and the most common 2500 characters.

Online Chinese Flashcards
www.yellowbridge.com/chinese/flashcards.php
The characters in Beginners Chinese and Intermediate Chinese are ready made on this site.

Semanda Mandarin Chinese Flashcards
www.semanda.com
It provides basic Mandarin Chinese flashcards and vocabulary exercises for children and beginners. The wordlists cover a wide range of basic concepts, such as colors, animals, fruits, vegetables, vehicles, furniture, etc.

Ting Flashcard Reader
http://hua.umf.maine.edu/Chinese/FlashCardReader/Tingflash-cardNetEnglish.html
Free download and you can study off-line.

Chinese Grammar

Basic Chinese Grammars
www.rci.rutgers.edu/~rsimmon/chingram
A slide show that reviews the basics of spoken standard Chinese grammar.

Grammar Index
www.ctcfl.ox.ac.uk/Chinese/grammarlist.htm
A list of grammatical items with examples. Also provided are Vocabulary Index and Character Index.

Learn Chinese Grammar
www.csulb.edu/~txie/grammar.htm
A list of links to various sites about Chinese grammar.

Chinese Podcasts

ChinesePod
http://chinesepod.com
Online service that provides daily podcasts, with accompanying text expansion exercises and other extensive tutoring aids available to Chinese users.

CSLPod
www.cslpod.com
Free Chinese courses offered at three levels: beginners, average, and advanced.

iMandarinPod
http://imandarinpod.com/hoola
Designed to teach Chinese by introducing topics about Chinese culture or what is happening in China today.

Serge Melnyk
www.melnyks.com
100+ audio lessons in a daily theme-based and progressive manner together with PDF transcripts and worksheets in both traditional and simplified Chinese characters, along with pinyin and English translations.

Pronunciation and Listening Comprehension

BBC Chinese
www.bbc.co.uk/languages/chinese/games
Online drilling games for Chinese learners. One game is for practicing the four tones and the other for learning how to write Chinese characters.

Beginning Chinese Listening Comprehension
www.wellesley.edu/Chinese/Listening/contents.html
An interactive website with 18 audio lessons followed by listening comprehension questions.

Learning Oral Mandarin
www.pthxx.com
Resources for studying pinyin, including flashcards, pictures and graphs, pronunciation skill, tongue twisters, etc.

Mandarin 123
www.mandarin123.com/pronunciation.html
An online multi-level mandarin learning resource that includes pronunciations, vocabulary, grammar and reading.

Pinyin Font Converter
www.foolsworkshop.com/pfc.html
In order to input romanized Chinese in pinyin using the 4 tones of Mandarin Chinese, special fonts are used to mark vowels with tones. A variety of these fonts are available online. The Pinyin Font Converter converts texts between some of the most popular pinyin fonts that are available for Windows and Macintosh.

Pinyin Info
http://pinyin.info
This site presents rules for using pinyin as well as tools for writing pinyin with tone marks.

Pinyin Practice
http://pinyinpractice.com
The site provides ample Mandarin pronunciation exercises and learning components.

Chinese Input Devices

Chinese Input Method Editor
www.chinese-tools.com/tools/ime.html
This tool allows users to write simplified Chinese characters online in pinyin without installing any software.

Chinese Online Input Tool
www.newconcept.com/Reference/chinese_pinyin_input.html
This online Chinese input tool allows users to type Chinese characters through their web browser without installing any Chinese input software. It accommodates both simplified and traditional characters.

InputKing
www.inputking.com
Browser-based Chinese input method editor. It supports both simplified characters and traditional characters.

Dictionaries

Chinese Dictionary Web
http://zhongwen.com/zi.htm
Contains more than a dozen dictionaries.

Chinese-English Dictionary
www.mandarintools.com/worddict.html
This dictionary provides a searchable interface. Searches can be conducted by characters, pinyin, or English. Results will show the Chinese word, the pinyin representation of the word, and the English definition. You can also click on the pinyin to hear how it is pronounced.

Chinese-English Talking Dictionary
www.yellowbridge.com/chinese/chinese-dictionary.php
Integrated word and character dictionary on the web lets you

search by word, pinyin, or English. Unique features include: handwriting recognition, fuzzy pinyin that matches words even when you are unsure of the exact pronunciation, word and character decomposition, character etymology, and stroke order.

Online Tutorials, Courses & Programs

ActiveChinese
http://activechinese.com
Its interactive lessons use multimedia to engage students of all ages, which can be taught from CD-ROMs, mobile downloads, or through online access.

BBC Chinese
www.bbc.co.uk/languages/chinese/real_chinese
A lively introduction to Mandarin Chinese in 10 short parts. Each topic contains: a slideshow with the key language, tips on pronunciation and grammar, cultural notes, a challenge, video clips from Real Chinese (broadband, UK only) and a shorter video clip from Real Chinese for narrowband or non-UK users.

Chinese Multimedia Tutorial
http://otal.umd.edu/chintut
A tutorial on greetings, expressing thanks and food terms, including characters and sounds.

Chinese Online
www.hanyu.com.cn/en
Free e-class, webcast, e-magazine, culture and entertainment.

Learn Chinese Online
www.csulb.edu/~txie/online.htm
Large index of links for learning, studying, or practicing Chinese online. Links include pronunciation, conversation, grammar and characters, literature, dictionaries, software, and more.

Learn Mandarin Chinese
www.chinese-tools.com/learn/chinese
40 free online lessons with audio, including reading, speaking,
writing, vocabulary, grammar, calligraphy, examples and exercices.
All texts and dialogues are in mp3 format for download.

Chinese Study Programs

Study Chinese in China
http://clta-gny.org/studyabroad.html
A comprehensive list of scores of study programs in China.

www.studyabroadlinks.com/search/China/index.html
Another comprehensive list grouped by such categories as College
Year & Semester Programs, College Summer Programs, High
School Study Abroad in China, Chinese Language Programs,
Field Studies Programs, Internships and Experiential Programs,
Homestay Programs, Martial Arts Programs, and Cooking
Schools and Programs.

Software Programs

ChinesePlus
www.biderworld.com/chineseplus.asp
A comprehensive Chinese text input software. It allows for the
two-way conversion of traditional to simplified Chinese text. The
software converts character to pinyin with tone marks, and pinyin
back to character. The software also features an interactive
stroke-by-stroke demonstration of Chinese character writing.

Chinese Software-related Homepage
www.gy.com/www/chlist.htm
A web of webs.

Key

www.cjkware.com

Text editing and inputting software that enables Chinese text entry through standard pinyin and other methods. It has a Chinese/ English and English/Chinese dictionary, Text To Speech functions, and allows for the conversion of Chinese text to pinyin with tone marks.

NJStar

www.njstar.com

Word processing software which reads, writes, edits and prints Chinese text in English Windows environment. It includes English-Chinese /Chinese-English dictionary and has the function of converting a block of Chinese text to pinyin with tone.

Wenlin Software for Learning Chinese

http://wenlin.com

A CD-ROM software, Wenlin tackles the most frustrating obstacles for students of Chinese with its versatile and easy-to-use interface. Wenlin combines a high-speed expandable Chinese dictionary, a full-featured text editor, and unique "flashcard" system all in one intuitive environment.

More Hippocrene Titles for Learning Chinese

Intermediate Chinese with Audio CD
ISBN 0-7818-1096-5 · $21.95 pb

Chinese through Tone and Color with 2 CDs
ISBN 0-7818-1204-7 · $24.95 pb

Introduction to Chinese-English Translation
ISBN 978-0-7818-1216-0 · $19.95 pb

Chinese-English/English-Chinese Practical Dictionary
15,000 entries · ISBN 978-0-7818-1236-8 · $19.95 pb

Hippocrene Children's Illustrated Chinese Dictionary
500 entries · ISBN 978-0-7818-0848-4 · $14.95 pb

Chinese-English/English-Chinese Pocket Legal Dictionary
6,000 entries · ISBN 0-7818-1215-1 · $19.95 pb

Chinese-English/English-Chinese Dictionary & Phrasebook
4,000 entries · ISBN 0-7818-1135-X · $12.95 pb

Chinese-English Frequency Dictionary
A Study Guide to Mandarin Chinese's 500 Most Frequently Used Words
500 entries · ISBN 0-7818-0842-1 · $18.95 pb

Emergency Chinese Phrasebook
200 entries · ISBN 0-7818-0975-4 · $5.95 pb

Dictionary of 1,000 Chinese Proverbs
ISBN 978-0-7818-0682-4 · $11.95 pb

Dictionary of 1,000 Chinese Idioms
ISBN 978-0-7818-0820-0· $14.95 pb

Prices subject to change without prior notice. **To purchase Hippocrene Books** contact your local bookstore, visit www.hippocrenebooks.com, call (718) 454-2366, or write to: HIPPOCRENE BOOKS, 171 Madison Avenue, New York, NY 10016.